PERGAMON INTERNATIONAL LIBRARY
of Science, Technology, Engineering and Social Studies

*The 1000-volume original paperback library in aid of education,
industrial training and the enjoyment of leisure*

Publisher: Robert Maxwell, M.C.

New Methods
of Mental Health Care

THE PERGAMON TEXTBOOK
INSPECTION COPY SERVICE

An inspection copy of any book published in the Pergamon International Library will
gladly be sent to academic staff without obligation for their consideration for course
adoption or recommendation. Copies may be retained for a period of 60 days from
receipt and returned if not suitable. When a particular title is adopted or recommended
for adoption for class use and the recommendation results in a sale of 12 or more copies,
the inspection copy may be retained with our compliments. The Publishers will be
pleased to receive suggestions for revised editions and new titles to be published in this
important International Library.

New Methods
of Mental Health Care

Edited by

MOLLY MEACHER

MENTAL HEALTH FOUNDATION, LONDON, U.K.

PERGAMON PRESS

OXFORD · NEW YORK · TORONTO · SYDNEY · PARIS · FRANKFURT

U.K.	Pergamon Press Ltd., Headington Hill Hall, Oxford OX3 0BW, England
U.S.A.	Pergamon Press Inc., Maxwell House, Fairview Park, Elmsford, New York 10523, U.S.A.
CANADA	Pergamon of Canada Ltd., P.O. Box 9600, Don Mills M3C 2T9, Ontario, Canada
AUSTRALIA	Pergamon Press (Aust.) Pty. Ltd., P.O. Box 544, Potts Point, NSW 2011, Australia
FRANCE	Pergamon Press SARL., 24 rue des Ecoles, 75240 Paris, Cedex 05, France
FEDERAL REPUBLIC OF GERMANY	Pergamon Press GmbH, 6242 Kronberg-Taunus, Pferdstrasse 1, Federal Republic of Germany

First edition 1979

British Library Cataloguing in Publication Data

New methods of mental health care.
1. Mental health services — Great Britain
I. Meacher, Molly
362.2'0941   RA790.7.G7   78-40285

ISBN 0-08-022264-1 (hardcover)
   0-08-0237150 (flexicover)

Printed in Great Britain by
William Clowes & Sons Limited
London, Beccles and Colchester

Contents

Foreword   ix

Introduction   Robert Loder   xi

PART I.   **THE MENTAL HEALTH SERVICE: DEVELOPMENTS SINCE THE 1950s, PROBLEMS AND PROSPECTS**   1

Chapter 1   Integration or Disintegration of the Mental Health Service: Some Reflections and Developments in Britain since the 1950s
KATHLEEN JONES   3

Chapter 2   Joint Approaches to Community Care
PETER M. JEFFERYS   15

Chapter 3   Drug Research and Mental Health Services
MALCOLM LADER   33

PART II.   **PREVENTION**   47

Chapter 4   The Use of Community Care in Prevention
COLIN MURRAY PARKES   49

Chapter 5   The Primary Health Care Team: The Way Forward for Mental Health Care
GEOFFREY MARSH and MOLLY MEACHER   69

Chapter 6   The Role of Social Work in Relation to
             General Practice in the Mental Health Field
             MATILDA GOLDBERG   83

Chapter 7   The Development of an Action and
             Counselling Service in a Deprived Urban
             Area
             SUSAN HOLLAND   95

Chapter 8   The Libra Project — An Experimental
             Community-based Self-help Group Analytic
             Approach into Alcohol Abuse
             RONALD MAGGS
                                                        107

Appendices to Part II

Appendix I   A Model of Emergency Management
              ROLF OLSEN   127

Appendix II   An Experimental Crisis Centre
              JOHN GLEISNER   133

PART III.   CARE   AND   AFTER-CARE   IN
             PSYCHIATRY   137

Chapter 9   A Brief Hospitalisation Policy: the Effect
             upon Patients and their Families
             STEVEN R. HIRSCH, STEPHEN PLATT, ANN
             WEYMAN and ANGELA KNIGHTS   139

Chapter 10   Employment Problems and Prospects for
             Chronic Patients
             PHILIP COOPER   157

Chapter 11   The Employment Patterns of Former
              Psychiatric Patients
              NANCY WANSBROUGH, PHILIP COOPER and
              BETTY MITCHELL   171

Chapter 12   A Positive Approach to the Care of Old
              People with Mental Disorders
              TOM ARIE   187

Chapter 13   All is not Lost: New Approaches to the
              Management of Old People with Mental
              Disorders in Continuing Care Settings
              DAVID JOLLEY   195

Chapter 14   Comments and Conclusions
              J. K. WING   209

Appendix   The Case for Low Cost Solutions
              HUGH FREEMAN   221

Name Index   227

Subject Index   231

Foreword

This book has been written by some of the main contributors to a Conference which was organised by the Mental Health Foundation and held in Magdalen College, Oxford, in September 1977.

The aim of the Conference was to provide an independent forum for a number of forward-looking practitioners in the mental health field, to enable them to consider some of the more significant recent developments in psychiatry which could substantially affect the future shape of services. Speakers were selected for their unique contribution to a particular aspect of mental health care and delegates were invited who were in a position to affect the future development of services whether as senior personnel in the DHSS, health authorities, social services departments, hospitals or voluntary organisations.

For the purposes of the book it has been necessary to select some of the main themes of the 1977 Conference and to develop these in greater depth than was possible within the confines of a weekend of discussions. Important contributions to the Conference by such eminent figures as Professor Linford Rees and Professor David Goldberg have necessarily been omitted from the text because their subject matter fell outside the more limited terms of reference of the book. We are, nevertheless, indebted to these speakers whose papers were essential to the success of the Conference in providing introductory material, a breadth of vision and a wit which will be remembered by all those present.

The following pages include a discussion of many important developments in the prevention of mental disorders and the aftercare of patients but this volume is not comprehensive in its coverage. In particular, housing and day-care services for the chronic patient are not discussed here (except in relation to the elderly) and yet these services will play an essential role in the care of patients in the future. Despite such glaring omissions, we hope that readers will benefit from sharing the experience of those who have tried with varying degrees of success to improve the care of patients, whether by introducing preventive counselling schemes, self-help initiatives, improved methods of assessment or radical approaches to institutional care. The intention of the Foundation is that this should be one of a series of discussions which will contribute to the formulation of a mental health policy much more closely geared to the needs of the patient and in which he and his family and community play an increasing role.

MOLLY MEACHER

Introduction

Neglect of the mental health services by central and local government for many years and confusion and conflict within the services have produced a situation in which the patient is all too often bewildered and his family close to despair as they search for the "right" method of treatment, appropriate services and a meaningful human response to their needs.

In the following pages a number of experienced practitioners in the field examine what has gone wrong; ways in which the administrative structure could be improved; preventive techniques developed and after-care services planned to meet the needs of patients and their families more effectively.

The Patient versus the Bureaucracy

For the individual patient or his family the lack of a unitary organisation is one factor which can pose severe practical problems as he is referred from one department to another in search of someone within the health or social services able to give an effective response. Is it the case as Kathleen Jones suggests (in Chapter 1) that successive changes in the organisation of the health services for the mentally ill have failed to provide a structure comprehensible to the individual patient or one which is readily accessible to him?

Today a psychotic patient may be in hospital for no more than two weeks and find himself discharged but still in need of a range of services provided by his doctor, his social worker, a housing officer, a disablement resettlement officer and a social security officer in no less than five separate departments or authorities. Peter Jefferys analyses some of the problems of collaboration at the planning and individual levels, and suggests ways in which health and local authorities can facilitate joint planning. But whatever the management arrangements, argues Jefferys, effective partnership ultimately rests on personal understanding and co-operation by individual doctors, nurses, social workers and increasingly volunteers.

Nowhere is this more apparent than in the primary health care team where genuine collaboration between GPs, health visitors, social workers and marriage guidance counsellors has in at least one area improved patient care while reducing the need for hospital referral (Chapter 5).

The Case for a Redeployment of Resources

Writers have consistently referred to the wholly inadequate response of Government and local authorities to the increasing proportion of chronic psychiatric patients who spend most of their lives *outside* hospital and whose needs for housing, day care and social support have simply not been met. The new joint financing arrangements introduced in 1977 have provided a boost to the development of such services jointly funded by .health and local authorities, but a number of speakers at the 1977 Mental Health Foundation Conference, notably Professor Linford Rees and Professor David Goldberg, urged the need for funds to be earmarked for mental health projects by the DHSS if the whole success of the Health Service is not to be seriously jeopardised.

Even given a serious attempt by the Government to provide the infrastructure of services needed by chronic psychiatric patients in the community, Tilda Goldberg argues that sufficient social support will only be provided for such patients in the event of a radical redeployment of social work resources and a change in the orientation of social work in the mental health field (Chapter 6). Social workers of the future will, says Tilda Goldberg, need to play a quasi-community worker role as initiators of voluntary support groups and self-help projects. A number of such groups have developed spontaneously amongst problem drinkers and drug abusers, "battering" mothers, the relatives of schizophrenics, compulsive gamblers and agoraphobics, but the support of social workers for such movements is essential if they are to provide a stable and nationwide service.

The practical difficulties associated with the stimulation of a self-help approach in a deprived area are illustrated in harsh terms by Susan Holland in her description of her work in Battersea (Chapter 7); and the potential and problems of a self-help group of problem drinkers are outlined by Ronald Maggs, the initiator of the Libra group, in Chapter 8.

In the absence of self-help and counselling opportunities for patients suffering from more minor disorders, the GP turns to his prescription pad for the cheapest and quickest way to deal with symptoms of social and psychological stress. Malcolm Lader's recommendations for changing current methods of treatment for such disorders also have significant implications for a reallocation of resources (Chapter 3).

Care and After-care in the Community

Professor Hirsch's study of a brief hospitalisation policy (discussed in Chapter 9) gives further impetus to the rapid discharge policy of psychiatric hospitals. Reassuring statistics which seem to suggest that neither patients nor families suffered as a result of the administrative shortening of the average stay in hospital will no doubt be received with scepticism in some quarters, however. With the very uneven and inadequate level of provision of alternative services in the community, any further reductions in hospital care will need to be balanced by a major Government spending programme on community services. The problems of establishing hostels, day centres and support services in the community have by no means yet been solved, however. It is a sad reflection that already many of the worst features of our old mental hospitals are being reproduced in some community based facilities. A closer partnership between the statutory and voluntary services in the future will, it is hoped, do much to remedy this situation.

Employment is surely one of the basic needs of any individual and yet the finding of a job presents very real problems for the psychiatric patient not least because of the prejudices and fantasies of employers and employees about the behaviours to be expected from an ex-patient. In Chapter 10 we examine the employment prospects of the very small proportion of patients for whom open employment will perhaps never be a realistic option and in Chapter 11 Nancy Wansbrough provides the first results of a major six year study examining the position of those ex-patients who have succeeded in finding a job in open industry, the nature of complaints about them, the types of work undertaken, the pattern of communication and causes of stress. It remains to be seen just how far the prospects for ex-patients can be improved, to what extent enclaves can enable quite severely disabled patients to hold a job in open industry and what role could or should be played in the future by specialised sheltered factories for psychiatrically disabled people. Our contributors provide valuable material relevant to these questions but point to the need for further experimentation and research in this important field.

New Methods of Care for the Elderly

In Chapters 12 and 13 we turn to the special needs of the growing numbers of elderly and infirm people — the biggest single users of institutional care and probably the biggest single trigger of social and medical crises. Professor Arie outlines the principles of a positive approach to the care of the elderly mentally infirm while David Jolley examines the results of a number of experimental projects in this area, notably one in which the educational techniques generally associated with the teaching of ESN children were employed by nursing staff on a psychogeriatric ward to remarkable effect.

These two chapters suggest that much can be achieved *with existing resources* to improve the quality of life of the elderly mentally infirm, whether within hospital, within Part III homes or in less institutional settings. At the same time, the job satisfaction of staff can be dramatically improved.

THE MENTAL HEALTH FOUNDATION

While presenting a somewhat gloomy picture of the present state of the mental health service, our contributors point to many important research developments and new methods of care or treatment which, if applied generally, would greatly improve the preventive and after-care services provided. Some of the more encouraging developments, perhaps stimulated by the absence of any clear sense of direction within the statutory services, have been those initiated by voluntary organisations such as the National Schizophrenia Fellowship, local Associations for Mental Health, the Psychiatric Rehabilitation Association and the Guideposts Trust. These initiatives have been taken in direct response to the real needs of patients and their families and often provide a more meaningful response than can be given by an overworked and committee-bound employee of the local authority or hospital. The essential feature of these voluntary organisations is that they provide an environment in which a patient can achieve a sense of belonging to society, and where he is encouraged to help himself and others in a similar situation. The Mental Health Foundation has as one of its main aims the support of such community initiatives, particularly where they set new trends or provide improved methods of care.

At a time when considerable controversy exists between practitioners who emphasise the value of chemotherapy and those with a psychotherapeutic orientation; between environmentalists and geneticists, between behaviourists and analysts and so forth, the Foundation fulfils the need for an entirely independent body which includes on its two professional grant-giving committees representatives from all the more important schools of thought. Only through extensive further research in all areas can we become more clear about the complex causes of mental disorders and the relative success of different methods of prevention and treatment. Only by bringing together those with different, and in some cases conflicting, theories and ideas will the benefits of each be better understood by their opponents.

If this volume serves to increase the level of understanding and co-operation between professionals, volunteers and patients and if it stimulates a more effective response from the community and from the statutory services to the needs of the individual patient and his family, this publication will have made a significant contribution to the immense task of improving the prospects for sufferers from mental illness.

ROBERT LODER
Trustee, Mental Health Foundation
and
MOLLY MEACHER

PART I

The Mental Health Service: Developments since the 1950s, Problems and Prospects

CHAPTER 1

Integration or Disintegration of the Mental Health Service: Some Reflections on Developments in Britain since the 1950s

KATHLEEN JONES

Mental health administration — the system by which some people are defined as mentally ill and their care and treatment is prescribed — derives its strengths and its weaknesses from the values of the society in which it is practised. What we define as mental illness depends on the norms of society, what it is prepared to tolerate, and what it finds intolerable. Modes of care and treatment evolve out of complex interactions between rival philosophies. The nature of the administrative model used may be taken for granted, or obscured by the accretion of detailed plans which never ask the basic philosophical questions: who are the mentally ill? What are their special needs? Why do we handle their problems in the way that we do?

The traditional model of administration, which developed in the nineteenth century, involved a heavy investment in bricks and mortar. Institutions, variously called madhouses, asylums or mental hospitals, served — and still serve — a variety of purposes: custody, asylum (in its original sense of sanctuary, a place of shelter from the pressures of the outside world), treatment, rehabilitation. But we now have plenty of evidence that such institutions can be highly damaging. Separation from the outside world leads to the creation of a tight social system which imposes its own curious and sometimes pathological imperatives on those who live within it. Patients often suffer from a social stigma which deters others from seeking treatment, and which intensifies the difficulties of rehabilitation. The negative effects of a purely hospital-based system have been widely publicised in recent years. The writers of the "literature of protest"[1,2] do not tell the whole truth about mental hospital life, and in many respects offer a distorted picture but there is no reasonable doubt that they have some unpalatable truths to tell us. In policy terms, the flight from the closed, monolithic mental hospital system is general.

Two facts stand out clearly: first, that, despite its relatively poor public image, the mental hospital system is remarkably tough, and seems to survive all onslaughts. Rising admission rates mean that the chances of being admitted as an in-patient at some time in one's life may well be increasing rather than decreasing. Second, that despite some twenty-five years of experiments in community-based psychiatry, we are still much clearer about what we are running away from than about where we are running to.

The Multiplex Model

By the early 1950s, there was a distinct shift in mental health policy (if not in practice) in many countries from a system largely or exclusively based on mental hospitals to one which provided some flexibility and diversity of provision. A basic description of a multiplex model occurs in a World Health Organisation Report.[3] The report contrasted the "classical" or traditional model of the isolated and self-sufficient mental hospital with a "modern" community model containing a number of related elements: in-patient treatment in either a specialist psychiatric hospital or a general hospital, according to the patient's requirements; day care, whether in a unit attached to the parent hospital or a detached unit; out-patient care; hostels, workshops and domiciliary care. Much interest was aroused at this time by the development of mobile psychiatric teams in Amsterdam and Rotterdam;[4] by the concept of the "shift hospital", taking patients by day or by night, at the weekend or during the week, according to domestic and occupational necessity;[5] and by Professor Lambo's village-based community service in Nigeria, which offered some hope that the developing countries might avoid the mistake of building large mental hospitals in the first place.[6]

This was a time of hope. Looking back, we can see that, despite some brave experiments and some valuable gains in knowledge, the hopes have not been fulfilled as widely as many people expected. The WHO Report talked of "a range of tools in the hands of the community" which could be employed to meet the needs of individual patients; but there were two major snags to the realisation of this vision. The first was that "meeting the needs of the patient" meant that there must be some choice of provision available to the psychiatrist, and that meant that there must be over-provision — an excess of supply over demand. In fact, no country has ever made psychiatric provision on a scale which allowed any but the richest patients and their doctors any element of choice in treatment. The question is not usually whether to use a bed or a day place or a visit from a social worker, but whether any of these can be made available. The second snag was that the very requirements of flexibility and diversity made it difficult to spell out the administrative mechanisms appropriate to the new model. Were the hospitals to control the new community agencies? Was some outside agency to control the hospitals? If the system were to be split — part hospital-based and part community-based — how was coordination to be achieved? What guide-lines were to be used for planning — what, for instance, was an appropriate ratio of day places to in-patient beds, or of social workers to nurses? Such questions were probably incapable of international solution, because the answers depended on the kind of administrative machinery available, the extent of existing provision, and the relative availability of different kinds of trained staff.

Thus the principles of the "modern" system were clearly laid down, and in theory applicable to any country; but there is a gap between this kind of meta-policy and the day-to-day running of a mental health service. The hospitals had more than a century of unitary organisation behind them, while the community agencies, where they existed at all, were relatively fragmented. Doctors, belonging to a prestigious and highly-organised profession, took professional pre-eminence over less established professional groups, like nurses, psychologists and social workers. So a system which on paper allowed for considerable flexibility between agencies of equal availability and personnel of equal prestige ran into difficulties of unequal financing, unequal prestige, and the unequal exercise of power.

In the past twenty years, the WHO multiplex model has been abandoned. The medical and social care of psychiatric patients has been sharply divided between the Health Services and the Social Services (with consequent administrative problems in trying to link them up again) and there is now no entity at central or local government level which can be called a Mental Health Service. The story of how and why this happened is worth reconsidering.

Policy in the 1950s

Up to 1961, observers from the United States and other countries were able to come to Britain, and to find new developments of immediate relevance to their own work. After a trip organised by the Milbank Memorial Fund[7] for psychiatrists from the states of New York, New Jersey and Connecticut, Dr. Robert C. Hunt of New York reported:

> "Those of us who have had a good 'take' from the British 'vaccine' underwent a revolutionary upheaval and emerged with a whole new set of concepts about our patients, about our institutions, about our professional roles, and we see almost every detail of our work from a radically different point of view."

The Milbank group was particularly excited by the development of the open door system in British mental hospitals — both the freedom which many in-patients had to enter and leave the hospital, and the ease of admission and discharge under the new Mental Health Act of 1959, which meant that very few patients were compulsorily detained. They were quick to see that this policy implied a variety of other provisions in the community, and Dr. Hunt thought that the unitary organisation of the British National Health Service would make this particularly easy to provide:

> "The major differences which might limit what we can do (in the States) related not so much to our hospitals as such, but rather concern the organisation of a total service program. The nationalisation of all health and welfare services in Britain gives them the machinery for pulling all the needed things together in one package. Because we do not have this machinery in our society, we are faced with the problems of communication and of organisation between diverse, separate agencies so as to pull them into a continuum. . . ."

During the late fifties and early sixties, successive groups of overseas visitors were to beat a path across England, viewing the show places where hospital/local authority coordination worked: Portsmouth, Worthing, West Ham in London, Nottingham, Oldham, York. Within the hospitals, there was the developing therapeutic community system — a series of sustained attempts to break down the stereotyped relationships of "doctor", "nurse" and "patient".[8,9,10]

Time was to show that many of the hopes raised by this experimentation were unfounded. Each of the success stories in hospital/local authority coordination was based on a double accident: an administrative situation where hospital and local authority boundaries were roughly coterminous, or at least easily assimilable, and an accident of personality which provided them with psychiatrists willing to reach out into the community and to experiment with a community-based service.

The therapeutic community system did much good in showing other hospitals how to humanise relationships and lessen institutionalism; but it gradually lost its intensity as the mental hospital system came under attack and the pace of admission and discharge increased to the point where short-stay patients were not in hospital long enough to sustain the kinds of depth relationships it sought to create.[11]

The Run-down of the Mental Hospitals

The intention of the framers of the 1959 Act had been to create a multiplex system in which mental hospitals would play a part, though a less dominant one than in the past. In 1961, Enoch Powell, then Minister of Health, announced a policy of a different kind. On some rather shaky statistical evidence, it had been decided that the mental hospital population would be halved by 1975, and that most of those psychiatric in-patients remaining would be treated in units in general hospitals. In a somewhat intemperate speech, the Minister spoke of "setting the torch to the funeral pyre" and "the defences we have to storm". A number of commentators pointed out that there was little or no research on the respective merits of specialist psychiatric hospitals and psychiatric units in general hospitals; and that while an emphasis on community care was welcome, they would like to see some guarantee that the necessary community services would be provided, and that the aim was not simply treatment on the cheap.[12] No guarantees were forthcoming. Morale among mental hospital staff was severely affected. About the same time, they began to lose their Physician Superintendents, who were replaced by a system of tripartite management — medical, nursing and administrative — which was excellent in theory, but contributed to the general insecurity, and provided some remarkable interprofessional battles in practice.

The Reorganisation Period: 1968–74

By the late sixties, nobody was very interested in the Mental Health Services. The period of excitement and experiment was succeeded, as so often by a trough of unconcern. Dr. Jack R. Ewalt had noted earlier in the US Government Report *Action for Mental Health*[13] that, over a period of two centuries,

> "While each reform appears to have gained sufficient ground to give its supporters some sense of progress, each has been rather quickly followed by backsliding, loss of professional momentum, and public indifference."

The spotlight in health and social policy had switched to two general issues: reform of the personal social services and reform of the health services. Each of these measures was immense in its repercussions, and from many points of view highly desirable in modernising an outdated administrative system. Each in turn almost absent-mindedly knocked another nail into the coffin of the Mental Health Services.[14]

The Report of the Seebohm Committee in 1968 recommended the creation of free-standing Social Services Departments in local authorities, with broad responsibilities for meeting social need in their areas. This involved initially bringing together the work of the Welfare Departments largely concerned with the disabled, the chronic sick and the elderly, the Children's Departments, which dealt with children in need of care and with preventive family case-work, and the Mental Health Departments, then under medical control as sub-departments of the Health Departments. When the recommendations were implemented, it was also decided that hospital social workers, including those in mental hospitals, should be transferred to the local authority for the purposes of pay and deployment. Meanwhile, in anticipation of the new generic approach to social work which would be needed, most training courses for social workers "went generic" and ceased to provide special types of training, including training for psychiatric social workers. The Association of Psychiatric Social Workers itself ceased to exist in 1971, when, together with other specialist organisations, it was merged into the new British Association of Social Workers.

By the time the Local Authority Social Services Act of 1970 was implemented in 1971, Medical Officers of Health and hospital psychiatrists had lost their administrative contact with social work for the mentally ill. The new Social Services Departments faced many problems, and faced them in a period of financial stringency. To the present writer's knowledge, none of the Directors of Social Services appointed in 1971 had a background in the Mental Health Services — the majority were Chief Welfare Officers or Children's Officers, who brought with them other models of care and other preoccupations. Psychiatrists who had taken considerable interest in community care, and played a considerable part in developing it, found the door firmly slammed in their faces. When they requested social work help from the new departments, they were likely to be sent a social worker with a different kind of training and no knowledge of the special clinical or legal problems of mental health work. In Portsmouth, Worthing and the other well-known centres, hospital/local authority coordination ceased to exist.

Meanwhile, on the Health Service side, moves were afoot to develop a new and integrated hospital/community service. The "Cogwheel" reorganisation of doctors' work in hospital resulted in the creation of "divisions" for medicine, surgery and some other specialisms — and psychiatrists were swept into the system of divisions, with no separate organisational framework. "Psychiatry" said Sir Keith Joseph, the minister responsible for Health and Social Security, "is to join the rest of medicine".[15] He explained that the reason for this was that:

> "The treatment of psychosis, neurosis and schizophrenia have been entirely changed by the drug revolution. People go into hospital with mental disorders and they are cured. . . ."

The nursing profession was also reorganised on lines which applied equally to mental and general hospitals, despite their different structure in the past. All three professions — medicine, nursing and social work — were tightening their professional organisation, stressing those factors which their members shared, and minimising those aspects of professional knowledge and practice in which they differed. The result was that general medicine, general nursing and generic social work took precedence over psychiatric medicine, psychiatric nursing and psychiatric social work. The psychiatrists at least kept their own professional body, the Royal Medico-Psychological Association, which became the Royal College of Psychiatrists; but with this exception, specialist professional organisations ceased to exist.

The reorganisation of the National Health Service involved the creation of Regional Health Authorities, Area Health Authorities and District Management Teams responsible for all hospital and community health services in their areas. Again, there was no special representation for mental health interests at these senior levels. The only possibility of a body with such an interest was at the comparatively low level of a Mental Health Care Planning Team within the district. Though the National Health Service Reorganisation Act came into operation in April 1974, these planning teams have been curiously slow to develop in many areas.

Thus two major measures designed to improve the health and social services had between them destroyed the administrative structure of the mental health services. The extraordinary thing is that it had all been done in the name of "integration". Psychiatric social work had been "integrated" with generic social work. Psychiatrists had been "integrated" into general medicine. Psychiatric hospitals had been "integrated" into a general hospital system. The only people who remained unintegrated were the mentally ill, who were now required to carve their needs into neat parcels labelled "medical" and "social", and to apply to the appropriate authority for care and treatment. But for both health and social service authorities, mental health has become a minority interest, rather than a major part of their work.

The White Paper of 1975

By 1975, changes in administrative definition and in the modes of collecting official statistics had made it impossible to say with any certainty whether Enoch Powell's predictions about halving the mental hospital population had been fulfilled or not. A Government White Paper[16] made no mention of the predictions. It did, however, make it clear that mental hospitals, though somewhat reduced in beddage, deal with a mounting volume of work, and "some will continue in use for many years". There is now no question of their abolition. Comparatively few psychiatric patients are in general hospital units − building has lagged seriously behind earlier plans. Community care facilities − hostels, day centres, group homes and domiciliary care "have to be built up from their present minimal levels". So much for the promises of 1961.

In spite of the many problems and the shortfall on expectations, the Department of Health and Social Security is convinced that:

> "The failures and the problems are at the margin, and that the basic concept remains valid. We believe that the philosophy of integration rather than isolation which has been the underlying theme of development still holds good."

There is an honest attempt to draw a balance-sheet − to answer the question "How far have hopes been fulfilled, and how far frustrated or disappointed?" On the credit side, it is argued that improvements in drug treatment have made it possible to treat many more patients in the community, and to cut the length of stay of many others − the pharmacological revolution of the fifties has brought positive advances; but it is admitted that the effects of drugs are imperfectly understood, and that many of them are merely palliative, masking severe psychological and social problems. The open door policy has been maintained with considerable benefits to the majority of patients − but against that must be set the growth of acute problems with violent patients who need to be kept in a closed environment, and for whom it is no longer available. (There have been several recent cases of patients who have been sent to prison rather than mental hospital by the courts after the commission of an offence because no mental hospital had the facilities to hold them.) The integration of psychiatry with general medicine is seen as an advance − "psychiatry is coming in out of the cold". The ideal service of the future (and it is said that it may not be achieved for another twenty-five years) is delineated as one in which the family doctor and the home nurse form the basis of the "primary care team", assisted by the social worker, and the psychiatrist works alongside his colleagues in general medicine, usually in a general hospital setting.

The Meaning of "Integration"

The whole policy rests on the concept of "integration" and it is here that some clear administrative thinking seems to be needed. "Integration" is repeatedly contrasted with "isolation", and seen as something good in itself; but this view can be challenged.

Both "integration" and "isolation" are emotive words. "Integration" has a value connotation in such fields as psychology and human relations, where an individual is said to be "integrated" when the various elements in his personality are held in balance and control, forming a harmonious whole. The same idea has been carried over into race relations. Integration between black and white is desirable, non-integration is undesirable; but when the term "integration" is used in administrative theory and practice, it has no value connotation. It is a basic fact of administration that one cannot integrate in all directions at once. Much of the art of administration consists of breaking down large units into smaller, socially meaningful units, and then finding some suitable means of coordination between them. One does not ask "Is integration good?" or assert that it is. One asks, "Is *this* kind of integration meaningful — at the cost of destroying some other kind of integration?" There must be some subdivision. It will always be partly artificial; and attempts must always be made to link up again what has been separated; but there is no such thing as total integration; and no value, except the purely pragmatic one of what works best, in one kind of integration rather than another. The only feasible question is not "Is this good in some absolute sense?" but "Does it work?".

In the mental health field, we have attempted four kinds of integration — between mental hospitals and general hospitals, between psychiatrists and general physicians, between the administrative structure of the mental health services and that of the services for physical health, and between mental health social workers and other kinds of social workers. The cost is the destruction of the unity of the mental health services, and of the common understanding of professionals working in the mental health field.

It is difficult for observers in Britain, to whom the changes of the past few years have come piecemeal, and often without explicit analysis, to realise how far services for the mentally ill have travelled from specialisation (which may be a more appropriate term for what the White Paper calls "isolation"). The fact is that *Britain now has no Mental Health Services*; and there is a serious question of whether, and for how long, psychiatry can retain its distinctive skills and knowledge without an administrative base. There are services for the mentally ill; but they have no distinctive framework, no senior administrative staff appointments, no clear and integrated statistics on which to base monitoring and evaluation,[16] and no specialised administrative training. At the primary care level, they rest on the concept of using a team trained in the care of physical illness, without mental health skills for the care of conditions they do not understand. The White Paper admits that "much mental illness, some of it serious, goes untreated".

We have not only lost knowledge and skill, we have sacrificed good working relationships between medical and nursing personnel and social workers. Patients' needs do not come in packages neatly labelled "medical" and "social". They come in a tangle of emotions and insupportable situations in which physiological, psychological and social factors overlap and interact.

What is happening to people who are mentally ill? The short answer is that we have little idea. Though there are some elaborate schemes for record-linkage between hospitals, and a good deal of clinical research is in progress, there is little or no work on tracer studies. As the length of stay in hospital gets steadily shorter, and patterns of care diversify, the value of a purely service-oriented view of the course of the patient's illness steadily diminishes. We know what happens while he is in hospital, or while he is in touch with a social worker. But in many cases, these periods are now comparatively brief, and separated by long spells of non-contact. The patient becomes visible for a few days or weeks, gets treated or case-worked, and goes away again. What happens during the periods of official non-contact? Who helps him? Who rejects him? What factors in community life aid or retard his recovery? If community care is ever to be seen in terms of care *by* the community in any real sense, it is on this sort of knowledge that policy will depend.

References

1. Goffman, E. (1962) *Asylums*, Doubleday, New York.
2. Kesey, K. (1972) *One Flew Over the Cuckoo's Nest*, Methuen.
3. WHO (1953) World Health Organisation, *Third Report of Expert Committee on Mental Health*, Technical Report Series No. 73, Geneva.
4. Querido, A. (1968) *The Development of Socio-Medical Care in the Netherlands*, Routledge & Kegan Paul, Chapter 6.
5. IHF (1963) *International Hospital Federation, Proceedings of the Thirteenth International Hospital Congress, Paris.*
6. Lambo, T. A. (1968) Patterns of Psychiatric Care in Developing African Countries: The Nigerian Village Program, in H. O. David (ed.), *International Trends in Mental Health*, McGraw-Hill.
7. Milbank Memorial Fund (1960) *Steps in the Development of Integrated Psychiatric Services*, New York. Quotations are from pp. 18 and 76.
8. Main, T. F. (1946) The hospital as a therapeutic institution, *Bulletin of the Menninger Clinic*, 10.
9. Jones, M. (1952) *Social Psychiatry*, Tavistock Publications, London.
10. Rapoport, R. (1961) *Community as a Doctor*, Tavistock Publications, London.
11. Manning, N. P. (1976) What Happened to the Therapeutic Community, in K. Jones (ed.), *Year Book of Social Policy in Britain*, Routledge.
12. NAMH (1961) National Association for Mental Health, *Report of Annual Conference*, London.
13. Joint Committee on Mental Illness and Health (1961) Final Report, *Action for Mental Health*, Basic Books, New York.
14. Jones, K. (1972) *A History of the Mental Health Services*, Routledge & Kegan Paul. Chapters 13 and 14 give a fuller account of this process.
15. Hansard (1971) *House of Commons Reports*, HMSO, London 879, 280-1.
16. DHSS (1975) Department of Health and Social Security, *Better Services for the Mentally Ill*, Cmnd. 6233, HMSO, London.

CHAPTER 2

Joint Approaches to Community Care

PETER M. JEFFERYS
Northwick Park Hospital and Shenley Hospital and Division of Psychiatry,
Clinical Research Centre, Harrow

We have seen in the previous chapter the effects of successive attempts to "integrate" the psychiatric services into general medical or social work divisions. In the following pages, we will be examining the administrative barriers to cooperation between services and ways in which these can be overcome even within the existing legislative framework. A reference to the many departments and individuals involved in community mental health care gives an indication of the size and complexity of the problem.

Community Care

In the United Kingdom, Community Care for people with psychiatric disorders is provided at primary and secondary levels. The bulk of psychiatric disorder is treated in the community at primary level,[1] by a variety of primary carers including: family doctors, social workers, health visitors, clergymen, friends, families and volunteers. At the secondary level, community care is the community provision for those people with severe psychiatric disorder, whom psychiatrists would otherwise treat in hospital. Secondary community psychiatric care involves psychiatrists and other members of their specialist teams, but also relies on many of the personnel working at primary level. In addition to personnel, facilities such as day hospitals and day centres and residential accommodation for the mentally ill are required. Improvements in psychiatric services in the 1980s will depend largely on the provision of high quality secondary community care. Constructive collaboration and sharing between Social Services, specialist psychiatric services, housing departments, voluntary agencies and primary carers is required together with the necessary staffing and funding for all these services.

Community Psychiatry

Community psychiatry has many definitions. A traditional view is that it refers to the provision and use of resources outside the hospital for the care and treatment of the mentally ill. But in common with most members of the Working Party on Services of the Community and Social Psychiatry Group of the Royal College of Psychiatrists,[2] I favour Sabshin's definition: community psychiatry involves "the utilisation of the techniques, methods, theories of social psychiatry and other behavioural sciences to investigate and to meet the mental health needs of a functionally or geographically defined population over a significant period of time, and the feeding back of information to modify the central body of social psychiatric and other behavioural science knowledge".[3] In other words, the place *where* care is given is less important than testing out and evaluating new methods and changing *what* care is given as a result. This means a continuous process of shared care, with an acknowledgement that the provision of continuing care where needed is more important than *where* (i.e. hospital or outside) care is given.

The personnel and facilities from a variety of services or agencies must be used in a coordinated way effectively to meet these needs. How to achieve this goal of coordination between services is our challenge.

Joint Approaches

Joint approaches to community psychiatric care can be at a variety of levels. These range from shared involvement at a personal level between members of a multidisciplinary team treating an individual client or family through various ways of sharing facilities or resources to meet the needs of certain patient or client groups, through to genuine joint planning and development perhaps involving joint financing and formally shared responsibility. The commitments, problems and benefits of collaboration at these different levels are not the same and need to be distinguished. A recent paper on *Collaboration between Health and Social Services* by Brunel[4] provides a particularly thorough analysis of many of the problems in this area, placing particular emphasis on distinguishing different levels of multidisciplinary interaction. I intend to outline some key problems, starting with those related to joint planning and continuing with the problems of collaboration at an individual patient care level.

Joint Planning

The circular recently issued by the Department of Health and Social Security[5] on Joint Care Planning suggests that effective joint planning between health and local authorities should "secure the best balance of services and make the most effective use of the resources available for the elderly, the disabled, the mentally handicapped, the mentally ill, children and families and for socially handicapped groups such as alcoholics and drugs addicts". The aim of the Secretary of State is to "encourage joint planning by health and local authorities in which each authority contributes to all stages of the other's planning, from the first steps in developing common policies and strategies to the production of operational plans to carry them out". This circular and its predecessor in 1976[6] followed clear recognition that services had not developed in a coordinated manner; "the balance of existing facilities − health and social services − bears increasingly less relation to acknowledged needs".[7] Professor Goldberg has commented strongly on the inadequacy of community provision for the mentally ill and handicapped.[8]

(a) *Health and local authority reorganisations*

It is painfully clear to many of us that reorganisation in itself can hinder progress in joint planning even when intentions are the opposite. Both health and local authorities have suffered recently. Organisations preoccupied or overwhelmed by internal change are unlikely to be well equipped for negotiation or collaboration with other organisations or services.

According to Sir Keith Joseph[9] National Health Service Reorganisation was undertaken "solely in order to improve the health care of the
public" and the White Paper stressed that "the Health Services depend
crucially on the humane planning and provision of the personal social
services and therefore on effective and understanding collaboration with
local Government". The Government was concerned "to see that
arrangements are evolved under which a more coherent and smoothly
interlocking range of services will develop for all the needs of the
population". National Health Service Reorganisation in 1974 created a
new level of authority — the Area Health Authority — with responsibility
for one or more Health Districts including family practitioner services and
former local authority Community Health Services as well as the hospital
services. New management and planning structures were introduced at a
variety of levels.

The "grey book" entitled *Management Arrangements for the
Reorganised National Health Service*[10] appeared to suggest a planning
function for almost everyone. "All levels in the reorganised NHS have a
part to play at all times in the planning process" (para. 33). More
specifically it was suggested that the AHAs would set policies and
standards for their Areas as a whole, allocate resources to Districts, plan
services to be provided in Districts, plan directly certain Area-level services
and collaborate with local authorities in planning.

Regional Health Authorities would be responsible for developing a
strategy for the development of services in their Regions, in particular for
major building developments and for allocating resources to AHAs. The
Secretary of State would be ultimately responsible for determining the
overall objectives and priorities of the NHS and for allocating resources to
RHAs. In addition, Districts were to prepare and implement their own
plans but with involvement by higher authority levels in a variety of ways.

Local authorities experienced a radical internal restructuring of their
social service departments following Seebohm, and outside London many
have been amalgamated into larger authorities. However, the responsibilities of the larger local authorities are not uniform across the country. In
Metropolitan districts (outside London), Personal Social Services, School
Health, Environmental Health and Housing are the responsibility of a
single local authority, but in non metropolitan centres although the
County Council has responsibility for Personal Social Services, and School

Health, many smaller District Councils are responsible for housing. In Inner London, Personal Social Services and some housing are Borough responsibilities, but education is run by an Inner London Education Authority and the Greater London Council also has major housing and environment responsibilities.

Transfer of hospital social work responsibility from the health service to local authority in 1974 accompanied the more substantial changes and many psychiatrists and hospital social workers were very unhappy about the transfer.

Some joint ventures in mental health suffered as a consequence of social services reorganisation and the fragmentation of mental health departments. Some former mental health departments possessed sufficient political and professional expertise to persuade both their local authority and their psychiatric services to invest resources in joint developments, and developed model services, which have since been disrupted.

(b) *Geographical factors*

In spite of the boundary changes following NHS and local authority reorganisation, coterminosity has not been achieved at many levels, and hinders joint planning approaches, specially at district level. The catchment area of an Area Social Services Office is larger than that of a health centre and commonly smaller than a health district. Many health district boundaries, particularly in urban areas cross either local authority or area social services boundaries. Mental hospital catchment areas traditionally followed local authority boundaries but the combination of local authority changes, moves towards the provision of a district based service and the pressure to conform to health district boundaries have complicated the picture. Geography can also create major difficulties for local authority social service departments trying to provide services for the mentally ill in collaboration with the health services. County authorities probably have most problems. They often cover enormous areas, sometimes with difficult topography and personal contact between hospital staff, patients and social workers can be difficult to maintain because of time spent in travelling.

(c) *Priorities*

Over the past five years few local authorities have awarded provision for mental illness a high priority faced with competing legislative and public expectations for services for children, young people and the elderly. One contributing factor may have been that few Directors of Social Services had extensive previous mental health experience. Despite the priority formally given by the DHSS for some years to mental health services, this has not been reflected in the spending of health authorites.[11] In 1973-74, for example, both the amount in real terms and the share of overall resources for mental illness had actually dropped over the previous decade. Central guidelines on priorities[12,13] are likely to continue to be largely ignored at local level in health and social services, with their eagerness for local autonomy. Mental illness and handicap services are most likely to suffer because of their low status and MIND[11] therefore argues that these services have to receive special consideration.

(d) *Planning and management structures*

There are major differences between the management structures of local authorities and the health service. Management relationships and responsibilities are particularly complex in the health service at district level with its emphasis on consensus. Decisions about finance and other resource allocations are made in different ways in the two services. Planning programmes and cycles do not coincide, and there is no uniform local authority planning system. Few managers based in one service adequately understand planning procedures in the other. There has been little data sharing between planners, and health districts have been short of planning expertise.

Communication between managers and planners within the different components of the Health Service has often been either complicated or inadequate. Similarly liaison and communication between different local authority departments such as Education, Housing and Social Services has often been cumbersome or inadequate.

Within the health service there has been confusion about the levels for planning between district, area and region. Part of the confusion has arisen because strategic and operational planning and consultation have not been clearly distinguished, but rivalries have also played a part. Multidistrict areas and those with complicated management arrangements for mental hospitals have had particular problems. Social services input to district health service planning teams has often lacked top management commitment, and been rather passive. Social service planners have rarely invited contributions by health service professionals in their planning processes.

Joint Consultative Committees were established with Health Service reorganisation specifically to provide a planning forum in which health and local authority could consult each other and collaborate. They were created at Area Health Authority level because local authority boundaries were more often coterminous with AHA boundaries than health district boundaries. It is perhaps too early to judge the effectiveness of this forum. Because it is only a consultative forum it has a limited role. Joint Consultative Committee proposals and plans have no more strength than the collective willingness and abilities of all the interested statutory authorities concerned to implement their own posts.

Although psychiatrists can often legitimately complain that they have not been consulted by Social Service Departments on mental health developments, it should be recognised that Social Service Departments commonly face a dilemma over whom to consult. Because of the autonomy of individual consultants full consultation between them all and social services can be a lengthy and frustrating experience. Since 1974 most AHAs have appointed a Specialist in Community Medicine (Social Services) with responsibility for collaboration between health and social services. The specific job descriptions for these Area-based staff show considerable variation reflecting widespread differences in their training and previous experience, as well as differing strategies toward Social Services liaison. Few have so far played a substantial role in Local Authority planning teams, although most have been involved with health service planning at one or more levels. Personal liaison between the Specialist (Social Services) and clinicians at district level is not easy in most district areas and many psychiatrists are still unsure of their potential contribution in community care.

Many local authorities have nominated an officer for health service liaison for mental illness, but the level of seniority has varied. In some authorities the appointment has been at Assistant Director level and the holder has been well equipped to participate in collaborative planning activities, but elsewhere more junior appointments have been made.

Voluntary organisations previously had no place in either health or local authority planning structures even though the resources or facilities they provided were essential for high quality community care.

Collaboration for Individual Care

Whatever the management arrangements or resource allocation effective partnership in the care of patients rests on personal understanding and cooperation by individual doctors, nurses, social workers and increasingly volunteers. But within psychiatry in particular, the nature of teamwork is changing quite fast as well as the membership of the team and the experience and expectations of its members. The St. Augustine's Enquiry[14] highlighted for many the questions of authority and responsibility within psychiatric teams.

Effective collaboration in individual cases can be undermined by lack of clarity in agreed referral patterns between health and social services and also as to who is supposed to be carrying prime responsibility at any time. Should a psychiatrist without an attached team social worker make a direct referral to a day centre manager or hostel warden, or ask an Area-based social worker to make the referral for him? Should an experienced social worker refer a client with a major psychiatric illness direct to the specialist services or first to the general practitioner with a hint that specialist referral would be helpful?

Whether working closely together in a team or more casually, the prime responsibilities of health and social services staff are distinct and need to be understood. The Brunel Working Party[4] suggests the following distinction:

(i)   There is prime responsibility for the case seen as one of actual or potential "social distress" and thus coming within the aegis of the Local Authority as the responsible body.

(ii) There is prime responsibility for the case seen as one of actual or potential "ill health".

The Royal College of Psychiatrists[15] recently discussed multidisciplinary teamwork in a policy statement entitled "The Responsibilities of Consultants in Psychiatry". It comments on the confusion between team functioning at management and administrative levels and at clinical levels and on the variety of interpretations about teamwork at a clinical level. Rejecting the idea that each member of a team should have equal status in all matters, the College suggests that the legal, professional, ethical, diagnostic and prescriptive responsibilities of the medical profession cannot be delegated to a multidisciplinary group when treating an individual patient. The relationship of hierarchical management to multidisciplinary teams at ward level is discussed in the context of questions such as "Can the authority of any one person override the team decision? Has a team decision any real authority when opposed to hierarchical management authority?" After warning about idealistic, impractical and irresponsible approaches to multidisciplinary teamwork the College recommended that "Multidisciplinary team functioning should be seen as an option, not as a rigid pattern and there should be discretion at ward level".

To some extent the College statements can be seen as a cautious reaction against the simplistic prescription of "multidisciplinary teams" as a solution for all the inadequacies of the mental illness services in this country. Perhaps a clearer and more positive description of multi-disciplinary teamwork comes in the Trethowan Report: [16]

> "As we understand it, multidisciplinary teamwork implies the mutual recognition, by the members of the different professions concerned, of a shared responsibility for patient care. This does not, we must emphasise, mean that every decision affecting a patient will necessarily be a team decision. Each profession has its own sphere of competence and its members are responsible for the decisions within that sphere. They are also individually responsible for recognising the limits of their own competence and enlisting the involvement of their colleagues when this becomes necessary. The decisions which involve the team as a whole are those concerning the patient's care as a whole which involve a choice between different forms of professional intervention." (para 5.2.4).

For social workers in a team the doctor's authority can be a sensitive issue. While it is generally recognised that a senior doctor will often lead the team, any attempt by the doctor to tell the social worker what to do and how to do it (i.e. exercising, prescribing or managerial authority),[4] is likely to be seen as a challenge to the professionalism of social work. Certainly some doctors find the increasing professionalism of social workers difficult to accept or understand. An untrained or experienced junior Social Worker is unlikely to impress the senior doctor who questions the professionalism of social work and runs the risk of either trying to work "for" the doctor or becoming alienated. In multidisciplinary hospital teams it is probably particularly important to have a competent and experienced social work input.

Social workers have additionally had to cope with a fashion for generic social work which disturbed many psychiatrists. Controversy about attachment arrangements for social workers (following transfer of hospital social workers to local authorities) has often confused several distinct, albeit overlapping issues. Some of these issues are geographical location, professional autonomy and accountability, status, specialisation, team-work and training. Many of these issues have been discussed at length by various working parties,[17,18,19] and I shall not discuss them in great detail. As a consequence of some of these changes personal collaboration has sometimes been less successful or more complicated than previously.

Poor psychiatrist/social worker liaison in some areas has resulted in attempts being made to plug the gap with nurses from the rapidly growing community psychiatric nursing teams. Insufficient attention has been given to the evaluation of community psychiatric nursing services, and some enthusiasts have failed to recognise that nurses do not possess the skills of professionally trained social workers. It is also unfortunate that liaison developments between general practitioners and social workers at the primary level which could have relevance for improved psychiatric community care have received comparatively little attention.[20]

Voluntary Organisations

Voluntary organisations, particularly those linked to MIND (National Association for Mental Health) and leagues of friends associated with mental hospitals have established a variety of services and facilities to complement health and social services provision in the community.[21]

These range from hostels for the mentally ill to group homes, sheltered workshops, clubs, day centres, counselling[22] and befriending schemes.

Many of these developments have been innovations from which professionals have learnt much. Coordination with health and social services has usually been casual, and relevant professionals have often been members of the voluntary groups. Few voluntary service coordinators or organisers within the health service or local authority have yet focussed on joint approaches specifically for psychiatric patients living outside hospital.

Voluntary organisations have made some important contributions to central health service policy, often using a variety of political channels, and are beginning to have more say at local level through community health councils and involvement of individual AHA and LA members.

Proposals

Agreement on objectives

For the 1980s there cannot be a single joint approach to psychiatric community care. A variety of approaches are needed at different levels. An essential ingredient is that there should be broad agreement on objectives and the desired pattern of provision and service for people with psychiatric disorders in a district or area. In my view the White Paper *Better Services for the Mentally Ill* is a most useful starting point for the strategic discussions.[9]

The Government's broad policy objectives for mental illness services are as follows:

"First is an expansion of local authority personal social services to provide residential, domiciliary, day care and social work support. The second is the relocation of the specialist services in local settings. The third is the establishment of the right organisational links: between area social work teams and the social work staff in day centres and residential care, and between the multiprofessional therapeutic teams and the primary care services; between the health service and local authority social services administrators and planners; between professional and lay people. The fourth is a significant improvement in staffing to enable individual patient needs to be assessed and reviewed on a multi professional basis and to provide for earlier intervention and preventive work. A coordinated strategy meeting all four objectives should minimise the risks of fragmentation and selectivity."

Joint planning

The provision for genuine joint planning between health and local authority services must be made clearer and be supported by both services. The limitations of district health care planning teams must be acknowledged. Professionals at district level are likely to be best equipped for discussion of day to day problems or short term plans, and district planning teams rarely include members with any substantial experience of strategic planning. But I see an important watchdog role for district mental health care planning teams serving as a committed multidisciplinary group helping to identify problems in local services, initiating and assessing local developments and trying to ensure that mental health services receive priority. Elsewhere in this volume Godber[23] describes the development of an experimental sheltered housing scheme in Southampton which was first designed and planned in a district health care planning team. This planning team for the elderly included a senior representative from the Housing Department as well as social services and medical staff. The close collaboration and cooperation first demonstrated at the district planning level was followed by the formation of a joint steering group responsible for the running of the project.

Where planning expertise is available or concentrated at area level I think areas should give specific support and guidance to districts and improve training for planners at district level. I welcome the suggestion[5] that voluntary organisations should be able to participate in district planning either by direct representation or via Community Health Council nomination.

District Management Teams must take the initiative in developing personal links with Directors of Social Services and other senior officers and learn to consult them constructively, particularly on topics where health and social service provision overlap.

Assuming that personal social services remain the responsibility of local authorities then the joint forums at area level assume major importance. The Joint Care Planning Teams at area level must include the most senior officers from the local authority relevant to the task. Area officers and specialists and district representatives must be involved and I think there should be a subcommittee for mental health.

Area Health Authorities and local authorities need to make a major effort to facilitate joint planning. Radical reappraisal of their planning structures is needed to avoid excessive duplication of work and increase in committee hours. Realignment of planning cycles to facilitate joint planning should receive a high priority. In many areas unless some of the coterminosity issues are resolved authorities are not likely to invest time and effort in joint planning.

Stockport[24] appear to have modified and linked their health and local authority planning structures in an imaginative way to improve joint planning. Particular features in Stockport have been the participation by The Area Health Authority (who fund two staff members) in a joint research and intelligence unit within the local authority's corporate planning unit and the formation of an area planning team comprising three AHA officers with special responsibility for planning together with the Council's coordinator of central units. The latter group has the broad function of advising the area management team on matters connected with planning generally and briefing and coordinating the work of all health care planning teams. In addition the area planning team links with specific local authority programme teams to serve as a joint care planning team providing advice to the joint consultative committees via a combined officers group. Similar initiative and experiment should be encouraged in the recognition that effective planning systems designed to facilitate joint planning are likely to vary in composition between districts according to local circumstances. Health authorities should not be expected to form absolutely identical planning systems.

Joint financing

Joint financing is an important development, especially relevant for community care for the mentally ill. The expansion of the scheme and its increased flexibility[5] are welcome developments, and I hope it provides a stimulus for authorities to use existing resources and services more flexibly and imaginatively. It will probably be necessary for the joint finance to be the major permanent revenue source for selected projects. Joint financing appears to have stimulated increasing interest in the health service among local politicians, which should help community psychiatric care.

Earmarking for psychiatry

Political and financial devolution is a current fashion and likely to work to the disadvantage of the low status mental health services where they have to compete at district level with acute specialties for scarce resources. Area Health Authorities and local authorities should be obliged to insist that health districts and social services departments spend a specific proportion of revenue and capital on mental health and handicap services. The specific allocation would of course need to be related to the quality and level of existing services, but would in effect be an "earmarking" of funds for these services. Earmarking may not be politically popular at the present time, especially with economic recession, but may be essential for the development of community psychiatry in the 1980s. Provision of community facilities for the mentally ill should also be made mandatory. I envisage a central directive asking health and local authorities to reach a minimum tolerable level of provision as a first step. With time, an increasing fraction of mental health revenue would be routed through joint financial arrangements.

A joint corporation?

In their evidence to the Royal Commission, the BMA and several other groups have suggested the reorganisation and incorporation of personal social services within the health service. A variety of motives lie behind these proposals, including mistrust of politicians both in local government and centrally. In the immediate future reorganisation would be too costly and in any case mental health has not done particularly well so far out of either local authority or health service reorganisation. But if local authorities and the health service prove incapable of working together constructively in joint care planning teams and joint consultative committees and fail to improve community facilities for the mentally ill such radical proposals will need re-examination within the next five years.

Joint projects

Joint financing should be used to sponsor or fund a variety of ventures to which health, social services and voluntary services might contribute to varying extents. Flexible use of personnel and resources should be the key note. It should be possible, for example, to second a trained psychiatric nurse to work within a day centre or hostel or designated home for the elderly mentally infirm. Most innovations in community psychiatric care have relied on skilled personnel working in a novel setting. Voluntary associations have often been most imaginative and joint funding and flexible staffing could enable more of their ideas to be tried. The expertise to evaluate developments in this area also needs to be developed.

Social work developments

Brunel[4] have usefully summarised some of the possible strategies which could be used to improve collaboration between social workers and health workers at the case level. One of the most important changes often needed is in the personal attitudes of the staff concerned, and formal educative or re-educative programmes may have particular relevance. The Working Party on Social Work Support for the Health Service[18] placed particular emphasis on the training responsibilities of health service staff for social services personnel. The subsequent Working Party Report on Manpower and Training for the Social Services[19] has an important chapter on relationships between social services and other public services. The report devotes only seven paragraphs to health and manages to discuss penal services in the same seven paragraphs. It is unfortunate that this important training report largely ignored the positive contribution of health service personnel to social services training.

The three major strategies for linking social workers to health service institutions are alignment, outposting or attachment. With an alignment arrangement all hospital social work referrals would be dealt with by one Area Social Work Office. Alternatively, one or more full or part time social workers could be outposted from an area team to a hospital. Still closer links could be established by the attachment of a social worker to a specific clinical team, creating a multidisciplinary team in which a high degree of personal identification, commitment and permanency is called for. A variety of factors such as availability of social work staff, size of hospital, volume of referrals and the character of the social work task inside and outside the hospital will have a bearing on the most desirable model.

There are strong arguments for social work attachment to psychiatric units and services because of the need for close liaison in psychiatric treatment. But special arrangements will need to be made to ensure continuity of social work care for people with mental illness within and outside the hospital. Various permutations need to be tried and evaluated. Hospital attached social workers could maintain responsibility for selected patients following discharge; area based social workers could follow clients into hospital and out again; joint appointment social workers with sessional attachments to both hospital teams and area offices could either maintain personal continuity of care or supervise less experienced colleagues in area offices.

The health service has been preoccupied with the question of how to get better social work for the health service. Much less attention has been given to the ways in which the health service can provide help for social services in residential settings, day centres or area offices. Psychiatrists provide support on a sessional basis for many local authority children's homes and a growing number now attend psychiatric day centres and residential homes for the elderly. Their time has been used in two main ways. Most commonly psychiatrists have seen individual children or adults for assessment or treatment, but increasingly they have joined in staff meetings or groups in which advice and supervision is given by the psychiatrist who may not himself see the child or adult under discussion. These latter sessions are likely to have a strong educational and training component. Similar sessions are provided by psychiatrists in some Area Social Work Offices with field work staff. These developments need to be evaluated but their expansion is likely to improve collaboration in the health care of the mentally ill.

Community nurses (district nurses and health visitors) are likely to play a larger part in caring for the elderly in residential homes for old people,[25] and it is possible that psychiatric nurses may work more closely with local authority day centres and hostels for the mentally ill. Many of the Group Homes for the mentally ill established by Social Services Departments or Voluntary Associations are successfully supported by community psychiatric nurses in association with social workers and volunteers.

Whatever the formal links or arrangements between health and social services, in a district psychiatric service personal acquaintance and contact between individuals are essential ingredients, and efforts must be made in both services to facilitate these.

Elsewhere in this volume Miss Goldberg discusses the nature of the Social Work task and stresses the need to analyse the possible contribution of social workers at Area Offices, GP surgeries and in hospital. Following such analysis and research it should be possible to make more rational decisions about the allocation of specific tasks and the place of the specialist social workers. Specialisation in mental health should be encouraged both for some area based social workers as well as those attached to psychiatric teams.

References

1. Shepherd, M., Cooper, B., Brown, A. C. and Kalton, G. W. (1966) *Psychiatric Illness in General Practice*, OUP, London.
2. Corbett, J. A. (1977) *Models of Community Psychiatry*, Report of the Working Party on Services of the Community and Social Psychiatry Group of the Royal College of Psychiatrists, (Unpublished draft).
3. Sabshin, M. (1966) Theoretical Models in Community and Social Psychiatry, In *Community Psychiatry*, L. M. Roberts, S. L. Halbeck & M. D. Loeb (eds.), University of Wisconsin Press, Madison.
4. Brunel Institute of Organisation and Social Studies (1976) *Collaboration between Health and Social Services – A Working Paper*, Brunel University, Uxbridge, Middlesex.
5. DHSS (1977a) *Joint Care Planning: Health and Local Authorities*, HC(77)17, LAC(77)10.
6. DHSS (1976b) *Joint Care Planning: Health and Local Authorities*, HC(76)18, LAC(76)6.
7. DHSS (1975) *Better Services for the Mentally Ill*, Cmnd. 6233, HMSO, London.
8. Goldberg, D. (1977) Technological Developments in Social Psychiatry: Implication for Services, In *New Methods of Mental Health Care*.
9. DHSS (1972a) *National Health Service Reorganisation: England*, Cmnd. 5055, HMSO, London.

10. DHSS (1972b) *Management Arrangements for the Reorganised National Health Service*, HMSO, London.
11. MIND (1977) Mind's evidence to the Royal Commission on the NHS with regard to services for mentally ill people, National Association for Mental Health, London.
12. DHSS (1976a) *Priorities for Health and Personal Social Services for England*, HMSO, London.
13. DHSS (1977b) *The Way Forward*, HMSO, London.
14. South East Thames Regional Health Authority (1976) Report of Committees of Enquiry, St. Augustine's Hospital, Chartham, Canterbury, SETRHA, London.
15. Royal College of Psychiatrists (1977) The responsibilities of consultants in psychiatry within the National Health Service, *Bulletin of the Royal College of Psychiatrists*, September 1977, 4-7.
16. DHSS (1977c) *The Role of Psychologists in the Health Services*, Report of the Sub-Committee, HMSO, London.
17. DHSS (1973) *Reorganisation of the National Health Service and Local Government in England and Wales*, Report from the Working Party on Collaboration between the NHS and Local Government on its activities to the end of 1972, HMSO, London.
18. DHSS (1974) Report of the Working Party on Social Work for the Health Service, HMSO, London.
19. DHSS (1976c) *Manpower and Training for the Social Services*, Report of the Working Party, HMSO, London.
20. Goldberg, E. M. (1977) The Role of the Social Worker in General Practice, In *New Methods of Mental Health Care*.
21. Ennals, D. (1977) The Role of the Voluntary Services in a Future Mental Health Service. (Unpublished paper).
22. Hatswell, V. (1977) The Case for Counselling, In *New Methods of Mental Health Care*.
23. Godber, C. (1977) An Experiment in Sheltered Housing and Collaboration, In *New Methods of Mental Health Care*, Chapter 13.
24. Paine, R. E. and Epps, B. M. (1977) Local and Health Authority Joint Planning: Stockport's Approach (Mimeographed), Stockport Metropolitan Borough.
25. DHSS (1977d) *Residential Homes for the Elderly, Arrangements for Health Care, A Memorandum of Guidance*, Welsh Office.

CHAPTER 3

Drug Research and Mental Health Services

MALCOLM LADER
Institute of Psychiatry, University of London

Introduction

As with most other branches of medicine, some of the most important advances in psychiatry have concerned the discovery, development and introduction of new drugs. Evaluation of the effectiveness and safety of these drugs is particularly difficult in psychiatry where objective measures of improvement are unavailable so that subjective impressions by psychiatrists, nurses, social workers, patients and their relatives must suffice. Indeed, "improvement" itself may be a value judgement. For example, increased activity and initiative by a schizophrenic patient may gratify the social worker attempting to find him a job but may be less welcome to harrassed nursing staff in a ward of disturbed patients.

Because of these and other factors, much controversy among psychiatrists often surrounds the introduction of new compounds. The enthusiasts hail each apparent innovation as a break-through miracle about to revolutionise psychiatry; the pessimists recall many such false dawns and await change in their patients with cynicism. The experienced point out that it may take years (if ever) before the full balance-sheet of each drug becomes apparent. They catalogue the list of drugs which have raised false hopes of therapeutic advance only to prove more trouble than they were worth. Bromides and amphetamines are prime examples, thalidomide a chilling reminder of the catastrophes that can be unleashed by professional gullibility and industrial cupidity.[1]

Even when drugs have been introduced, found acceptance and gained respectability, their effects in practice may be unclear. The classic test for new drugs is to administer them in a controlled fashion, comparing them with placebos or with the standard medication, if any. Usually, neither the patient nor the assessor is aware which treatment is being administered at any time. This is a far cry from the hurly-burly of hospital wards or out-patient departments or the general practitioner's surgery. Here, many other factors operate — the relationship with the doctor, the patient and the doctor's attitude to the drug, previous experience, future expectations, compliance in taking the prescribed remedy, and so on. Extrapolation is not easy from the rigorous but artificially sterile conditions of the double-blind trial to the dust of the therapeutic arena.

The purpose of this paper is not to review all the advances (real or claimed) in pharmacotherapy and then to draw implications from them concerning the future requirements of the mental health services. This would necessitate a rare dual expertise in psychopharmacological research and epidemiological practice. Rather, certain illustrative examples of drug developments will be discussed, but from the viewpoint of the clinical scientist. The dangers of relying too heavily on such data in planning mental health services will be stressed. It is hoped that those concerned with such services will assess the claims of our therapeutic optimists with more realism and the proverbial grain of salt.

The Antipsychotic Drugs

Our first example concerns the antipsychotic drugs, also termed "major tranquillisers" or "neuroleptics". The prototypal member of this class was chlorpromazine introduced in 1953 to clinical practice. Its administration to disturbing patients resulted in marked improvement in the general climate of the wards as evidenced by a drop in such measures as hours of seclusion, number of broken windows, assaults on staff and use of restraint. Despite occasional dissident expression of distaste for this "chemical straitjacket", the use of chlorpromazine, and its allied compounds, has steadily increased. Indeed there have been allegations that these drugs have been used to quieten and render malleable inmates of non-medical institutions such as prisons and detention camps.

As well as this general "tranquillising" property, these drugs are widely used in acutely schizophrenic patients. There seems little doubt that their action is broadly "antipsychotic", that is, they lessen such phenomena as hallucinations, delusions and paranoid ideas. Claims that they are "antischizophrenic", i.e., have specific actions on the course of the schizophrenic illness, are not generally accepted. The consensus has emerged that these drugs curb the progress of the condition by curtailing the acute, initial attack and subsequent relapses. Both the personal and social sequelae of such relapses are attenuated. The effectiveness of antipsychotic medication is well-established. In one large American trial[2] thirteen areas of psychopathology were rated significantly more improved on drug than on dummy control treatment: social participation, confusion, self-care, hebephrenic symptoms, agitation and tension, slowed speech, incoherent speech, irritability, indifference to environment, hostility, auditory hallucinations, ideas of persecution and disorientation.

In chronically hospitalised schizophrenic patients, however, antipsychotic drugs have less effects on symptoms and behaviour than in more acutely ill patients.[3] Indeed, some studies have failed to show any significant advantages of drug over placebo.

Elucidation of the type of action of these drugs has obvious implications for psychiatric research. If these drugs were judged specific remedies for schizophrenia, finding out how they acted would tell us much about the disease itself. As relatively nonspecific "antipsychotics", their mode of action is of correspondingly less theoretical interest. Nevertheless, their use had profound practical implications for mental health services, in particular the hospitals. If drug therapy can rapidly improve acute schizophrenic patients and can expedite the rehabilitation of chronic schizophrenics, then the need for large custodial institutions would diminish. The advent of the major tranquillisers was most enthusiastically welcomed by psychiatrists working in huge, overcrowded hospitals which offered little more than custodial care. In New York State, for example, the resident population of the State hospitals, with schizophrenics as its core group, had increased steadily for fifty years until the mid-1950s. From this time, coinciding with the introduction of chlorpromazine, the numbers of long-stay patients have declined.

However, other work has suggested that this reversal of trend is not necessarily due to drug factors alone. Much regional and temporal variation in the discharge-rates from state mental hospitals in the USA was reported by Kramer.[4] Similarly, Lewis[5] has detailed the British experience in the 1950s. In December 1951 143,196 men and women inhabited the mental hospitals of England and Wales; in 1953, 146,643 and in 1957, 143,220. These fluctuations cannot be regarded as significant, certainly not with respect to the introduction of the antipsychotic agents in 1953-4. In many hospitals the decline in resident population was striking but was evident by the late-1940s, before the advent of the drugs.

Also, the size of the population inside the mental hospitals is not a good index of changing conditions. The quittance rate (the ratio of discharge and deaths in any year to total number of patients in hospital at any time during the year) was rising steadily from 1950 onwards. Lewis[5] identified potent influences other than the new drugs. He attributed much of the change to a vigorous reforming influence, chiefly characterised by an increasingly active out-patient and domiciliary service and a determined effort at rehabilitating chronic patients.

Shepherd, Goodman and Watt[6] found that the impact of pharmacotherapy on the population changes in an English county mental hospital was very small; the major amelioration of such indices as the death-rate and the duration of in-patient stay occurred between 1931-47 and probably followed an enlightened administrative policy. Essentially similar findings were described by Ødegard[7] in Norway.

Thus, it seems we must look for an interaction between social and pharmacological factors. In smaller, better-staffed institutions with intensive treatment regimens and vigorous rehabilitation programmes, drug effects were less easily discernible than in large custodial institutions. For example, Ødegard[7] found a significant negative correlation between pre-drug discharge rates from Norwegian mental hospitals and the improvement in discharge rates with drug therapy, i.e. the poorer the hospital originally, the greater its change. Furthermore, Linn[8] has shown that the introduction of antipsychotic medication can be followed by an increased discharge rate not only among the treated but also among the untreated patients. In wards where especially favourable conditions had been created, such as energetic social and occupational therapy, drug effects were not very evident.[9] In fact, disturbances on the ward were not related to the administration of drug or placebo but more to whether the nursing staff believed they were giving active medication.

This controversy of the early 1960s is not merely of historic interest: the implications for mental health services are profound. If the important issue is a concatenation of pharmacological and social factors, establishing optimal conditions is obviously complex. Is it better to concentrate on ensuring that hospitalised patients get effective medication or should the ward milieu be overhauled? If both are essential then the question is meaningless — both must be improved. However, in an imperfect world, economic and political considerations obtrude uncomfortably. Drug administration is much cheaper than scrapping our Victorian lunatic asylums situated fortress-like outside our county towns and cities. Their replacement can be justified on humanitarian, aesthetic, moral and medical grounds but the antipsychotic drugs cannot be used as a cheap substitute for proper institutional or community care.

We have seen how the importance of the antipsychotic drugs in fundamentally altering patterns of health care for schizophrenic patients has been exaggerated because it coincided with changes in public attitudes, legislation and social reform in our hospitals. This is not to gainsay the real therapeutic advances facilitated by these drugs. It is probable that some of the social changes could not have occurred or could not have been taken so far without the new drugs. It is much easier to discharge a chronic schizophrenic to the care of community services when he is no longer shouting back at his "voices".

The most telling evidence that the antipsychotic drugs control symptoms but not diseases comes from the realisation that "new" long-stay psychiatric patients are accumulating in the mental hospitals.[10] At the end of 1971, a census showed that nearly 23,000 people had been continuously resident from 1–5 years, constituting 21 per cent of the total mental hospital population. Of the remainder, 27 per cent had been in hospital less than a year, 52 per cent over 5 years, the "old chronics". Thus, on average, over 5,000 patients per year are failing to be maintained outside hospital. Mann and Cree estimated that a third of these people needed continuing hospital treatment, a third were capable of discharge if suitable accommodation in the community were forthcoming, and a third needed "asylum" on an indefinite basis.

These data should give pause to those policy-makers who urge that mentally ill people should stay in hospital only for medical or nursing reasons during the acute phase of their illness and then be discharged and maintained in the community. These recommendations seem based on an uncritical analysis of antipsychotic drug effects and potentialities, as well as unwarranted and unsophisticated extrapolations over time. The logical outcome was to press for the complete closure of the big mental hospitals with all that implied for staff morale, forward planning, etc. The lesson to be learned is that drug effects are easy to determine in the artificial context of a clinical trial but difficult to disentangle from social, economic and political influences in the larger epidemiological framework. Wishful thinking about the effectiveness of new medications is no substitute for a cautious appraisal of their practical usefulness, and should certainly not be the basis for major policy decisions.

Long-acting Antipsychotic Drugs

As well as being used in controlling symptoms in patients hospitalised for schizophrenia, the antipsychotic drugs are vital in preventing, or at least postponing, relapse in patients living in the community. The term "maintenance therapy" has been applied to this long-term treatment with antipsychotic drugs of schizophrenics in remission. Early studies (reviewed by Gittelman, Klein and Pollack, 1964)[11] used a variety of indices of patient adjustment including re-hospitalisation rate, work record, residual symptoms and social functioning. An analysis of over 20 controlled studies of antipsychotic medication administered for periods longer than one month concluded that patients taking drugs were much less likely to relapse than those maintained on placebo.[12] For example, Pasamanick and his associates[13] found that over 80 per cent of schizophrenics were able to remain outside hospital for 18 months or more when maintained on drugs whereas half of a control group given placebo relapsed. Similarly, Leff and Wing[14] reported that during the course of one year's maintenance therapy with phenothiazines, about a third of patients relapsed compared with four-fifths on placebo. Patients admitted to the study seemed to be drawn from the middle third of the range of schizophrenic patients with respect to prognosis. Patients with better prognosis did well without drugs; those excluded from the trial on the grounds of poor prognosis did badly in spite of standard drug treatment.

A complicating factor in such studies is that an undetermined proportion of patients who relapse either cease to take their drugs or reduce their dosage.[15] It is uncertain whether patients cease taking their drugs and then relapse or become more ill and then decide to stop their medication.

Another problem concerns the metabolism of antipsychotic drugs. When given by mouth, chlorpromazine and fluphenazine both undergo extensive metabolism in the liver after absorption from the gut.[16] About 85 per cent of chlorpromazine on average is broken down before it can reach the general circulation and thence the brain. The proportion with fluphenazine is over 90 per cent. Also, these proportions seem to vary from patient to patient, "rapid metabolisers" breaking down almost all of the drug given orally which thus cannot exert any useful effect.

A significant advance in the maintenance therapy of the remitted schizophrenic patient followed the introduction of the "long-acting depot" antipsychotic drugs.[17] Existing drugs, fluphenazine and flupenthixol, were formulated in such a way as to be soluble in vegetable oil. The drug can then be administered by the intramuscular injection of a few millilitres of the oil every 2–4 weeks. These drugs have such a prolonged action because they are only slowly absorbed from the depot into the circulation.

The rationale for the use of these drugs is threefold. Firstly, as the drug is injected, problems of drug defaulting can be minimised. The main reasons for drug defaulting are unpleasant side-effects or unpleasant expectations of side-effects, the patients' attitude to the use of drugs in their illness, and problems of communication between patient and prescriber. With the injectable antipsychotic agents, drug defaulting can never be covert — the patient either attends the clinic and has his injection or he defaults.

The second concerns the metabolism of the drug. By depositing it in a muscle, the drug is absorbed into the systemic circulation without running the gauntlet of first-pass metabolism in the liver. Thus, even rapid metabolisers of phenothiazines may show a gratifying response to the injections.

The third factor is the social supervision which a properly organised depot antipsychotic clinic can provide. The support can greatly decrease the defaulting rate. Thus, in one investigation, defaulting rates were as high as 34 per cent when non-psychiatrically trained community nurses were responsible for the injections and many agencies were involved in the supervision. When a single master register was instituted and all injections given by fully qualified psychiatric nurses trained to evaluate mental state and side effects, the defaulting rate fell to 14 per cent. Also, vigorous steps can be taken if social crises occur or if the patient reacts adversely to home, social or work circumstances.

It must not be thought that the depot antipsychotic drugs are a cure-all for schizophrenic patients in the community.[19] Social functioning often remains poor and the burden on the family may be onerous.[20] Probably about a third of patients on depot medication will relapse over a two-year period of whom a half will require hospital re-admission.[21] Nevertheless, this represents a clinical gain over oral medication of about 50 per cent, i.e. only half as many relapse on injections as on oral drugs. Thus, what might have been construed as a minor formulation variation, primarily for convenience, has had definite implications for mental health services. Special clinics have been set up to supervise patients on depot injections and the re-admission rate has been appreciably lowered.

Tranquillisers in General Practice

Our concern with mental hospitals and with special services for the mentally ill in the community should not blind us to the fact that most patients with psychological symptoms never see a psychiatrist nor contact the specialised agencies. The general practitioner copes with by far the largest proportion of mental illness in the community. For every psychotic patient mainly schizophrenic receiving care, there are a score of neurotic patients, anxious and depressed, consulting their family doctor for support and medication, and probably another thirty who struggle on with their anxiety, depression, insomnia and despair without seeking medical advice. The majority of those seeing their doctors receive drug treatment, primarily anxiety-relieving drugs, the tranquillisers (sedatives, anxiolytics). The introduction of new members of this class of drugs has been associated with an increase in their prescription to an alarming extent.

This has been treated as a novel phenomenon but mankind has used drugs affecting the mind for all recorded history and probably for many preceding millenia. Some of the drugs used have been highly dependence —

producing, for example, the opiate narcotics; others such as alcohol have proved disastrous for a vulnerable minority of the population. The twentieth century has witnessed a rapid growth in organic and pharmaceutical chemistry culminating in the introduction of drugs with profound effects on emotions, especially anxiety. Among the most widely used have been barbiturates, now being rapidly superseded by the benzodiazepines (e.g. chlordiazepoxide, "Librium", and diazepam, "Valium"). The benzodiazepines are ousting the barbiturates because: (1) they are more effective in alleviating anxiety and stress responses; (2) they are much safer in overdosage, accidental or deliberate; (3) they are less liable to induce physical dependence; and (4) they have less effect on liver metabolising enzymes and thus are less likely to interact adversely with other drugs given at the same time.

What is the extent of tranquilliser usage? A cross-national survey interviewed samples of individuals in nine Western European countries about such drug-taking and about their attitudes to these drugs.[22] In the United Kingdom 14 per cent of the adults admitted to taking tranquillisers at some time during the previous year. Male rates were about half those of the female. Regular daily use for one month or more was admitted by 8 per cent of adults, i.e. half of people taking tranquillisers. In general, usage was greater in North European countries than in Mediterranean countries. In the UK, 37 per cent of non-users but only 15 per cent of users thought the tranquillisers did more harm than good.

The prescription of psychotropic drugs has risen steadily. In 1965 in the UK, 38.5 million prescriptions were written for psychotropic drugs, the bulk being for tranquillisers and hypnotics; in 1971, 48.0 million, and by 1975 the total had reached 66 million. As a percentage of total prescriptions those for psychotropic drugs rose from 15.8-18.0 over these seven years.[23]

A recent survey of the prescription of medicines in general practice revealed that psychotropic drugs were prescribed more often than any other group, accounting for 17 per cent of prescriptions.[24] Diazepam was the most frequently prescribed of all drugs — 4.3 per cent of all prescriptions. During one year 9.7 per cent of the adult male population and 21.0 per cent of females received a prescription for at least one psychotropic drug. Nor do these figures include "hidden psychotropics", preparations containing sedatives combined with more important amounts of other agents for treating conditions such as dyspepsia or asthma. Psychotropic drug prescription was commoner for females than for males and increased sharply with age.

The extent of chronic drug usage can be gauged from figures for repeat prescriptions. Again psychotropic drugs head the list, comprising a quarter of all medicines taken for a year or more.[25] The commonest complaints for which these drugs were administered were "sleeplessness", "nerves" and depression.

The prescribing of tranquillisers, in particular the benzodiazepines, is obviously very extensive. Does this reflect genuine symptomatic distress in the recipients or are the drugs being used indiscriminately or even for recreational purposes?

Studies of minimal psychiatric morbidity vary widely in their estimates. One group of six general practitioners collaborating with a psychiatrist estimated that about one-fifth of patients seen in one day in an urban practice suffered from "stress disorders".[26] Quite clearly, such figures depend crucially on the definition of and the criteria for the condition under study. Thus in Kessel's[27] study of a London general practice, 50 per 1,000 of the adult population were diagnosed as suffering from a formal psychiatric illness. If the criteria were widened to include all patients with psychological disturbance, the prevalence rate rose to 90/1,000; if patients with physical symptoms for which no organic cause was detectable were added, the figure reached 380/1,000.

In an extensive study of London general practice, Shepherd and his colleagues[28] found that psychiatric morbidity was one of the commoner reasons for consultation. During the course of a year, on average 139 per 1,000 adults visited their doctor with psychological problems. Most patients with formal psychiatric illness fell into the neurotic category, mainly anxiety states; morbidity was twice as prevalent in females as in males. The mean of 139/1,000 for total morbidity prevalence conceals a range from 25/1,000 to 300/1,000 at risk. True differences in prevalence related to social class and mobility were discerned but the most important factor was the attitude of the general practitioner, those sympathetic to emotional problems having a high prevalence rate. Not only did emotionally disturbed people tend to gravitate to such doctors but also these doctors were more ready to diagnose psychological problems and to apply psychiatric labels.

However, the whole story is not disclosed by the numbers of patients seeing their family doctors. In the household survey of Taylor and Chave,[29] the prevalences of nervous symptoms were recorded in a satellite New Town and compared with data for a dormitory suburb and for a decaying inner area of London. The New Town was a socially planned community with full local work opportunities; the dormitory housing estate had good living and recreational facilities but poor social planning and few local work-places; the old area had poor housing usually with shared bathrooms, multiple occupancy and an above-average number of widows.

Nervous symptoms ("nerves", insomnia, depression and irritability) were reported by about a third of the subjects. The percentage of females reporting such symptoms was about twice that of the males; the percentage of positive responders tended to be highest in the lowest social class. The incidence of complaints, of what was dubbed "subclinical neurosis", was the same in all three milieux and Taylor and Chave acknowledge the importance of constitutional factors. The step from this subclinical syndrome to overt neurosis occurs when the patient becomes distressed and consults a doctor. This overt neurotic group varies in size according to the quantity and quality of general practice and specialist psychiatric services available.

These astonishingly high figures for the prevalence of subjective distress were confirmed in a survey using a standardised self-assessment for anxiety.[30] About 30 per cent of adults fell into the anxious range.

A survey combining self-reports of anxiety and questions about the use of tranquillisers confirmed the close relationship between them (Stoll and Lader, unpublished data). The use of tranquillisers was clearly linked to high anxiety scores, especially in women. Professional and managerial workers and their wives were the most likely to have taken tranquillisers but chronic usage was more firmly established among manual workers. When a person consulted his doctor about anxiety, insomnia and stress, a tranquilliser was prescribed in three-quarters of cases. In general, patients were quite pleased with the effectiveness of the benzodiazepines and regarded their prescription as a legitimate way for the doctor to deal with their problems.

From the above and other data, it would appear that the prevalence of anxiety and emotional distress is very high in the general population and that these problems are primarily treated symptomatically with tranquillisers. Many agencies are involved: the pharmaceutical industry discovers, develops, markets and promotes its drugs; the government exercises some control through expert committees, especially with regard to safety; the doctor primarily the general practitioner prescribes the drugs; the medicines are dispensed by pharmacists; the patient consumes the medication, or wastes them; and in the UK the taxpayer very largely foots the bill. The doctor is the keystone of this edifice: he is the cornucopia providing the drugs for the patient; he is the focus of the drug industry's promotional efforts; he is the government's bulwark against unwarranted or exaggerated claims. As the mixing of so many metaphorical roles extends to reality, the doctor is often bewildered and unsure what to prescribe.

The doctor is confronted by cohorts of patients complaining of physical and psychological symptoms which are manifestly the result of social or psychosocial stress. The doctor, unfitted because of inadequate training or unsuited because of lack of psychological empathy, "medicalises" the problem by concentrating on the symptom rather than the cause. He rounds off this inappropriate management by writing a prescription for a tranquilliser which reinforces the patient's belief that he is "ill". Thus is set in train a perpetual process with a chronically "ill" person receiving repeat prescriptions until death.

The social implications concern the consequences of treating symptomatically stress reactions to the common problems of living. More appropriate measures would seek to lessen the social difficulties of the individual. Instead the "patient" is persuaded to tolerate his problems and his responses are attenuated pharmacologically. In cost-effectiveness terms, tranquillisers are cheap. It costs less to sedate distraught housewives living in vertiginous isolation in tower blocks with nowhere for their children to play than it is to rehouse these families adequately.

The mental health services must recognise that the bulk of mental "disease" is seen by the general practitioner. It is neither appropriate, advisable nor feasible for community mental health services to assume responsibility for such a large segment of the population. Rather, people with special expertise should assist in the education of doctors, nurses, social workers and the general public. Tranquillisers should be relegated to temporary expedients while counselling services, self-help groups, relaxation classes and other approaches are mobilised. Not only will human distress be lessened but nemesis in the form of a widespread dependence problem may be avoided. Already, official moves have been initiated in several countries to curtail the prescribing of tranquillisers because of increasing problems of psychological dependence. Mental health professionals must instruct their colleagues in the best methods of dealing with their patients' problems.

Finally, the economics of alternative methods cannot be forgotten. As an extreme example, formal psychoanalysis — five 50-minute sessions per week for 3–5 years — even if proven effective could never be more than an expensive way for the rich to buy a sympathetic listener.[31] Brevity and economic feasibility must combine with effectiveness.

References

1. Sjöström, H. and Nilsson, R. (1972) *Thalidomide and the Power of the Drug Companies*, Penguin, Harmondsworth.
2. Goldberg, S. C., Cole, J. O. and Clyde, D. J. (1963) Factor analyses of ratings of schizophrenic behaviour, *Psychopharmacology Service Center Bulletin*, 2, 23-38.
3. Prien, R. F. and Klett, J. C. (1972) An appraisal of the long-term use of tranquillizing medication with hospitalized chronic schizophrenics: a review of the drug discontinuation literature, *Schizophrenia Bulletin*, 5, 64-73.
4. Kramer, M. (1959) Public health and social problems in the use of tranquilising drugs, In J. O. Cole & R. W. Gerard (eds.), *Psychopharmacology, Problems in Evaluation*, National Academy of Science, Washington, 108-42.
5. Lewis, A. (1959) Discussion of Dr. Brill's paper, In P. B. Bradley, P. Deniker & C. Radouco-Thomas (eds.), *Neuropsycho-pharmacology*, Elsevier, Amsterdam, 207-12.
6. Shepherd, M., Goodman, N. and Watt, D. C. (1961) The application of hospital statistics in the evaluation of pharmacotherapy in a psychiatric population, *Comprehensive Psychiatry*, 2, 11-19.
7. Ødegard, Ø. (1964) Pattern of discharge from Norwegian psychiatric hospitals before and after the introduction of the psychotropic drugs, *American Journal of Psychiatry*, 120, 772-8.
8. Linn, E. L. (1959) Drug therapy, milieu change and release from a mental hospital, *Archives of Neurology and Psychiatry*, 81, 785-94.
9. Rathod, N. H. (1958) Tranquillisers and patients' environment, *Lancet*, 1, 611-13.
10. Mann, S. A. and Cree, W. (1976) "New" long-stay psychiatric patients: a national sample survey of fifteen mental hospitals in England and Wales 1972/3, *Psychological Medicine*, 6, 603-16.
11. Gittelman, R. K., Klein, D. F. and Pollack, M. (1964) Effects of psychotropic drugs on long-term adjustment, a review, *Psycho-pharmacologia*, 5, 317-33.

12. Davis, J. M. (1975) Maintenance therapy in schizophrenia, *American Journal of Psychiatry*, 132, 1237-45.
13. Pasamanick, B., Scarpitti, F. R., Lefton, M., Dimitz, S., Wernent, J. J. and McPheeters, H. (1964) Home versus hospital care for schizophrenics, *Journal of the American Medical Association*, 187, 177-81.
14. Leff, J. P. and Wing, J. K. (1971) Trial of maintenance therapy in schizophrenia, *British Medical Journal*, 3, 599-604.
15. Mason, A. S., Forrest, I. S., Forrest, F. M. and Butler, H. (1963) Adherence to maintenance therapy and rehospitalization, *Diseases of the Nervous System*, 24, 103-4.
16. Curry, S. H., D'Mello, A. and Mould, G. P. (1971) Destruction of chlorpromazine during absorption in the rat *in vivo* and *in vitro*, *British Journal of Pharmacology*, 42, 403-11.
17. Johnson, D. A. W. (1977) Practical consideration in the use of depot neuroleptics for the treatment of schizophrenia, *British Journal of Hospital Medicine*, 17, 546-58.
18. Johnson, D. A. W. and Freeman, H. (1973) Drug defaulting by patients on long-acting phenothiazines, *Psychological Medicine*, 3, 115-19.
19. Watt, D. C. (1975) Time to evaluate long-acting neuroleptics? *Psychological Medicine*, 5, 222-6.
20. Stevens, B. C. (1973) Role of fluphenazine decanoate in lessening the burden of chronic schizophrenics on the community, *Psychological Medicine*, 3, 141-58.
21. Johnson, D. A. W. (1976) The expectation of outcome from maintenance therapy in chronic schizophrenic patients, *British Journal of Psychiatry*, 128, 246-50.
22. Balter, M. B., Levine, J. and Manheimer, D. I. (1974) Cross-national study of the extent of anti-anxiety/sedative drug use, *New England Journal of Medicine*, 290, 769-74.
23. Cooperstock, R. (1974) *Social Aspects of the Medical Use of Psychotropic Drugs*, Alcoholism and Drug Addiction Research Foundation of Ontario, Toronto.
24. Skegg, D. C. G., Doll, R. and Perry, J. (1977) Use of medicines in general practice, *British Medical Journal*, 2, 1561-3.
25. Dunnell, K. (1973) Medicine takers and hoarders, *Journal of the Royal College of General Practitioners*, 2, 23, 2-8.
26. Finlay, B., Gillison, K., Hart, D., Mason, R. W. T., Mond, N. C., Page, L. and O'Neill, D. (1954) Stress and distress in general practice, *Practitioner*, 172, 183-90.
27. Kessel, W. I. N. (1960) Psychiatric morbidity in a London general practice, *British Journal of Preventive and Social Medicine*, 14, 16-27.
28. Shepherd, M., Cooper, B., Brown, A. C. and Kalton, G. W. (1966) *Psychiatric Illness in General Practice*, OUP, London.
29. Taylor, L. and Chave, S. (1964) *Mental Health and Environment*, Longmans, London.
30. Salkind, M. R. (1973) The construction and validation of a self-rating anxiety inventory, Ph.D. Thesis, University of London.
31. Tancredi, L. R. and Slaby, A. E. (1977) *Ethical Policy in Mental Health Care*, Heinemann Medical, New York.

PART II

Prevention

CHAPTER 4

The Use of Community Care in Prevention

COLIN MURRAY PARKES
The London Hospital Medical College

Among the wide range of activities which have been included under the rubric of "community care" virtually every one can be regarded as a form of Preventive Psychiatry. In fact Gerald Caplan regards Preventive Psychiatry and Community Mental Health as terms which are almost synonymous.[1]

For the purposes of this chapter, however, I propose to limit myself to what are generally termed primary and secondary prevention, the prevention of mental disorder by measures which modify its causes or facilitate intervention before the full picture of mental illness has emerged. I shall not discuss tertiary prevention, the prevention of recurrence or the limiting of harmful secondary consequences of mental illness nor shall I examine the claims of those who believe that they can foster *positive* mental health. The former are discussed elsewhere in this volume and the latter remain the province of political and religious theorists rather than pragmatic psychiatrists.

In psychiatry multiple causes are the rule and it is rare to find a simple relationship between a mental illness and the life events which precede it. In a given case hereditary factors, intrauterine influences, the circumstances of birth and early childhood, the effects of upbringing and the events and circumstances which obtain in the life of the adult person all contribute to a particular outcome which we call a "mental illness". Conversely a particular life event such as retirement may be capable of contributing to a number of possible outcomes some of which we call mental illnesses, some psychosomatic disorders and some increments in health and

49

maturation.

Because of the complexity of these causal chains we should not expect the prevention of mental disorder to be simple. But that does not mean that we are not already in possession of a great deal of knowledge about a wide range of circumstances and events which contribute to increase the risk of mental illness in a population.

Most of these causal factors are social circumstances and events which impinge upon vulnerable sections of the community. It is therefore, reasonable to suppose that the increased focussing of psychiatric resources in the community (community care) will begin to make it possible for psychiatrists to work with other community agents to develop preventive intervention programmes. To some extent this is already happening and I shall refer to a number of projects which illustrate practical approaches to preventive intervention. But these are just the beginnings, the first awkward gropings towards new disciplines and new fields of study. We are only now able to glimpse the implications of these approaches. These are so wide and they call in question so many of our traditional assumptions that we view them with apprehension and we must proceed with caution to develop and evaluate by the most rigorous scientific methods at our disposal, each new programme of intervention.

In any form of preventive medicine the first step is to identify those members of the community who are at special risk of illness. The identification of high risk groups is possible with respect to both primary and secondary prevention. In the former case we must locate persons who are exposed to situations known to increase risk, in the latter case we must locate individuals who are showing early symptoms of incipient mental disorder.

A systematic list of high risk situations is given in the report of the Council of Europe's working party on The Organization of Preventive Services in Mental Illness.[2] The secretary of this group is its British representative, Rudolf Freudenberg. The Council of Europe's report is a most useful document, which not only helps us to identify sections of the population at special risk but also lists the front-line workers who are in a position to intervene to reduce that risk.

The high-risk situations are subdivided into those impinging upon Children, Adolescents, Adults and the Aged.* In each case the situation is

*See Appendix I at end of this chapter.

listed on the left, persons in a position to detect risk in the middle column and persons in a position to intervene to reduce risk in the right hand column.

To take one example, the battered baby is obviously at risk. It can be detected by neighbours, health visitors, general practitioners or hospital staff who are aware of the implications and who can notify an appropriate intervention service such as the local authority social workers or the NSPCC inspector. The action which he takes will usually include psychiatric consultation for the mother and a close liaison between the community worker and a psychiatrist is essential.

Another publication which will be of value in the planning of preventive services is the report of a working party of the Royal College of Psychiatry's Social and Community Psychiatry Group.[3] This was a mixed disciplinary working party which was set up to examine the use of psychiatric resources for indirect service to patients. It recognised from the outset that psychiatrists will never be able to provide direct support to more than a tiny proportion of those individuals who are psychologically disturbed let alone those at risk of becoming mentally ill and it discusses the ways in which the members of the district psychiatric team can work together to help plan, select and support front-line services. It urges a greater emphasis on the teaching of consultation skills to psychiatrists in training and outlines some of the pilot schemes that have already been set up to demonstrate how these preventive intervention services can operate.

Granted that we can now identify high risk groups and front-line workers who are in a position to help them, what type of help do we expect to be effective and what evidence do we have that preventive intervention can work? Here it seems to me that two overlapping conceptual models come into their own, these are the Developmental Model and the Psycho-social Transition Model.

The Developmental Model proposes that, at each stage of human development, there are certain physical and psychological circumstances which must obtain if the individual is to mature in a healthy manner. A great deal of research in recent years has demonstrated the damaging effects upon the young child of absent or inadequate parenting. The scientific literature in this field has been well reviewed by Wolff[4] and by Rutter[5] and a closely reasoned theory of parent-child interaction developed by John Bowlby in his three volume opus *Attachment and*

Loss.[6] Work in this field has already given rise to important changes in the care of children in institutions and foster care but its implications for community psychiatry have not been fully realised. It is important to recognise that we are not talking about medical fashions in child rearing which are likely to change when the next Truby King or Benjamin Spock comes along. Research into child development has achieved a high scientific standard and has implications which will outlast the anti-family fad and the wilder offshoots of the sexual revolution. Of particular importance is the discovery, in recent years, of the extent to which the damaging effects of parental separation and deprivation are reversible given appropriate substitute parenting. It remains to be seen whether education or therapeutic programmes can be devised which will improve the quality of parental behaviour where this is clearly inadequate.

The Psycho-social Transition Model proposes that any life event which requires a person to abandon one set of well-established major assumptions about his world and to develop another carries with it an increased risk to mental health. It provides a frame of reference within which the empirical findings of Brown,[7] Rahe[8] and Paykel[9] can be systematically studied and which includes many of the concepts described by Caplan and others (1964) under the rubric of "crisis theory" (but without some of the imprecision of that concept). For a fuller exposition of this field my paper *Psycho-social Transitions: A Field for Study*[10] can be consulted.

Transitions range from accidental changes, the fortunes and misfortunes of an uncertain world, to maturational changes, the milestones of life. Insofar as these are realistically anticipated and prepared for they will seldom prove difficult; but changes which are unexpected or for which no appropriate world model exists, changes which make redundant the basic assumptions which give life its meaning and upon which a person's sense of direction and self-esteem depends, may well give rise to intolerable affective disturbance and even cause psychiatric or psychosomatic illness.

Preventive Intervention can be attempted prior to a transition as anticipatory guidance or after the point of transition as what Shneidman has termed "Postvention".[11] Some exciting research results in recent years have concerned the evaluation of both of these types of intervention. As evidence for successful Anticipatory Guidance one can cite studies of preparation for operative surgery by Egbert and others,[12] preparation for childbirth by Carpenter, Aldritch and Boverman[13] and preparation for release from prison by Sinclair, Shaw and Troop.[14] Each of these studies involved random allocation of subjects to experimental and control groups and revealed significantly fewer subsequent psycho-physical problems in the experimental (i.e. supported) groups after the transition. In each case the anticipatory guidance provided opportunities for cognitive and emotional rehearsal of the life situation which could be expected after transition.

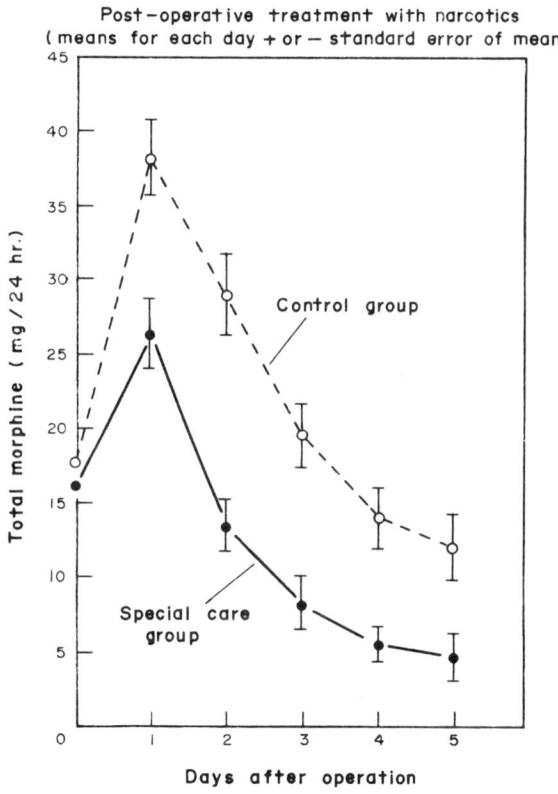

Fig. 1.

Egbert *et al.*, 1964[12]

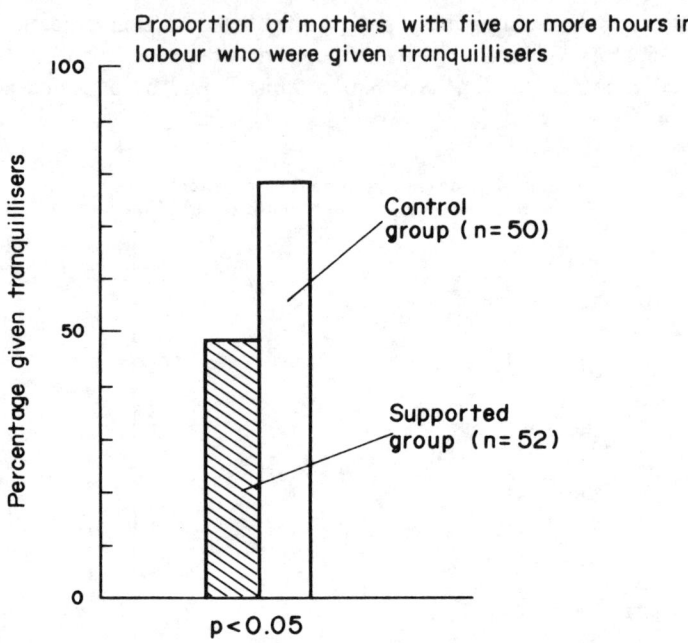

Fig. 2.

Carpenter, Adritch and Bovesman, 1968[13]

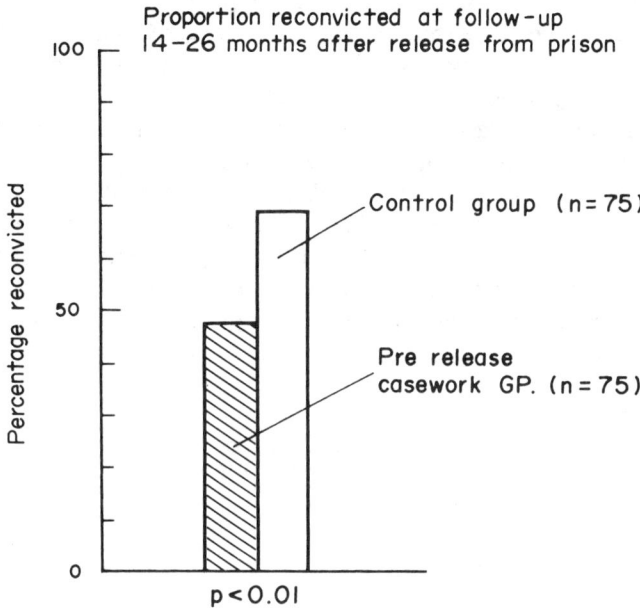

Fig. 3.

Sinclair, Shaw and Troop, 1974[14]

The evaluation of Postventive Guidance can best be illustrated by studies of bereavement counselling. Most impressive is Raphael's study of widows.[15] These women were screened using methods of predicting poor outcome after bereavement developed by Maddison and Viola.[16] From among 200 widows who were screened, 64 were assessed as being at high-risk for psychological and psychosomatic problems. These 64 were then randomly assigned to experimental and control groups and the experimental group provided with weekly postventive counselling for 2 hours per week from about the 6th to the 12th week of bereavement. Thirteen months after bereavement follow-up interviews of both groups revealed significant differences favouring the experimental group. *Inter alia* Raphael found significantly fewer visits to doctors in her experimental group ($p < 0.001$), lower consumption of alcohol, tranquillisers and tobacco and fewer psychosomatic symptoms than in her control group.

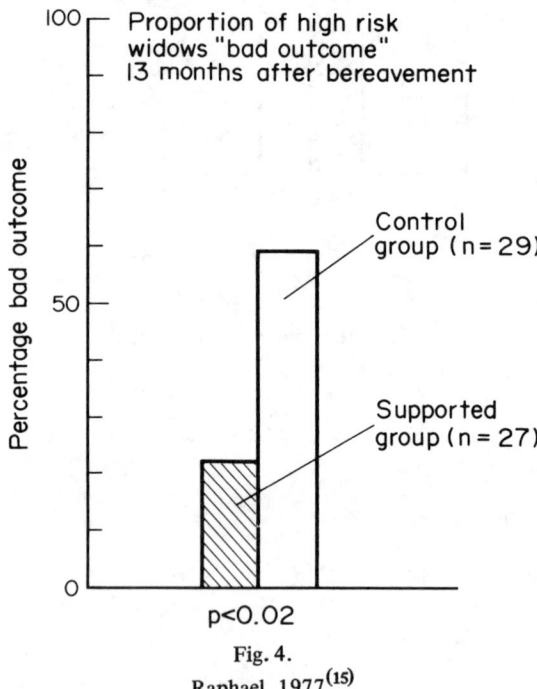

Fig. 4.
Raphael, 1977[15]

Somewhat similar findings, though at rather lower levels of significance have been found in two other random-allocation studies of bereavement counselling.[17,18]

Each of these studies adopted the same basic approach to bereavement counselling — the provision of a small number of lengthy interviews in the homes of the bereaved subjects and focussed on facilitating the expression of grief, reassurance and help with cognitive appraisal of the new life situation faced by the bereaved. It remains to be seen whether similar approaches will be successful after other types of psycho-social transition but an example can be cited of the effects of combining anticipatory guidance with postventive counselling in Lazarus and Hagen's study of 54 patients who were undergoing open-heart surgery.[19] The 21 patients who were supported in this way had significantly fewer episodes of post-operative psychosis than the rest.

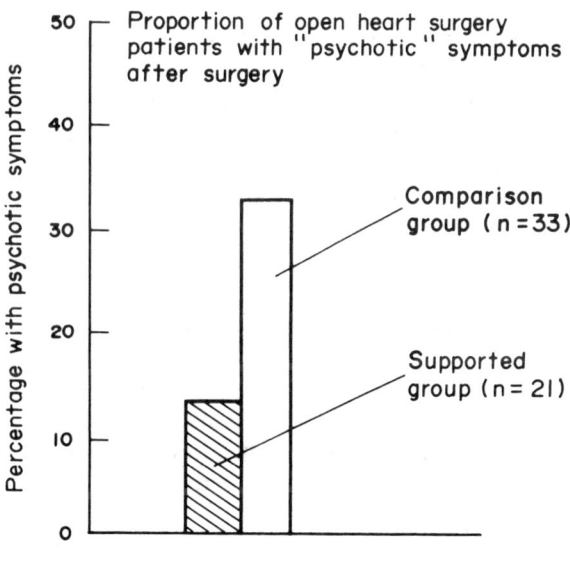

Fig. 5.

Lazarus, 1968[16]

There are, of course, many other approaches to the primary prevention of mental illness these include public education, genetic counselling, encounter groups, transcendental meditation and a wide range of political and social activities aimed at improving the lot of the disadvantaged. Unfortunately most of these are of unproven value and there is not space to discuss them further here.

I would like to turn instead to consider some recent approaches to secondary prevention which have important implications for the future of community care. These are all services for people in emotional crisis and they range from counselling for those tempted to suicide to mobile crisis teams which visit distressed families in their homes.

An impressive evaluation of crisis intervention has been carried out by Langsley and his colleagues[20] who randomly assigned 300 people who were referred for acute psychiatric care and who were living with a family within one hour's journey of Colorado to an experimental and a comparison group. The experimental group were supported by a family crisis team who used a variety of approaches to help the family through the crisis and to turn a situation of threat into an opportunity for improved functioning. The comparison group were admitted to Colorado Psychiatric Hospital and treated by traditional methods.

The experimental group lost on average 10 days away from their usual roles during the period of support and 26 days during the 6 months after support had terminated. The hospitalised group, on the other hand, were away from accustomed roles for 32 days during treatment and 48 days during the first 6 months after it.

Similar results have been obtained in Barnet and Edgware where the multidisciplinary teams developed by Dennis Scott have produced a sharp drop in the admission rate to Napsbury Hospital.[21] A further extension of the concept is now in pilot stage in Bethnal Green. Here an attempt is being made to widen the range of family crises for which help is offered by accepting referrals from social service departments and a wide range of community workers as well as from General Practitioners. Although psychiatrists have an important role to play in this service there is no need for any individual to be seen as "the patient" and most crises are treated as problems in living rather than as evidence of mental illness. Full details of one such centre are given on pages 133-5.[22]

This review of recent developments in preventive psychiatry is by no means comprehensive, and in singling out a few evaluative studies which have had positive results I do not intend to conceal the fact that there may be others which have proved negative. I have simply tried to lay the ghost of the simplistic claim that "preventive services have never been shown to prevent anything".

How can the implications of these approaches be developed without a major financial investment at a time of economic stringency?

While it is generally true to say that prevention is cheaper than cure the onus is still on the proponents of preventive services to demonstrate that their proposals are economically viable. The success or failure of intervention programmes must, in the end, depend upon the development of reasonably low-cost services. Fortunately there is already much evidence that highly trained, and expensive, professionals are not necessary if preventive programmes are to be effective. Carpenter's service for pregnant women was provided by medical students without special training. Most of the counselling for high-risk bereaved people in my own service at St. Christopher's Hospice is provided by selected volunteers who require very little supervision from a psychiatrist and Lazarus and Hagen's service to cardiac patients was mainly provided by ward nurses.

Even when psychiatrists have to be involved in a service capacity the overall costs are likely to compare favourably with traditional approaches. Thus Langsley and his colleagues found that the cost of their family crisis service was one sixth that of the psychiatric service provided to the comparison group and this takes no account of the costs to the community of the 44 extra days during which the average patient in his comparison group was out of commission.

In moving psychiatry out of the mental hospital into the community we are changing the very nature of psychiatry. From dealing only with the most severe forms of manifest mental illness we are increasingly concerned with the emotional crises and neurotic behaviour patterns which often precede "breakdown". The more familiar we become with these the closer we get to the situational crises and other life events which precede them and which so often act as precipitating factors. We are inevitably moving from traditional clinical psychiatry to secondary prevention and from secondary prevention to primary prevention. And as we move out of the mental hospital into the community we find ourselves becoming familiar with the community agencies which are already practising preventive psychiatry; with the teachers and health visitors who are attempting to mitigate the effects of unfavourable childhood environments, with the clergy and general practitioners who are supporting families through the crises of death and bereavement, with the social workers and members of voluntary agencies who are trying to improve the lot of underprivileged or incapacitated members of the community. These professionals know that what they are doing has important implications for psychiatry and they are increasingly turning to us for advice and support. Whether we like it or not they expect us to answer their questions, to share with them our understanding of psychopathology and to emerge from the privacy of our consulting rooms. We have to choose whether to develop the skills to meet these expectations or to dissociate ourselves from their efforts. There is much to criticise in the activities of many of these "front-line caregivers" and we are right to insist that proper standards of ethical service must be attained if we are to associate ourselves with them.

An ethical service is essentially one the user can trust. One which offers the client effective help by individuals who have been properly selected, trained and supported and who will respect the trust which is placed upon them. All of these standards can be attained by individuals who are not psychiatrists although psychiatrists may have a part to play in bringing services into existence and ensuring that standards will be maintained. It follows that we should seek to develop the knowledge to do this effectively, carry out systematic research to set up and evaluate ethical programmes, learn the skills of consultation and inter-disciplinary collaboration and disseminate the findings of work which is already completed.

Conferences such as that held by the Mental Health Foundation in 1977 are a step in the right direction but much more encouragement is needed from Government and University sources if real progress is to be made. The Council of Europe Working Party recommends that "Health Services must make a clear and open commitment to preventive work co-equal to its emphasis on remedial work, and this spirit must be actively cultivated in all professionals and administrators". The Committee of Ministers itself adopted a resolution [(76) 40] to the effect that "all professionals working in the mental health team should engage themselves in all three areas of prevention" and recommends to governments of member states that they legislate to promote a wide range of preventive services. Let us hope that their recommendations will not be ignored.

References

1. Caplan, G. (1964) Principles of Preventive Psychiatry, Basic Books, N.Y.
2. Council of Europe (1977) *The Organization of Preventive Services in Mental Illness: Report of a Working Party* (1974–75), European Public Health Committee, Strasbourg.
3. Royal College of Psychiatry (1978) *On the Use of Psychiatric Resources for Indirect Service: Report of a Working Party*, Awaiting publication in *Bull. Roy. Coll. Psychiat.* February, pp. 29-32.
4. Wolff, S. (1973) *Children Under Stress*, Penguin, Harmondsworth.
5. Rutter, M. (1972) *Maternal Deprivation Reassessed*, Penguin, Harmondsworth.
6. Bowlby, J. (1969) Attachment, Vol. 1 of *Attachment and Loss:* (1973) Separation: Anxiety and Anger, Vol. 2, Hogarth, London & Penguin, Harmondsworth.
7. Brown, G. V. (1974) Life Events and the Onset of Depressive and Schizophrenic Conditions, In *Life Stress and Illness*, E. K. E. Gunderson & R. H. Rahe (eds.), Charles Thomas, Illinois.
8. Rahe, R. H. (1975) Epidemiological studies of life-change and illness, *Internat. J. Psychiat. in Med.,* 6, 133.
9. Paykel, E. S. (1974) Life Stress and Psychiatric Disorder, In *Stressful Life Events: Their Nature and Effects*, B. S. Dohrenwendt & B. P. Dohrenwendt (eds.), John Wiley, N.Y.
10. Parkes, C. M. (1971) Psychosocial transitions: a field for study, *Soc. Sci. & Med.,* 5, 101.
11. Shneidman, E. S. (1973) Suicide, *Encyclopedia Britannica*, William Benton, N.Y.
12. Egbert, L. D., Battit, G. E., Welch, C. E. and Bartlett, M. K. (1964) Reduction of postoperative pain by encouragement and instruction of patients: a study of doctor-patient rapport, *New Engl. J. of Med.,* 270, 825.
13. Carpenter, J., Aldrich, C. K. and Boverman, H. (1968) The effectiveness of patient interviews: a controlled study of emotional support during pregnancy, *Arch. Gen. Psych.,* 19, 110.
14. Sinclair, I. A. C., Shaw, M. J. and Troop, J. (1974) The relationship between introversion and response to casework in a prison setting, *Brit. J. Soc. Clin. Psychol.,* 13, 51.
15. Raphael, B. (1977) Preventive intervention with the recently bereaved, *Arch. Gen. Psychiat.* (in press).
16. Maddison, D. and Viola, A. (1968) The health of widows in the year following bereavement, *J. Psychosom. Res.,* 12, 297.
17. Parkes, C. M. (1977) Evaluation of Family Care in Terminal Illness, In *The Family and Death*, E. R. Pritchard *et al.* (eds.), Columbia Univ. Press, N.Y.
18. Gerber, I., Wiener, A., Battin, D. and Arkin, A. M. (1975) Brief Therapy to the Aged Bereaved, In *Bereavement: Its Psychosocial Aspects*, B. Schoenberg *et al.* (eds.), Columbia Univ. Press, N.Y.
19. Lazarus, H. R. and Hagens, J. H. (1968) Prevention of psychosis following

62   *Colin Murray Parkes*

open heart surgery, *Amer. J. Psychiat.*, **124**, 1190.
20.   Langsley, D. G., Flowenhaft, K. and Machotka, P. (1969) Follow-up evaluations of family crisis therapy, *Amer. J. Orthopsychiat.*, **39**, 5, 753.
21.   Scott, R. D. (1973) The treatment barrier, *Brit. J. Med. Psychol.*, **48**, 45.
22.   Gleisner, J. (1977) Supplementary paper prepared for Mental Health Foundation Conference.

Appendix I

(a) *Children*

	High-risk situations	Detection	Management
(i)	Under-privileged families (health, size, poverty, criminality, resettled families, migrant and itinerant families).		Action by social and welfare agencies, non-professional voluntary groups; organisation of support groups; community planning
(ii)	Pre-school and school problems	Pre-school and school personnel	Day nurseries, kindergarten, and community planning, training of personnel
(iii)	Separation from parents: – absence of parents from home – children in institution and frequent change	Medical teams (general practitioner, gynaecologist, obstetrician, midwife, nurse, social worker, pediatrician etc.) and services such as family planning, MC centres, and family counselling	Home help; assessment and advice to institutions
(iv)	Peri-natal problems		Better coordination of services; improved information from all health personnel and services to (pregnant) mothers

Appendix I cont.

High-risk situations	Detection	Management
(v) Single parenthood		Specially trained personnel within social services; adequate supporting facilities for single mothers; support groups
(vi) Sisters and brothers of handicapped		
(vii) Battered baby		Possibility of referral to a "confidential" crises intervention service
(viii) Poor somatic health of child		Screening facilities and their accessibility to be improved

In general, community and all existing services should:
(1) cooperate more closely;
(2) be made more sensitive to primary prevention of mental illness.

Appendix I cont.

(b) *Adolescents*

	High-risk situations	Detection	Management
(i)	Isolated from peer group contact	Parents	Parents' school
(ii)	Belonging to under-privileged families	Teachers	Students counselling
		Tutors	Career counselling
(iii)	Departing from home (social identification)	Police	Youth clubs with advisory facilities
		Youth leaders	Psycho-social youth service
(iv)	In difficult situations: school work	Social workers	Peer support groups
		School nurses	Ideological (e.g. religious) groups
(v)	Drop-outs (from school and work)	Vocational guidance and occupational medicine	Sport clubs
(vi)	Gang identification	Peers	
(vii)	With extreme development ("The Different")	Clergy, sport trainers, police	
		For Group 6: the general practitioner	

Appendix I cont.

(c) *Adults*

	High-risk situations	Detection	Management
(i)	Bereaved and divorced (loneliness)	Civil register, hospital staff, general practitioner, clergy, voluntary organisations, lawyers, relatives, friends, neighbours	Voluntary groups (Samaritans) Support groups, clergy
(ii)	Experiencing psycho-social and psycho-physical changes (menopause, bereavement, retirement, first child, loss of job etc.)	General practitioner, gynaecologist, social services in work places, registration offices for residents	Social services and support groups
(iii)	With chronic somatic diseases, their environment, included	General practitioner, hospitals, public health nurse	Psychiatric consultants in general hospitals, support groups, sheltered workshops
(iv)	With former mental illness or family of mentally ill or handicapped	Patients' clubs, relatives, friends, public health nurse, social services, general practitioner, psychiatrist,	Support groups, psychologist, follow-up case by multi-disciplinary specialised teams, adequate community facilities

Appendix I cont.

High-risk situations	Detection	Management
(iv) cont.	community psychiatric nurse, psychiatric hospitals	
(v) Young married	Family planning, general practitioner, public health nurse, lawyers	Family counselling, support groups
(vi) Unemployed	Labour exchange, social services	Labour law social services within trade unions
(vii) With excessive workload	Occupational health services	Education of heads of personnel, labour law
(viii) Minorities	Schools, relatives, occupational health services, consulates, clergy etc.	Social services and support groups

(d) *The Aged*

High-risk situations	Detection	Management
(i) Isolation	GP hospitals	Outside hospital services (clubs, day care centres, day hospitals)
(ii) Chronic somatic diseases (including sensory defects and other somatic handicaps)	Voluntary organisations	Telephone services, alarm systems, home help
(iii) Recent bereavement	Social services	Integration housing
(iv) Severe, acute disease calling for sudden hospitalisation	Family	Part-time work
(v) Discharge from hospital	Clergy	Legal advice
(vi) Previous mental illness	Neighbours	Comprehensive diagnostic services
(vii) Poor finances	Peer groups	

CHAPTER 5

The Primary Health Care Team: The Way Forward for Mental Health Care

GEOFFREY MARSH
Stockton-on-Tees

and

MRS. MOLLY MEACHER
Mental Health Foundation

The greatest opportunities for preventive work in the mental health field are provided within general practice. A most important development in recent years has been the growth of health centres and medical centres incorporating health visitors and sometimes social workers into the primary health care team. The concept of group practice was put forward as long ago as 1920 in the Dawson Report[1] and today, albeit more than fifty years later, there are less than 18 per cent of general practitioners working in single handed practice.[2] Over the past decade in particular there has been a pronounced movement towards large group practices with supporting professional and lay staff, and a typical well developed primary health care team may now include a group of general practitioners and trainee doctors working with nurses, health visitors, midwives, receptionists, secretaries and filing clerks.[3] Of particular importance to patients with minor mental disorders are the less common experimental schemes which include social workers or counsellors within the team or, alternatively, bring a psychiatrist's skills to the surgery for perhaps a session or two each week.[4] The urgency for the need to extend such schemes lies in the number of patients receiving inappropriate treatment at

*This chapter is written on the basis of contributions of Geoffrey Marsh, George Adams, Valerie Hatswell, Henry Egdell and Campbell Murdoch to the Mental Health Foundation Conference, 1977.

the present time, whether in the form of psychotropic drugs or hospitalisation or both.

Psycho-social Problems Presenting to the Primary Health Care Team

Recent analysis of the complaints presented to a medical centre in Stockton-on-Tees showed that after respiratory disease, the second most common group of illnesses coming to the attention of the GP are psychiatric disorders. Analysis of individual disorders revealed that depression was the second most common in consultative frequency and anxiety state was third. These findings are supported by similar results in a study comparing mid-Western American general practice with 25 North-East England counterparts[5] and others referred to in Chapter 3. It can be deduced from the Stockton-on-Tees data that every twelfth time the consulting room door opens a patient enters who, whatever else may be the matter with him, is either depressed or anxious to such an extent that he will consult his doctor about it. Examining the figures by sex indicates that women consult more frequently about depression than they do about any other illness even including the ubiquitous upper respiratory tract infection.[6]

The Use of Psychotropic Drugs in General Practice

The normal response of a GP to a patient presenting symptoms of anxiety or depression is to prescribe a psychotropic drug. As we see in Chapter 3 there is nothing new in the use of mood-altering or psychotropic drugs. These have been used by man since the beginning of time. What is new is the sheer volume of such drugs consumed each year. More than 66 million prescriptions for mood changing drugs were issued in 1975 at a total cost of more than £40 million.[7]

The growth in the number and range of such prescriptions during recent years is discussed in some detail in Chapter 3. It remains for us here to refer to the parallel escalation in the number of cases of deliberate self poisoning,[8] often using the drugs prescribed by the general practitioner,[9] and to suggest that the GP's standard method of handling stress symptoms appears to have a direct bearing on the self poisoning propensity of patients. Several surveys have confirmed that the majority of patients who take an overdose of drugs have seen their GP within the preceding few weeks and about a third attend within the previous week.[10,11,12]

TABLE 1

Number of Prescriptions for Psychotropic Drugs in England in 1975

	Million
Antipyretic Analgesics	19.30
Hypnotics (Barbiturate)	6.74
Hypnotics (Non-Barbiturate)	9.74
Tranquillisers	20.54
Antidepressants	7.91
Stimulants and Appetite Suppressants	2.61
Total	66.84

Source: *Health and Personal Social Services Statistics for England,* 1976.

The fact that a prescription for psychotropic drugs is inappropriate in so many cases is underlined by the findings of Hawton and Blackstock in their Oxford study.[12] Sixty per cent of self-poisoning cases who had visited their GPs within the preceding year were troubled by a disturbance in a key relationship. In addition almost three quarters of the married couples in the Oxford study were experiencing chronic marriage difficulties. The impression of the authors was that in general the relationship problems were primary and the depression or anxiety secondary, in which case the correct approach would have been an attempt to deal with the relationship problems in the hope that some of the mood changes would thus have been reversed.

In general it is probably reasonable to assume that general practitioners do not have the time to counsel depressed or acutely anxious patients. However, the evidence suggests that time alone is not a decisive factor. In countries where private medicine operates and where patients are given more time, drugs are prescribed to no less an extent than they are under the British National Health Service. At least as relevant is the fact that the very qualities encouraged in those trained to practise medicine — to be objective, authoritative, and directive when necessary — are totally different from those required by a counsellor dealing with the relationship or marital problems which so often lie behind depression or anxiety.[13]

Training in General Practice

The training bias of general practitioners is a decisive determinant of their treatment response to patients with psychosomatic or neurotic disorders. Dr. Adams gives support to this view in his description of the effects of attachment to his practice of a Mental Welfare Officer: "The practice referral rate to consultant psychiatrists fell by about 75 per cent during the year and the admission rate to psychiatric hospitals fell by approximately the same proportion. Furthermore the doctors who took part in the experiment have maintained their referral rate of patients for psychiatric help at the new low rate in the absence of the MWO."[14] It appears that training in the skills of the MWO and confidence in dealing with the emotional problems of patients can enable the GP to handle the problems himself sufficiently satisfactorily to avoid, in many cases, the need for referral for psychiatric help.

Michael and Enid Balint after six years of research have shown that selected GPs can substantially improve the value of the average short interview with patients, given postgraduate training in psychotherapy.[15]

It remains unfortunately true, however, that despite the considerable amount of a GP's work which is essentially of a psychological or psychiatric nature, a student considering a medical training finds chemistry and biology valuable "A" level qualifications rather than psychology and sociology. The bulk of medical undergraduate training concerns the body rather than the mind. As a result, not only are GPs often ill-equipped to deal with emotional and interpersonal problems, but many of the people who opt to become general practitioners are likely to be those with more interest and aptitude for chemistry and physiology than they have for dealing with interpersonal relationship difficulties. It remains to be seen whether GP trainees who are insensitive can benefit from additional training, including perhaps the use of techniques such as videotape feedback.[16] There is not only a need for future general practitioners to be trained to diagnose in psychological and social terms as well as physical ones, but by the same token, nurses, midwives, health visitors and receptionists probably all need more appropriate training in the handling of patients with these problems, even if the clinical team does not play a major role in their continuing care.[6] A new development relevant to the future training of general practitioners, is the involvement of patients in the training process. This is being extended at the University of Dundee by Dr. Alec McQueen of the Centre for Medical Education.[17]

Extending the Primary Health Care Team

An alternative to the Balint approach – the training of GPs to counsel their own patients – is the involvement of social workers, counsellors or the Church in the work of the practice. But for referral to be made by the GP to such agencies or individuals he must be capable of making a diagnosis which is essentially environmental, financial, emotional, interpersonal, spiritual and so on. It is self-evident that those GPs who work effectively alongside counsellors and social workers are precisely those who would respond well to a Balint training and whose need for a social work or counselling support service is least pressing. Nevertheless, it is worth noting the effects of sharing patient care amongst members of a multidisciplinary team. In Stockton-on-Tees where all the caring disciplines already mentioned contribute to the team, the work of the doctors in the practice in consultative terms has been continued at a reasonable level while the list size has been enabled to rise to almost 3,500 patients per doctor, about 50 per cent above the average list size in the Country as a whole (2,365 in England in 1975).[18] The Stockton-on-Tees practice refers a very much smaller than average number of patients for in-patient care. In 1972 the average number of patients admitted per 1,000 in England and Wales was 112, but from the practice the number was only 76. Even more significant is the difference in referral to out-patient departments where the figures were approximately one third of the national average; 171 per 1,000 nationally but only 64 per 1,000 for the practice. Of 150 patients in 1972 who consulted Dr. Marsh about some type of depressive illness only five were seen at hospital, and of the 182 with anxiety none went for hospital psychiatric help. A patient satisfaction survey revealed very clearly that patients appreciate the service provided by the practice. Ninety-five per cent or more of the patients were satisfied or very satisfied with the overall treatment received.[19]

There seems a powerful case not only for improving the training of GPs but also for extending the team to include individuals whose special function is to help patients with emotional or relationship problems. It is probably desirable that the GP should see every patient who asks to see him in the first instance in order to ascertain whether or not any physical illness exists. Having established that a patient has an emotional or relationship problem and no physical illness, there is no need for the continuing care of that patient to be provided by a medically qualified person. The importance of making appropriate referrals cannot, of course, be over-estimated.

Overlapping Roles Within the Primary Health Care Team

A major problem concerns the definition of roles within the primary care team of health visitors, social workers, community psychiatric nurses and para-professional counsellors.

The contribution of the health visitor

Dr. Edgell has argued that "the potential use of the Health Visitor in Community Psychiatry has been insufficiently recognised by many mental health workers. Definitions of the role of the Health Visitor are no more rigid than those of other caring professions and include prevention and early detection of illness, and the counselling and support of the ill and their relatives."[20,21,22] The lack of rigidity in their work and outlook together with their ability to take independent initiative, and their experience of working independently in the community, make the health visitor highly suitable as a front line Mental Health Worker. The fact that health visitors are a body of 7,000 professionals already present in the community is one which we cannot afford to ignore.[23]

Basic health visitor training specifically includes acquiring skills in interpersonal relationships, knowledge of therapy, emotional factors in pregnancy and childbirth, detection of early deviation from the normal, assessing priority of needs of patients and assessment of high-risk groups, e.g. the elderly. Dr. Edgell suggests that:

> "The health visitor's involvement in the primary health care team could include recognition of onset and relapse of psychoses, neuroses, alcoholism, drug abuse and pathological grief; assessment

of the side effects of psychotropic drugs; counselling of psychiatric patients and their families (particularly of the recently discharged), general education of the public in matters relating to mental health; and problem family assessment and support. The education, guidance and counselling of families of patients in the community with longterm neuroses and psychoses is an area of need where the health visitor may develop a particular role."[23]

We believe that a number of these functions are more naturally fulfilled by psychiatric nurses and social workers, while others are quite clearly the province of the health visitor. For example, the health visitor who is responsible for monitoring pregnancy and childbirth, is in an ideal position to watch for early deviation from the normal during the first few years of a child's life. In the course of her repeated home visits to young mothers she is well placed to recognise the onset of psychiatric symptoms, in particular, symptoms of depression which may well otherwise remain undetected,[24] drink or drug problems and pathological grief. Having recognised these problems she will need access to other skilled workers or to specialist facilities for the on-going care of her patients. The role of the health visitor is essentially a preventive one and should probably remain so. Her skills could nevertheless be extended outside the field of young mothers and their children. The screening of old people for both physical and psychiatric disabilities, for example, can be effectively carried out by health visitors with considerable benefit.[25] It has been shown that, as far as old people are concerned, a service which depends upon the self reporting of illness will be seriously defective and that the only hope of success in dealing with the problems of morbidity in increasing numbers of old people lies in the development of effective preventive measures.[26] This issue is discussed at length in Chapter 14. Our only concern here is to emphasise the possible potential of screening and the use of the health visitor in this role. The screening of other high risk groups could usefully also be incorporated into the general practice routine; young mothers of handicapped children, for example.

The contribution of the psychiatric nurse

The psychiatric nurse deals mainly with the more severe psychotic

patients discharged from hospital. She is well placed to recognise the onset
or relapse of psychoses and to monitor the side effects of psychotropic
drugs administered to patients suffering from psychoses. It is also likely
that community psychiatric nurses, who are in touch with psychiatric
patients and their families, could provide guidance and counselling to
families or patients in the community. Specialist training for this latter
function should be made available, however, and the effectiveness of
nurses as family counsellors and their interest in this work should be
established before any national pattern of support is developed. The
National Schizophrenia Fellowship are examining the skills required by a
support worker for the relatives of schizophrenics. The study will be
completed in 1978 and the results will have a direct bearing upon the
future choice of personnel for this function.

General Practitioners are not well equipped to supervise the care of
chronic psychotic patients but more effort could be made to ensure that
they could recognise the early symptoms of schizophrenia and the
avoidable side effects of anti-psychotic drugs, for example. Attachment of
psychiatric nurses to the primary health team would facilitate the sharing
of information and skills in this area.

The contribution of the social worker

Dr. Edgell looks to the health visitor for problem family assessment and
support. However, problem families frequently need a variety of services
including help with social security claims, appeals to the housing
department, liaison with the probation service, support in the courts and
so forth. At present, social workers who are trained in the organisation and
functions of statutory authorities and their numerous departments and
subsidiaries, meet many of the needs of families with multiple problems.
Health visitors could nevertheless make a valuable contribution in this
area, working in close cooperation with their social work colleagues.

Social workers are also well equipped for social assessment and
evaluation of a patient's circumstances where the GP believes that his
health (whether mental or physical) is being affected by social or
environmental factors. Evidence of the incidence of such problems in
general practice is provided in the Caversham study.[27] Of 616 patients

presenting to their GP, 130 complained of family problems to the social worker, 89 revealed marital or sexual problems and 31 the need for a domestic service — problems which the GP could not have handled himself.

When the great majority of family problems come first to the general practitioner's surgery, often in the form of a physical presenting symptom, the need for immediate access to a social worker should need no explanation. Yet in 1973 only 16.9 full-time social worker equivalents, or between 0.1 per cent and 0.2 per cent of the social work force of 11,793 workers in Great Britain were attached to general practice. The majority of general practitioners remain indifferent to social work and have little understanding of the professional skills of trained social workers.[28] This despite the fact that social work in general practice dates back to 1948[29,30] and several enthusiastic reports of these experimental schemes point to the value of joint working.[6,31,32,33]

An experiment in Derby suggests that the apathy and hostility of general practitioners to the idea of medico-social teamwork can be overcome, and perhaps will only be overcome, by example and not by precept.[34] Is there a case for a statutory requirement that every general practice should have access to a social worker whether she be attached full-time or part-time to the practice, or (as may be more appropriate in rural areas) acting in a liaison capacity with the social services department? The evidence clearly points to the need for such a requirement.

The contribution of counsellors

How essential is a marriage guidance or generic counsellor to a team which includes, among others, social workers, health visitors and psychiatric nurses? The need for one of the team members to provide a counselling service is self-evident: an ever-increasing number of marriages in England and Wales end in divorce and a considerable proportion of the anxiety, depression and general "disease" presenting in general practitioners' consulting rooms is set against the background of disturbed inter-personal relationships.[35] In the Stockton-on-Tees practice where marriage guidance counsellors have been available to patients, their services have been extensively used. Their work has escalated from the tentative hour or two a week in the early months to two counsellors working approximately 24 hours a week in the counselling rooms at the surgery. "Their hour long consultations with patients cover a wide panoply of conditions, from sex problems to the problems of prisoners' wives; from patients contemplating a second marriage to lonely divorcees, and they have been the mainstay of many patients with depressive reactions. As a result it is the doctor's impression that the prescribing of psychotropic drugs by the practice has become less and the overall caring better."[6] Nevertheless, whether a practice can justify the appointment of a counsellor, will depend to some extent upon the skills and interests of the social worker and health visitor members of the team. If either has a particular interest and the necessary training in counselling, then the appointment of an additional worker may prove unnecessary.

It can be argued that the social worker's first duty is to represent the State and to fulfil her legal obligations. She has a divided loyalty which may inhibit a client in a counselling situation. Can he/she afford to be wholly honest with her social worker? If she admits her feelings of severe depression or tension she may fear that her children will be taken into care (however unrealistic such fears may be in practice). A further problem arises out of the social work function of advising the client about her statutory rights, and supporting the client in her requests for services. The provision of physical, financial and moral support tend to encourage dependence of the client upon the social worker. A counsellor, however, is free from all these duties and can concentrate upon helping her client to become self-reliant and autonomous — the principal objectives of counselling.

In the past, psychological and relationship difficulties have been catered for in a variety of settings by marriage guidance counsellors, student counsellors, the Samaritans and pastoral counsellors, but the focal point for these problems is the GPs surgery and it is here that the emphasis must surely be placed in the future. A further valuable development would be the amalgamation of these functions into a generic counselling service. With these objectives in view, a pilot counselling scheme was initiated by Mrs. Valerie Hatswell in association with general practices in Camden and Lambeth in London and in Alton, Hampshire. The objectives of the project have been threefold: (i) to reduce the workload of GPs, (ii) to reduce the number of prescriptions for psychotropic drugs and (iii) to reduce the distress and dysfunction of the patients.

Sixty-seven per cent of all the clients referred to the counsellors during the eighteen month period of the pilot study were prescribed drug users. The tentative evidence of the pilot study suggests that about half of the patients were using prescribed drugs less frequently at the end of the first phase of the project than at the beginning. It has not been possible yet to measure the effect of the service upon the workload of the GPs. The first task has been to prove to GPs themselves that a counselling service can be of value to them. More clear has been the effect of the service upon the patients themselves. It is rare in the health and social field for patients/clients to be given the opportunity of passing judgement on the professionals, but an essential ingredient of the project has been the questionnaire sent to each client when counselling ceased or at the end of the eighteen month period of the project, if the counselling were on-going. Sixty-three of the eighty clients participating in the project returned their completed questionnaires to an independent address and the results are encouraging.

Ninety-five per cent of the clients who responded to the enquiry felt that the counselling had been of help to them. This does not, of course, prove that the mental health of the clients had improved but merely that patients felt that they had been helped. General Practitioners' assessments were marginally less favourable than those of the patients themselves. Though tentative, the results are sufficiently favourable to justify continuation of the service for more rigorous evaluation, so that the effects of counselling upon patients can be measured as precisely as possible. It is hoped that the study will be completed by 1980.

Conclusions

The foregoing discussion accepts the incidence of neuroses in the adult population as given. In the longer run, the provision of a more secure environment for children and more careful preparation for coping with the pressures of modern industrial living could reduce the need for so much attention to be given to such problems by the primary health care team. However, such issues as housing policy, the case for a home responsibility allowance to encourage mothers to remain at home with their children, and education policy are beyond the scope of this book.

In any context, however, the introduction of multidisciplinary medical centres will be beneficial. Examples of highly successful teams already exist in which the potential role conflicts have been avoided through regular group meetings and a spirit of cooperation and mutual respect of each profession for the skills and contribution of the others. In general the division of responsibilities should probably evolve in each practice according to the personal strengths and interests of each team member, though more research in this area is needed as an indication of the relative strengths and weaknesses of each profession with different client groups.

References

1. Dawson Report (1920) *Interim Report of the Consultative Council on Future Provision of Medical and Allied Services*, HMSO, London.
2. *Health and Personal Social Services Statistics for England* (1976) HMSO, p. 60.
3. Marsh, G. and Kaim Caudle, P. *Team Care in General Practice*, Croom Helm, p. 13.
4. Brook, A. (1967) *College of General Practitioners,* **13**, 127-31.
5. Marsh, G. N., Wallace, R. B. and Whurell, J. *Anglo-American Contrasts in General Practice,* **1**, 1321-5.
6. Marsh, G. N. and McNay, R. A. (1974) Factors affecting work load in General Practice, *Brit. Med. J.,* **1**, 319-21.
7. *Health and Personal Social Services Statistics for England* (1976) 111.
8. Balter, M. B. *et al.* (1974) *New England Journal of Medicine,* **290**, 769-74.
9. Hawton, K. and Blackstock, E. (1977) Deliberate self-poisoning: implications for psychotropic drug prescribing in general practice, *Jl. RCGP.,* **27**, 182.
10. Davison, K. (1975) Management of patients at risk of suicide, *Medicine,* **12**, 566-8.
11. Barraclough *et al.* (1974) A hundred cases of suicide: clinical aspects, *B.J. Psych.,* **125**, 355-73 58.g.
12. Hawton, K. and Blackstock, E. *op. cit.*
13. Hatswell, V. (1977) Unpublished paper delivered at the Mental Health Foundation Conference.
14. Adams, G. (1977) Unpublished paper delivered at the Mental Health Foundation Conference.
15. *Six Minutes for the Patient: Interaction in General Practice Consultation*, Enid Balint & J. S. Norrell (eds.).
16. Goldberg, D. (1977) Unpublished paper delivered at the Mental Health Foundation Conference.
17. Murdoch (1977) Unpublished paper delivered at the Mental Health Foundation Conference.
18. *Health and Personal Social Services Statistics for England* (1976) 62.
19. Marsh, G. and Kaim Caudle, P. *Team Care in General Practice*, Croom Helm, p. 119.

20. *The Functions of the Health Visitor*, Council for the Education and Training of Health Visitors, Clifton House, Euston Road, N.W.1.
21. Health visitor in the seventies, *The Health Visitor*, September 1975, **48**, 322-31.
22. *World Health Organisation Technical Report* No. 167, WHO, Geneva, 1959.
23. Egdell, H. G. (1977) Unpublished paper delivered at the Mental Health Foundation Conference.
24. Goldberg, E. M. *et al.* (1968) Social work in general practice, *Lancet*, **2**, 552-5.
25. McCulloch, J. W. and Brown, M. J. (1970) *Medical Social Worker*, **22**, 300-9.
26. Paterson, J. (1949) *The Almoner*, **1**, 230-3.
27. Scott, R. (1949) *The Almoner*, **1**, 204-14.
28. Forman, J. A. S. and Fairbairn, E. M. (1968) *Social Casework in General Practice*, London, OUP.
29. Goldberg, E. M. *et al.* (1968) *Social Work in General Practice, op. cit.*
30. Ratoff and Pearson (1970) *Social Casework in General Practice: An alternative approach.*
31. Cooper, B. (1971) Social work in general practice: The Derby Scheme, *Lancet*, 539-43.
32. Brown, G., Brolchain, M. and Harris, T. (1975) Social class and psychiatric disturbance among women in an urban population, *Sociology*, **9**, 225-54.
33. Williamson, J. *et al.* (1966) The use of health visitors in preventive geriatrics, *Geront. Clin.*, **8**, 362-9.
34. Williamson, J. *et al.* (1964) Old people at home: their unreported needs, *Lancet*, **1**, 1117.
35. Marsh, G. and Barr, J. (1975) Marriage guidance counselling in a group practice, *Jl. RCGP*, **25**, 73.

CHAPTER 6

The Role of Social Work in Relation to General Practice in the Mental Health Field

E. MATILDA GOLDBERG

Many readers will be familiar with the table in the report of the Royal College of General Practitioners, *Present State and Future Needs of General Practice*, in which the psychiatric and social morbidity in an average general practice of 2,500 patients is computed from various sources:

TABLE 1
Psychiatric Disorders and Social Pathology
in a Hypothetical Average Population of 2,500

	Cases per annum
Acute Major Disorders	
Severe depression	12
Suicide attempts	3
Suicide	once every 3 yrs
Chronic mental illness	55
Severe mental handicap	10
Neurotic disorders	300
Social Pathology	
Chronic alcoholism (known cases)	5
Chronic alcoholism (unknown cases)	25
Juvenile delinquency	5-7
Problem families	5-10
Broken homes (one-parent families with children under 15)	60

Source: Royal College of General Practitioners (1973), *Present State and Future Needs of General Practice*, 3rd ed.

It will be seen that these cases amount to almost 500 – a prevalence rate of 20 per cent. As the Table shows, among them one would find 300 neurotic disorders, 55 cases of chronic mental illness, 12 cases of severe depression, some 30 chronic alcoholics (25 hidden from view) and about 60–70 disrupted families experiencing social problems of some kind. Have social workers a part to play in the alleviation of these problems?

If the answer is yes, then the next question is what should be their contribution, and what role should they occupy *vis-à-vis* the GP and other professionals and non-professionals involved – psychiatrists, psychiatric community nurses, health visitors, marriage guidance counsellors, bereavement counsellors, Alcoholics Anonymous, not to speak of a host of new and exciting informal and formal community mental health projects such as walk-in centres for adolescents, crisis centres and so on.

For some GPs the solution appears quite simple: since all social problems have a health context, they argue, and since everybody is registered with a GP, incorporate the majority of social workers into the primary health care team and either abolish the necessity for monolythic social services departments or reduce their functions drastically to certain service, statutory and residential care duties. Other GPs can see the potential, if not yet the reality, of an integrated social services department running "local surgeries", able to deal initially with all comers – like a GP – whether the presenting problem is delinquency, family disruption, frailty in old age, or gambling debts. But the primary physicians complain that they can never get hold of social workers and that it is a mystery to them how they actually spend their time, apart from being on the telephone or locked up in meetings and case conferences! They will concede that the elderly receive a variety of domiciliary services, that in crisis situations children can be taken into care, but they repeatedly observe that mental health problems appear to have a very low priority. As to receiving reports on what happens to patients referred to the social services, this has long since been given up as a utopian hope. What then is the reality that gives rise to these frustrations?

In order to answer this question it is essential to abandon emotive criticism on the one hand and an equally unrealistic inward-looking preoccupation with "communication", togetherness, support to team members and the like, often advanced as the solution to all problems.

It is more relevant and helpful to gain first of all a general understanding about how both trained and untrained social work resources are deployed in response to the multiple demands made on the social services. I shall then argue that until there is a fairly radical redeployment of these resources and a re-definition of appropriate social work tasks, there is very little hope of more positive, well informed collaboration between social work and medicine or psychiatry. I shall base this crude sketch of how social work resources are deployed at present on a year's monitoring exercise on all client referrals and ongoing cases in a fairly typical urban area office of a social services department in southern England, since no such information exists nationally. This exercise was made possible through the development of a computerised case review system, which records systematically, at intervals determined by the social workers, a client's problems and social situation, any past social work activities with and on behalf of the client, and intended future work and aims.[1,2,3] I shall then draw some comparisons between these data and similar data derived from studies in social work in general practice.[4,5]

The Clientele and the Social Work of an Area Office

It is safe to assume that about one-third of all clients referred or referring themselves to an area office of a social services department will be physically frail, elderly and disabled people of whom the majority will be over the age of 75. The proportion suffering from mental disorder will be at least 15 per cent,[6] but since much disorder except in its crudest and most obvious form goes unrecognised, the figure may well be around 20–25 per cent. Most of these elderly clients will get some form of practical service and their cases will then be closed from the point of view of active social work, though domiciliary services and aids to living will be delivered as long as seems appropriate. In the area office studied, some 10 per cent of very frail at risk elderly continued to receive occasional surveillance visits which usually were not able to forestall crises. A few very confused clients received very active and intensive social work support over longish periods, the social worker keeping their finances and domestic arrangements straight and thus undoubtedly enabling these clients to lead a reasonably worry-free life in the community.

The second largest client group (nearly a third) consisted mainly of young families, mostly self-referred, who came with financial, material and housing problems. They generally received information and advice, and the social workers were engaged in much time-consuming advocacy with the many agencies involved — DHSS, Electricity Boards, Housing Departments etc. This type of intervention has much in common with a Citizen's Advice Bureau type of service. A high proportion of these cases were referred on to other agencies and almost all were closed within a month of referral. Many of these families experienced other chronic stresses apart from material ones and a substantial proportion reappeared with other requests within a short time of closure.

The third main group of social service clients were highly disturbed families (some 16 per cent of the total referred) in which marital strife and violence, desertion, separation, divorce, child neglect, delinquency, and adolescent rebellion were common occurrences. Clearly this group contains many severely emotionally disturbed individuals. Usually a variety of other agencies are already involved (including psychiatric services in 25 per cent). A great deal of short term liaison and casework was undertaken with these families and 75 per cent of them were closed within three months of referral. But children coming into care, families at serious risk of neglecting a child and the most severely disturbed families remained open and tended to build up into a kind of chronic population consuming inordinate amounts of social work resources over years with few visible results. The social workers who deal with these cases are often caught in a vicious circle of crises arising, sorting out the most urgent causes such as debts, threats of eviction, parents running off or being in such a state that they might harm a child, only to be overtaken by the next crisis. It needs to be remembered that only 40 per cent of these social workers are professionally trained. Here is a snippet of a difficult and chronic problem situation in which a social work assistant consistently suggests in his case reviews that a qualified social worker should handle the case: this was a family in which a very much older hemiplegic man was married to an incompetent and unstable girl; there were three children, all of them reacting in disturbed ways to the home situation. One entry reads "incompetent mother, disabled father, financial problems, poor home, unlucky children", and under "changes to be aimed at" the social work assistant writes "visit weekly, hassle DHSS, get volunteer, review in six months, try to change above situation (ho-ho)", and the next entry reads "present situation a complete shambles" (seven problem areas were ticked with "child behaviour problem" as the most outstanding one).

In contrast there were an appreciable number of children – around 10 per cent of the long term population studied – who had become well settled in foster or residential homes and in whom a great deal of trained manpower was tied up, often for purely surveillance purposes. It seems that in general, because of the statutory responsibility involved when the local authority stands in *loco parentis*, trained workers are used wherever possible for the supervision of children in care, even if they are well settled.

Cases in which mental illness and emotional disturbance or mental handicap are identified as the main problem area comprise between 7–9 per cent of total referrals to social services departments, although it needs to be stressed that mental health problems – recognised and unrecognised – figure largely in the disrupted deprived families, among the elderly and the younger chronically disabled. It seems that a social services department deals roughly with five types of problems: (1) young people in an emotional crisis or with an incipient mental illness, usually dealt with on a short term basis and referred on; (2) cases in which the parents' mental illness affects the welfare of children, who may have to be taken into care; (3) the social services department also gets landed with some intractable problems such as older depressive alcoholics on the verge of homelessness; (4) the department may be involved in the after-care of patients discharged from hospitals, usually after a long stay, who have no families and who may live in hostels, group homes, or lodgings; (5) lastly there are the gross mental health problems of some elderly clients who require a great deal of supportive care to keep them going in the community.

In the field of mental handicap, social workers appear to be drawn in either at a point of crisis when the family, hostel or group home cannot cope any longer, or in relation to mentally handicapped children who are also in the care of the local authority.

The Social Workers' Tasks in Social Services Departments

To summarise the social workers' tasks; they are busy:
(1) Screening incoming demands, many of them for straightforward

practical services.

(2) Providing practical help and services of many kinds for the disabled and elderly.

(3) Acting as a kind of Citizen's Advice Bureau for a great variety of material and interpersonal problems.

(4) As a go-between or advocate *vis-à-vis* the DHSS, housing departments, and other statutory and voluntary bodies.

(5) With long term surveillance of the elderly and disabled (directly or through others) and of children in care.

(6) With crisis work among the frail elderly on the border-line of requiring residential care and among families in a chronic state of disequilibrium.

(7) And lastly with casework. Although this is usually taken to be the main activity of social workers, in the sense of helping people to engage in a clarifying and problem solving process in a calm atmosphere, it only constituted 20 per cent of social worker activities in the area studied. A caseload study in Suffolk[7] reported that only 5 per cent of clients received any form of individual casework.

Social Work in a Social Services Area Office and in General Practice

How does this picture of the social work task at primary social service level compare with the social work task in primary health care? We have some comparative data from two studies in which social workers were attached to general group practices, one in north-west London, the other in an outer London borough. In both these practices far fewer patients were referred for straightforward welfare services, such as home help and meals-on-wheels, since these services were arranged with the social services departments by the practice secretaries without using social workers as intermediaries. Significantly fewer clients were referred to social workers for predominantly material needs, such as financial or accommodation problems. In contrast, difficulties in family relationships, personality problems, and problems related to emotional and mental illness amounted to about half the referrals to the attached social workers in both practices whilst they comprised less than a quarter of the social services referrals. These very great contrasts in the kinds of social need reaching social workers in general practice and social services departments obtained despite the fact that demographically the two patient/client populations were very similar. One-third were elderly, the middle-aged were under-represented, and there were more women than men. Corney and Briscoe[5] suggest that the differences particularly in minor psychiatric morbidity and in presenting problems between clients coming to an intake team in a social services department and those referred to a social worker attached to a general practice, are due to differences in referral sources and in perceptions of the roles of local authority social workers. A high proportion of social service department clients are self-referred or are referred by friends and relatives, and thus possibly — so these authors argue — more in need of practical help and services. The clients of social workers in general practice are almost all referred by the primary health care team, and most of them by the general practitioners themselves. Furthermore, although there was evidence that a considerable proportion of social service department clients had discussed their problems with their general practitioner, only a very few had been referred for social work help to the area office, the social services department being seen as predominantly a welfare service agency.

Other hypotheses may be worth considering, for example that patients/clients with similar social and psychiatric morbidity present to both social services departments and general practice, but that the problems are presented and "dressed up" differently in the different settings, and that the social workers in the two settings select different facets for action or treatment. The other possibility is that the primary care team spots and selects earlier manifestations of social and psychiatric morbidity for referral to their social workers. The social services department on the other hand gets involved in situations which require statutory action (children in need of care or supervision orders) or with people who require domiciliary, day care or residential facilities, or with clients who have such longstanding and multiple problems that they need many different kinds of material, social and psychological support for an almost indefinite period.

A Redeployment of Social Work Skills

Having discovered in broad outline what social workers are facing in the social services, and that possibly in addition many cases of emotional disorder and "problems in living" can be identified in general practice, how are they to meet this challenge? (I am assuming that no additional manpower will be available within the next few years.) One answer is by a radical redeployment of social work resources, and by the reintroduction of certain forms of specialisation at a post-graduate and non-graduate level. Some of these developments have already begun. For example:

(1) Requests for specific domiciliary services might as a matter of routine be channelled directly to social service officers without using social workers as assessors of need; but some resources would be devoted to training the social service officers to spot those clients who appear to need help beyond the specific service requested. Only at that point would the trained social worker enter the case.

(2) Thought might be given to the development of an optimal information and advice service. Would it be more helpful to clients to create a special information and advice section manned by information officers with additional specialised training, either within the social services department or outside it by transferring some resources to Citizen's Advice Bureaux? Inherent in these suggestions is the concept of delineating clearer tasks in response to specific needs within the context of a social services team, abandoning the idea of the intake worker as a Jack-of-all-trades.

(3) Frail elderly and disabled clients might benefit by curtailing the endless round of occasional surveillance visits. Instead some social service input might go into the creation of neighbourhood support networks using both statutory (home helps, meals-on-wheels) personnel and volunteers. Those social workers who wish to develop such skills would then take on a quasi community worker role as initiators and advisors.

(4) It might prove more effective than hurried individual advice and advocacy to develop group and mutual help type of approaches to problems in home management, budgeting, child care, and

interpersonal relationships shared by a number of families – say in a housing development. Such activities would give some social workers a chance to become more expert in group work skills.

(5) It seems essential to devote some research resources to experimentation with different methods of intervention in chronically stressed families, and meanwhile to limit the social work resources going into this bottomless pit of endeavour.

Such a redeployment would give rise to a certain amount of specialisation (information, practical service delivery, neighbourhood work, group work) within the framework of an integrated social services department. These functional divisions would free social workers interested in casework from routine screening activities, straightforward service delivery and surveillance visiting. Such caseworkers could then devote themselves to the more complex material and non-material problems of the elderly and disabled, to the early problems of family disturbance, and the interpersonal manifestations of psychiatric disorder.

How would such developments affect the relationship between primary social care and primary health care, particularly in respect of social and psychiatric morbidity? The differentiation of recurrently highly generalised activities of social services departments into specialised functions, though not into the old fragmented specialties in terms of age or client categories, may help communication and ease referral decisions. For example, the primary health care team may wish to make more use of a streamlined and accessible information and advice service, both for their own benefit and the benefit of their patients, in order to find their way round the jungle of welfare state provision. General practitioners, aware of group work activities with mothers under material and emotional stress, may wish to use these facilities as a preventive measure for those young women identified by Brown and his colleagues[8] as being at high risk for the development of severe depression. Similarly the primary health care team may wish to notify confused and depressed elderly patients to the local neighbourhood schemes for close social support. The existence of a recognisable casework or counselling service may encourage general practitioners to refer emotional and family problems before they have reached crisis point necessitating some form of statutory action.

However, even a more differentiated social services department with more clearly defined functions may not always turn out to be the place to which people with mental health problems turn easily. Comparative studies of social service and general practice clients with socio-psychological problems may suggest that certain mental health problems are more easily tackled within the confines of general practice. For example, early counselling and support to parents who have produced a handicapped child; help in terminal care and bereavement; marital casework; work with people who have attempted suicide; social after-care of some schizophrenic patients who may find it easier to accept help within the familiar context of general practice. This still leaves for debate and experimentation which of these tasks should be carried out by which member of the ever-growing primary care team. There appears to be scope for considerable overlap in function between the health visitor, the psychiatric community nurse, the social worker and the most recent newcomer the "counsellor". Rumour has it that the clinical psychologist is also now turning an eye towards general practice.

Since skilled human resources are limited, experimentation and action research is badly needed to throw light on the specific contributions these different variants of the helping professions can make to the mental health problems arising in general practice. Not only would such research have to consider how the input differs as between the different types of helpers and whether there are any differences in outcome, but also what the consumer feels about these different forms of help, what their relative costs are, and above all what team size and level of complexity is manageable and tolerable in primary health care.

References

1.   Goldberg, E. M. and Fruin, D. J. (1976) Towards accountability in social work: a case review system for social workers, *Br. J. Social Wk.*, 6, No. 1.
2.   Goldberg, E. M., Warburton, R. W., McGuinness, B. and Rowlands, J. H. (1977) Towards accountability in social work: a year's intake to an area office of a social services department, *Br. J. Social Wk.*, 7, No. 3.
3.   Goldberg, E. M. *et al.* 1978. Towards accountability in social work: long term work in an area office. *Br. J. Social Wk.* 8, No. 3.
4.   Goldberg, E. M. and Neill, J. E. (1972) *Social Work in General Practice*, Allen & Unwin.
5.   Corney, Roslyn H. and Briscoe, Monica E. (1977) Social workers and their clients: a comparison between primary health care and local authority settings, *Journal of the Royal College of General Practitioners*, 27, May, 295-301.

6. Goldberg, E. M., Williams, B. T. and Mortimer, Ann (1970) *Helping the Aged: A Field Experiment in Social Work*, Allen & Unwin.
7. Booth, Tim (ed.), (1977) *Effectiveness and Priorities: Research Strategies for the Social Services*, Proceedings of the Annual Workshop of the Social Services Research Group held at Loughborough University of Technology, 30 March–1 April 1977.
8. Brown, George W. *et al.* (1975) Social class and psychiatric disturbance among women in an urban population, *Sociology*, 9, No. 2.

CHAPTER 7

The Development of an Action and Counselling Service in a Deprived Urban Area

SUSAN HOLLAND
Battersea Action & Counselling Centre

The following is a critical but descriptive account of the five years of life of a project which began with a realisation that a service which effectively tackled psychological or interpersonal relationship difficulties whilst at the same time helping the individual to affect his social or environmental problems, would contribute more to the wellbeing of a neighbourhood than a service which tackled only one side of these interacting forces. The problems of putting this ideal into practice are formidable and have only to some extent been overcome in this project. Valuable lessons have, however, been learned and the purpose of the following pages is to enable others to avoid repeating our mistakes.

1967-1973

This was a period of intense community involvement in the Battersea area. A group of us had been involved in tenants' organisations, various campaigns around public housing and land issues, and the production of a local newspaper. Although this was voluntary work, it took so much of our time and commitment that it was a constant reference point for our professional working lives as clinical psychologist and social worker. Conversely, we tended to bring our professional knowledge into our community actions. It was evident that social problems such as poor housing, low incomes, and unemployment not only have an effect upon the neighbourhood; there appeared to be a dynamic interaction between such problems and the prevalence of psychological difficulties. Social problems frequently included psychological problems, whilst the latter in turn disabled the individual from taking action to alter environmental difficulties. A vicious circle of powerlessness set in. During our community campaigns we had encountered many instances of psychological distress, usually in the form of incapacitating depression or anxiety states. Conversations with local GPs had confirmed that an increasing number of their patients were presenting psychological difficulties. One GP referred cynically to the "Valium Tonnage" of the locality, particularly on the new housing estates.

During 1973, the social worker and myself formulated the idea and produced a written proposal for a neighbourhood mental health centre based in the locality in which we had been most active in our community campaigns. We proposed to utilise our skills as both psychotherapists and social activists, by providing a counselling or therapy service in the context of a network of neighbourhood action groups both within and without the building. The basic assumption was that the root cause of mental problems was to be found in the interaction between interpersonal relationships and the social context in which they occurred. This approach to psychotherapy incorporated both the short-term aim of *alleviating* immediate individual suffering and the longer-term aim of utilising and developing neighbourhood structures which could have a *preventative* influence. In addition, we planned to set up a program of talks and open forums on mental health, social welfare, and environment. Finally, we incorporated the hope that, if successful ourselves, we could select and train local people to take on the work of counselling their neighbours. We did not, at that stage, devise *how* they could be selected and trained.

January 1974–September 1974

By the end of 1973 the project was functioning in skeletal form. We had rented a derelict three storey shop in a busy high street in Battersea, which we renovated and paid for ourselves, with contributions from community groups using the premises. Our employers (the Tavistock Clinic and Lambeth Social Services Department) gave us one afternoon a week off work to set up the centre. We then approached numerous charities for funding without success until the Mental Health Foundation agreed to support us for a pilot period starting in January 1974. There would be a salary for one worker plus running costs. During this period I would be employed as a therapist and general organiser for most of the week. If the project proved viable within a few months, we would approach the Council for funds for a second worker. In the meantime the social worker continued to be "loaned" from his Department for one afternoon a week.

Because this was the most crucially formative phase, it was also the most difficult and conflict-ridden. It was soon apparent that we had embarked on the project under-financed, and under-staffed. The building was in disrepair and under constant threat of early demolition. Space was limited because family members of our original community action group had taken up residence in the building, but soon found their needs and interests in conflict with those of a mental health centre. After their departure, another attempt to have residents in the building again proved untenable. It was only when all rooms became available for offices and group meetings that the place could start to be a neighbourhood resource and action centre. The lesson here was that although a resident "caretaker" seemed necessary, domestic interests tended to be incompatible with general development.

Much time was spent initially making contact with local groups and with people wanting to set up new groups. We offered the use of the premises to those we thought would support and contribute to the general aims of the centre. Our main criterion for selecting such groups was that they be actively involved in trying to improve the conditions of local working people, socially and/or psychologically. Examples of regular users of the premises during that period were: an adolescents' group, a claimants' union, a mental patients' union, a West Indian band and a street theatre.

Our aim in using the premises in this way was to encourage each group to have some interaction with the other groups and individuals in the building, even if only at the level of an exchange of information. We specifically told new users this and tried to discourage groups from using us merely as convenient premises. Achieving our aim was a tortuous exercise in group dynamics and extremely time consuming. The task was particularly difficult as therapy and social action tend to be in opposite, exclusive and mutually suspicious camps. Our task, which essentially aimed to interconnect the two, was bound to be conflictful. Before long it was possible to see which groups had been sympathetic to the general aims of the centre. Others had dissociated themselves but had opportunistically used the Centre's facilities. It was only possible to guess which groups had attracted the local people and which had alienated or frightened them.

By the end of this period we had expanded our own resources to include not only therapy and advice but a bookstall and low-cost printing service run by a volunteer printer. A non-profit green grocer stall was started by a disabled pensioner who had originally come to the centre for help. This was later to become one of the main, certainly the most visible aspects of the project. It continues to provide a useful service to pensioners and claimants, but has not lived up to our hopes of becoming a focus of OAP activity.

It was this original loose network of groups and services which was to influence the type of "consumer" or "client" who called at the centre for help of some kind. The reputation that the Centre developed in this formative period was conditioned by the fact that we had founded the place on our social action contacts rather than developing these out of therapy and advice services. This sometimes helped, sometimes hindered us in attracting local working people and their families.

We did not advertise except for a notice in the shop window. This was partly because the notion of therapy as a form of help in this kind of context was very difficult to communicate, and partly because our limited staff resources could not have coped with a great number of callers. For the same reason we did not at first make any formal approaches to the Social Services or Area Health Authority to accept us as a referral agency. Also, we wanted to try to get local people to use us independently even though we did not have the authority or respectability of a council department or National Health Clinic. Although this method meant a slower build-up of callers, it proved to be a good way to develop our identity as separate from the statutory agencies and what local people termed "the Welfare".

By the end of our pilot period we had had a substantial, although not huge, number of callers who were mainly self-referred and who had heard about us through neighbours or through members of groups using the premises. A small proportion of these had come asking for help directly with psychological and interpersonal problems mainly about difficulties with spouses, children, or parents. Many callers came asking for help with a specific material problem such as housing or social security and confined their request to this. On the other hand, frequently, people would come with a material problem but soon expand the discussion to interpersonal difficulties of a confidential nature but without making a direct request for help.

The help offered by our claimants' union linked in well with our therapy service. People coming with unemployment problems were often burdened with interpersonal problems, and vice versa. Some of our most useful work has involved the Claimants' Union officer and therapist working together on problems, in a threesome with the person. An example was a middle-aged Jamaican woman who had fainted in the Social Security office. Her GP was treating her for depression and had said she may have to go into psychiatric hospital. She would sometimes have to sit in a queue most of the day at the Social Security office and then be told when she got to the window "No, we can't do anything for you today". She would say nothing but go home and cry quietly in front of her young children (her husband had walked out some years before). As therapist, I focused on her rage which was habitually suppressed by her upbringing as a "good girl", but this was discussed in the context of what she and the claimants union officer could do in their struggle with the Social Security office. After that she had no recurrence of fainting. Since then she has come to see myself or one of the other therapists whenever there has been a particularly painful crisis in her life, and has tried to help some of her friends and neighbours by talking to them about the kind of things that we had discussed. This contact has been on-going for three and a half years.

The lesson we have learned is that skilled psychotherapy is useful in a neighbourhood setting where it can be accepted in short "doses" over a long period of time, and in the context of everyday life and its material struggles.

Because multi-faceted problems were so frequent, it soon became apparent that an essential skill demanded of therapists was to be able to make an initial judgement of which requests required practical advice and introduction to activist groups and which required *additional* psycho-therapy involving interpersonal issues. It became a basic rule that practical problems must never be overlooked due to our psychotherapeutic zeal.

Only when people saw that we tried to tackle their material problems with them would they trust us with their interpersonal difficulties. An example is Mrs. K. who came because her landlord had told her she and her small son must vacate their flat because he had sold the house. She had been preparing to pack her bags and go on the street because the landlord was, she said, "a nice man" and she didn't want to cause him any trouble. She went on to talk about her separation with her husband and the death of her last child at birth. Mrs. K. believed that the midwife had strangled the child. She was relieved to talk about this "unspeakable" event and it seemed as if her grief and hatred had made her indifferent and careless in her struggle with the landlord. After two sessions, Mrs. K. did not visit us again but kept her flat.

We had many problems connected with evictions during this phase, which reduced dramatically after the change in the Rent Act giving security of tenure to furnished as well as unfurnished tenants.

Another large group of "customers" during this phase were those who would drop in on errands or with questions concerning community politics. They would then go on to talk at length about psychological problems of some kind, usually interpersonal difficulties or "identity" crises. The "client therapist" nature of the interaction was not acknowledged, although they would be aware of the professional skills offered by the centre. It was as if an explicit recognition of the interaction would negate its usefulness or perhaps humiliate them. Some would specifically avoid the professionals but prefer to unburden themselves on the untrained volunteers. Any therapeutic orthodoxy or formality was anathema to them and yet they wanted to have something more profound and penetrating than a friendly chat. Although the project was not intended for this group who were generally young, educated, and socially active, the centre had unintentionally provided the kind of atmosphere that would attract these young people who rejected formal counselling agencies. This category of "consumers" could have increased had I personally wanted to give the time but I tended to discourage them in favour of using our limited resources for the less educated and more socially isolated. Ironically, the lesson was that for the educationally sophisticated the centre must not look too respectable and must espouse amateurism; and for the culturally underprivileged it must look more respectable and offer professional skills.

Since that time, there has been a growth of "radical" therapy and counselling groups which provide therapy for the young educated section of the population. With the recent increase in personnel at the Centre, we have ourselves become more flexible, but generally try to adhere to our original policy of putting our main effort into attracting the less well educated local people, particularly young mothers on the nearby council housing estates.

It was with this policy in mind that for the next phase of the project most of our resources and energies were put into setting up a nursery as an integral part of our establishment. This was not altogether uninfluenced by the fact that the project had earlier been interrupted for two months while I was on maternity leave. Both my clients and myself had a real need for help with toddlers.

October 1974–November 1975

By now, Wandsworth Borough Council had agreed to provide the salary for another psychologist or social worker, and eventually to take over the entire funding of the project from the Mental Health Foundation. A social worker started work with us in August 1975 but had left without notice by the beginning of December. We had by then extended our educational and public relations work by giving talks and receiving visitors at the centre by people who were interested in developing our kind of work.* We had taken on our first student social work placement trainee and had become actively involved in the local Community Health Council. The Secretary of the latter set up a temporary office in our premises, and has since been an active member of our Management Committee. From being entirely administered by myself and a part time social worker, we had developed a Management Committee made up of people working at the centre or contributing to its development. We had refused to have a borough councillor on this committee but had bowed to the council's demand to produce a constitution. Our "unofficial" administrative policy was that all those employed at the centre would automatically join the Management Committee. Inevitably, we were to grow and grow. The majority of that original committee has remained to the present day.

*M. P. Bender, *Community Psychology*, Methuen (1976).

December 1975–March 1976

Our nursery, or rather, toddler day-care unit was functioning by the beginning of this phase. We had renovated the top floor with the help of mothers who had been involved in the counselling due to marital violence or other family problems. The Child Minding unit of the Social Services had agreed to pay us the statutory rate per head for each child. This proved unviable financially but with the child payments plus the unused salary for a second counsellor we scraped together the funds to employ two local women who were registered child-minders. One of these women, Ann, was among the main pioneers of this very difficult venture, and although she is no longer employed by us, has kept her child in the nursery. The mothers themselves helped out voluntarily but this was always in conflict with their very understandable need to be relieved from the constant demands of their children. Pressure from us to get "involved" with the children would frequently increase their feelings of guilt or inadequacy. Alternatively, they would express resentment that the professionals were well paid whilst they were expected to work for nothing. We professionals, conversely, saw ourselves as very much underpaid compared with workers in the statutory services. In both groups, financial martyrdom had its limits.

We had been naïve when we had first embarked on our plan of attracting volunteers to the centre. *Giving* rather than selling one's labour is seen as a luxury for only the privileged or the eccentric, and something that most of our mothers were already oppressed by in the unpaid limbo of domestic labour. During therapy sessions with local people, it was shown that bitter and even violent arguments over money; who earned it and what it paid for, were often the basis of marital problems. Earning money equals power in domestic struggles. This fundamental fact has always limited the development of parent involvement and other forms of voluntary activity within the centre.

The lesson here was that in financing the project we should have obtained funds for paying local people who wanted to be involved in the work of the centre.

By the end of this phase we had a thriving although underfinanced and underequipped child care unit which we would develop towards registration as a nursery. The original bias towards being a meeting place for the mothers had given way to a less casual atmosphere of more individual attention to the children. The local child-minder staff had been replaced by nursery worker in the borough, and a local girl who had worked in a private nursery. A conflict was apparent between the kind of facilities that would alleviate the mothers' deprivations and the kind that would alleviate the childrens'. *Theoretically*, providing for the emotional and social needs of the mothers would enable them to better provide for their childrens', but this did not seem to happen within the same space. We found that the children needed to experience an *alternative* to their mothers, as much as their mothers needed to get a break from their children. Similarly, the need for alternative experiences prompted us to take on a male nursery worker. Many of our children had grown attached to a male figure in their household who had abruptly left or been left by mothers who took their children with them. Development of the nursery was greatly limited by lack of space and the deteriorating condition of our building as the bulldozers swept adjoining shops and houses away.

April 1976–October 1976

The appointment of a second counsellor (a social psychologist) marked the start of a new phase and a great leap forward in the individual and marital therapy provided at the centre. Most of the couples came to us through the local Women's Aid refuge and the neighbourhood Law Centres. Invariably the woman contacted us first because she wanted to have another try at living with her man. The man would come along unwillingly and with the mutual understanding that *he* was being given another chance. Our insistence that we as therapists were as much concerned with helping them to separate "rationally" and "knowledgeably" as with uniting them, proved to be an amorphous concept for either of them to grasp. *One* of them had to be blamed for the conflict. If the woman remained a resident of the Women's Aid refuge the counter-culture there of resistance to male oppression would confirm her in her "innocence" but if she returned to her man he would see this as an admission of her "repentance" for straying from home. Either way, our work with them rarely led to "happy" endings, but at best a recognition that mutual torture contributed nothing towards changing the miseries of their class and social situation.

November 1976-May 1977

In November 1976 we "opened shop" in new premises with euphoric activity which was soon to be squashed as we found ourselves in financial difficulties again. The renovations and fittings, particularly in the nursery had put us badly into debt and we were still being blocked by officials from receiving the disturbance costs due to us for having to move premises. In addition we had no secretary. It was not until a long time later, and after a display of considerable local support for the centre's work, that the council agreed to give us a bit more money.

In the meantime, we had taken on two social worker trainees to do placements with us. They became involved in some of the therapy work as well as general advice giving and duties in the nursery. This training commitment meant allotting some time for supervision but was very valuable in providing both Department of Health and Social Security funds and enthusiastic staff. Having now enough people to provide a rota for manning the nursery, we were able to take time out for staff meetings in which we could discuss theoretical and practical issues concerning therapy and child-care.

The method and content of educating ourselves and local people was soon to become one of the central concerns for future development within the project. Also during this time, there was an upsurge of parent involvement as they demanded more say in nursery policy. They wanted more cleanliness, better food, and more emphasis on structured play and "lessons". They did not want to spend more time with the children but they did offer to form a cleaning rota. Particularly, they wanted the nursery to open longer hours so that they could get jobs. An uneasy compromise would have to be made. Working mothers could not be "involved" in the nursery but "involved" mothers would turn the nursery into a very different place.

By the end of this phase, our reputation as a somewhat unorthodox and grubby looking but dependable service had brought enough of the local people to us to justify our existence. In therapy we had helped people of all ages and races with a wide range of interpersonal problems; sometimes to their satisfaction; sometimes not. Examples include a couple who despised and hit each other but mutually loved their children; a single mother whose seven year old daughter had started stealing from school; a divorcee who had brought up his children single-handed but now feared they no longer needed him; a single mother whose baby had been taken into care due to her boyfriend's violence; and a woman who wanted to go back to her teenage son but couldn't bring herself to leave her alcoholic lover. Many of these people showed us that they found one or two sessions useful but did not want to see us weekly over a long period. They wanted to come back when and if they needed to and they often did.

Besides these local people there had been a slowly increasing trickle of "outsiders", including a student who was unable to urinate in public lavatories; some couples who wanted to "communicate"; a homosexual who was annoyed that his GP would not prescribe him tranquillisers; and various people wanting an "alternative opinion" on their mental state from the one given by their GP or hospital psychiatrist. Several had been sent to us through the Community Health Council.

Although this latter category of people were not refused our services, they generally demanded a heavy commitment of our time and expected many and regular sessions. The lesson here was that once our psychotherapy service became more widely known and respected it would attract a more culturally privileged group who wanted psychotherapy but found it too expensive or unavailable. Because local people were not clamouring for our services, we were often drawn into spending time on this more "receptive" group rather than using it to go out into the neighbourhood and actively persuade local people to use us.

A lesson we learnt was the importance of using familiar language. We tended to speak of "mental" health whereas most of our clients spoke of physical or material health even when they meant such states as anxiety or depression. We had to find out more about ways of talking about mental health. It seemed that we needed to have someone who would spend most of their time *outside* the building on the local estates, talking to people about matters of everyday living.

October 1977

It is not clear what eventual direction the project will take. Our influence, if any, in preventing mental breakdown among local people and their families is not proven; but nor has it been researched.

My personal "do-it-yourself" blue-print for any future working-class mental health centre, would include the provision of finance for the payment of local "volunteers", as well as statutory rates of pay for the professionals. This *economic* basis would ensure that the project develops towards a real incorporation of local working class people in addition to the trained professionals serving them. "Good neighbourliness" should not be an excuse for the under-privileged to look after themselves on the cheap.

In addition, the basis of such a project should not depend on already existing political structures and groupings, but should try to develop its own arising out of the services provided and the local people using them. The reason for this is the need for local people rather than culturally privileged radicals to predominate.

It should be clear that I consider the Battersea Action and Counselling Centre, up to the present time of writing, to have failed in its original objective. Nevertheless, in terms of its less ambitious aims of helping a substantial number of local people to combat the mental and material sufferings of everyday life, it has been a unique and inspiring success.

CHAPTER 8

The Libra Project — An Experimental Community-Based Self-Help Group Analytical Approach into Alcohol Abuse

RONALD MAGGS

The results of treatment for alcoholism are such that there is much room for the use of new approaches. At best, somewhere between 16 per cent and one third of patients are likely to achieve abstinence, and as many as 66 per cent will either worsen or experience minimal improvement. Edwards and Guthrie,[1] have shown that there are no particular advantages to in-patient as compared to out-patient care, whilst Willems and his colleagues,[2] have demonstrated that there is little to be gained by prolonging the period of in-patient care. Most authorities are agreed that patients tend to arrive for treatment many years too late, very often after irreversible changes have taken place either within the individual or within his family and life pattern. Quite apart from the *late identification of the problem*, a *lack of motive* is often exhibited by alcoholics in a treatment programme and these factors reduce therapeutic prospects.

Probably one of the most effective approaches in people with drinking problems is that used by Alcoholics Anonymous. The method and style is however only suitable to a small proportion and, judged on the basis of consultant psychiatric practice, people are either driven away by the dominance of the principles or arrive on the scene far too late for help or need more understanding and support before they are ready for such a group experience.

The taking of drugs and alcohol indiscriminately is very much part of a man-made disease — if the condition is allowed to reach disease proportions. If, therefore, one approaches the situation afresh on the basis that we know very little and perhaps there is much to be learned from the sufferer so that he could be enabled to live a different pattern of life, some further progress in understanding the condition might result. There is, perhaps, no other condition besides alcoholism to which Sigerest's comments[3] are more appropriate: "Health cannot be forced upon the people. It cannot be dispensed to the people. They must want it and be prepared to do their share and to cooperate fully in whatever programme a country develops."

Attention was drawn recently[4] to the principle attributed to Illich[5] that: "Health is something people do, not something people get." The hypothesis upon which Libra is based is that, through participation in a community-based self-help scheme, people with drink problems can be helped more effectively than by other approaches. It was evolved out of a series of unsuccessful attempts to help a sufferer by in-patient/out-patient methods. He had experienced problems over a period of more than twenty years and had received treatment at two of this country's leading alcoholic units. Alcoholics Anonymous had been of limited use to him so what had we to lose? The patient *might* benefit from regular contact with others who, like himself, had not benefitted from treatment. The project arose out of a short list of names and telephone numbers given to the patient, on the basis of which he arranged a first meeting.

Whatever has been achieved in Libra has grown from the joint realisation of the psychiatrist and the patient that what had been tried in the past had been unsuccessful and that a new, cool look at ways in which the situation might be approached afresh could be advantageous. The methods that are being used and developed within Libra are ones based upon the belief that the sooner individuals can move from a sufferer to a helper role, the more likely are they to be motivated in therapy situations.

An analysis of the methods that have been used shows that a number of principles of therapy in the orthodox sense have been broken. Thus, whilst most units for the treatment of alcoholism are based upon a group or community therapy approach attached to an in-patient experience, Libra is predominantly community-based. It meets in people's homes although, if in-patient care is necessary, members of the group will maintain contact with the person during his stay and, thereafter, provide support after discharge from hospital. Libra, with its several patterns of group activity, both an open-ended and a closed group situation, ought not to survive for the division of group forces should have resulted in a weakening of the large group identity. In fact, the substantial growth of Libra over a period of four of its five years' existence occurred at a time when group activity consisted of a weekly large open-ended group experience. The emergence of pairing and small closed group activities, instead of weakening the large group identity, in fact strengthened it. On a number of occasions, it has been found that matters worked through within fairly small groups have been able to be brought back to the large group, which has been able to pursue matters further. The small group activity has, therefore, acted as a catalyst to the larger group experience. The weekly open-ended group, as it has become more confident, has slowly increased its functions and, indeed, modified them over a five year span. It is perhaps surprising to observe that it has been able to cope with all social groups and the extremes of intellect.

During the first year of the group, an attempt was made to limit it to eight people with the purpose of constructing a small purpose-defined experience. The aim was to select people who had expressed a desire for help and who seemed motivated towards therapy. This narrowly-defined approach was abandoned towards the end of the first year because it was observed that, owing to the high mobility of the people selected — some even moving overseas — the construction of the small closed group was impracticable. It was then planned to set no limit on the size of the weekly group meetings. The intention was to establish a small nucleus which would serve both as a continuous force within the larger open-ended group situation and also to develop this core for service in the community by involvement in crisis situations. At the end of the first year, the group had determined its attitude towards professionals and visitors (*vide infra*) and it became clear that a large open-ended group situation seemed to meet the needs of sufferers far more effectively. This basis was used and found most effective during the earlier formative years and existed at the time of the assessment of the group by Lucy Younger, a social worker having become interested in the group's activities and who saw the experience as the basis of a thesis. Subsequent growth and modification of the group functioning occurred as a result of her report and as a result of the further experience of the group. Most recently, a development has been the introduction of smaller, closed, purpose-built groups geared to specific patients or particular problems. Although practically effective, it is too early as yet to assess the significance of this development.

During the first year of Libra, persons with evidence of cortical damage or encephalopathy were excluded. As the group established its identity, this exclusive policy was relaxed. It was found that the group coped with this sole "organic" member well, eventually helping her to settle outside of hospital, and hopefully learning something from her in the process.

When the group was established, the intention had been to limit it to people with drinking problems. It has been shown, however, that nearly one third of the membership had co-existent problems with drugs, usually barbiturates. Libra has, therefore, been registered as a charity having an interest in people with alcohol and drug problems and problems of life. It has been unusual to encounter a person in the group who drank or took drugs indiscriminately for no obvious reason. Usually, some resistant problem in relationships, such as husband/wife interaction or say a dependency situation of the adult/child, was present. All too often, the group has found itself coping with a major disruptive experience involving a whole family.

The following are some of the more important factors associated with the group:

Functional description of unit

A community-based self-help system of therapy, using group analytical methods, for people with problem drinking, drug taking and life problems.

Group functioning

This is achieved by a weekly large open-ended session, backed by selected small, closed groups aimed at specific tasks. A telephone answering service provides 24-hour coverage and allows counselling of the acute crisis and earlier intervention.

Principles of the group

Membership involves acceptance of the following principles:

(1) An interest or involvement with problems of liquor and/or drugs.

(2) A desire to learn.

(3) An intention not to reject.

These principles are inherent within the individual and the group. They allow the patient who cannot at the moment declare his intention to abstain to be a member and encourage people *to move from a sick to a helper role.*

Leadership of the groups

This has evolved from the individual group structure. In the ordinary course of events, no group is led by a member of the caring professions. This has been the principle from the very early days of its formation, and indeed the founder and leader of the Libra project is a former teacher with personal experience of a drink problem over many years. The objectives of the group require that its leadership should be on a horizontal rather than a hierarchical basis.[6]

Role of the professional

This has been from the very start of the group maintained at a low key. The group expects that professional help will always be available whenever necessary, no matter what the hour of the day or night or day of the week. In group situations, professionals influence discussions as to what therapeutic prospects there are, using a traditional orthodox approach. There are abundant opportunities for professionals using their fundamental techniques to evolve, by new attitudes, an approach tailored for the individual. The fact that this is shared within the group means that the experience is available for all to learn from subsequently, i.e. if the approach fails, why did it fail? What other hypotheses can be constructed upon the failure? How can the future approach be modified?

Premises

These are preferably part of a person's home. Individual members of the group can invite the group to hold a weekly meeting in their house.

This encourages the involvement of friends and relatives and, situated as it is in the community, acts as a ready source of contact for others with similar' problems. Early involvement of patients is therefore encouraged and is possible.

A hospital setting for group sessions has been tried but found undesirable. This stems partly from the indirect implication of attitudes to care but also because of the relative isolation of the hospital from the community in which the problems are generated and present.

Basic goal

The basic goal of the Libra approach is to encourage the person to move from *a sufferer to a helper role*. This becomes possible when the state of health is more stable. The selection of group members for appropriate tasks is important.

Telephone answering service

A telephone answering service results in members being involved in crisis situations of any kind. Whilst this provides a unique opportunity for sufferers to learn, at the same time, basic knowledge to cope with such a situation is necessary.

Training programmes

These and the provision of library resources are an important part of the equipment of any counsellor. Subjects covered include such things as the chemical effects of alcohol and drugs upon the body, the nature of a dependent state, emotional and physical, withdrawal symptoms and some characteristics of emotional disturbance. Indications for special help are also part of the schedule. The group is in the process of establishing a library to be able to provide suitable reading lists.

Involvement of relatives and friends

This is invaluable. Supportive groups are of great relevance not only through physical assistance but also because the sufferer takes great comfort in knowing that relatives and friends get together to discuss difficulties and to provide practical help at crisis times. It is often found that such help is needed throughout a period of twenty-four hours and, although it may not be described as the kind of help that an experienced social worker would give, it is nevertheless vital in terms of allowing the family to survive at the time when one of its members is in great distress. Providing a safe place for children and making the home situation safe whilst the disturbed member is being helped through his toxic condition, possibly having to help cope with an overdose and to take appropriate action thereon — these are all examples of situations that have been encountered. A study of the Libra project (referred to below) revealed that in the context of the group, spouses could give each other valuable support or indeed can help other members to understand the reactions of their own wife or husband.

Continuing responsibility

A continuing sense of responsibility of the group was very much evident in the early days and there was agreement that, if a member failed to turn up, two other members of the group would be appointed to contact the absent member in order to ascertain intentions. As the group has grown in size, it has become less easy to fulfil this function. Some other method of dealing with the absentee is being formulated from our current experience.

Relationship with other bodies interested in alcohol and drugs

This is essentially a complementary one. Libra may become involved with a person and work through certain problems over a period of a year or two before that person becomes ready to cope with, say the AA. For a person to express verbally or even act upon a resolution of determined abstention is a state that is not very easily understood and the pathway towards this and the duration of time necessary is still very uncertain and often protracted. It has been our experience in Libra that discussions regarding any available form of treatment are of value because there is clear evidence that an approach which might be suitable for one is completely unsuited to the needs of another. There are at least two known instances where the Libra approach has been rejected because it has been seen and felt to be overwhelming. In the case of one male of labouring class, he recognised this within his first few meetings and, thereafter, moved over to AA which he found much more acceptable. The other was a highly intelligent man who had been doing battle with his drinking problems for many years and who had the intelligence to involve himself actively in an analytical process and would have been a great asset to the whole group situation but he, likewise, found the group too threatening. He had previously been involved with AA over a period of a number of years but all to no avail and, ultimately, he stole sufficient goods to ensure that he would be committed to prison, to a place of safety.

It has been the experience of some individuals involved in Libra who have in the past rejected AA that they have eventually evolved a better understanding of their condition through Libra and, after a period of a year or two, then find the approach of AA meaningful to them. Such people have tended to continue to involve themselves in AA and Libra with sustained benefit.

Insofar as the National Council for Alcoholism is concerned, again it is considered that the roles and methods of functioning are quite different both from the educational aspect and also from the attitudes that body has towards involving sufferers in the organisation and the treatment programme. But, nevertheless, there is a common ground between Libra and the Council and a complementary relationship exists between them.

Relationship with other professional and community organisations

Although Libra is an activity linked to a low professional input, it has actively sought to develop strong links with the professional bodies, thus in the visitors' book appear the names of general practitioners, community physicians, consultants, social workers, probation officers, police, and representatives of voluntary bodies. The open-ended nature of the weekly meetings has allowed this and, because of the involvement and situation of the group in the community, close links exist and allow direct referral from any of these bodies. This is advantageous to the community in the sense that it encourages earlier involvement of the sufferer in the caring programme for there is no need to wait for the customary referral from the general practitioner to the consultant.

Size of groups

The large, open-ended group varies in size from fifteen to thirty. It has been our experience that, in private homes, if the meeting runs to anything over twenty, physical problems exist in terms of ventilation and concentration of cigarette smoke. Once such a group size has been reached, this has been the signal for the establishment of another group in that community or in a neighbouring one.

With regard to the closed, small group situation, geared to a specific task, its size is rarely more than four and it has been interesting to observe that matters worked through in this group situation have become the basis of discussion in the larger group on more than one occasion. Indeed, one can see that the function on occasions of the small group is to act as a catalyst for the larger, open-ended weekly group and there has been no evidence, so far, to suggest that the existence of one has been at the expense of the other for their basic functions and goals are quite different. The large group concerns itself more with matters of general principle, educational sessions and, if necessary, the identification of individual problems. The small group, on the other hand, is geared to an analysis of individual problems linked specifically to understanding the individual's life situation and the relevance of that situation to the drinking problem. It also allows a formulation to be made of possible ways in which the sufferer could plan for his future and then for the group to provide support during the activation of those plans.

Quite apart from these two patterns of groups, other sub-groups are formed, sometimes spontaneously. Out of the large open-ended group, one hears of pairing activities in which two members of the group have been involved in matters of common interest between meetings. Other couples may have been involved in following up an absentee of the group but, mostly, these sub-group activities have been brought back to the parent group from which the secondary development arose.

Counsellors, who have been involved in crisis situations which they have been unable to contain individually, set up small groups suitably composed to meet the needs of the individual crisis. Thus, one member may be enlisted to cope with children whilst another supports husband or wife. Such a group will remain in existence until the crisis has been contained and, upon its dissolution, the group experience will be fed back to the main group situation.

Social group representation

All social groups appear in the large group situation and each seems to make the appropriate contribution within its capacity. Examples of this are as follows: some group members find it more appropriate to provide the coffee, victuals, help with the washing of dishes, whilst others seem more content to be responsible for the writing of the group diary. Each respects the other's position and all participate in common activities.

Results

Hill and Blane[7] have pointed out some of the problems concerned in assessing the efficacy of any particular approach regarding alcoholism. They argue that there are objections to making comparisons in a single individual and prefer an approach which will compare the results of different treatments in groups of patients carefully matched in their disorder. It is not the intention of this paper to attempt to give an objective analysis of the Libra group. Instead, one can give general impressions. These are as follows:

There have been a number of instances in the group whereby people who have not been helped following periods of in-patient care have responded much more favourably in the community-based group situation. This has been the case with patients of all ages and perhaps the most significant changes that we have seen occurred in one of our earlier members who had failed to respond to more than a year's in-patient therapy. The group has had its deaths — four in a period of five years but it is also true that the group has saved lives.

The group was privileged some two years ago to have a social worker member who became sufficiently interested in its activities to make the study of the group the basis of an M.Sc. thesis.[8] Lucy Younger was particularly concerned in analysing how the group seemed to function and the writer is indebted to her for allowing the inclusion of some of her observations.

The Effectiveness of the Group from Members' Points of View

"The following assessment of the effectiveness of the group is based upon interviews with nineteen regular attenders at group meetings and the personal experience of the author at group meetings. Of the group 13 were heavy drinkers, 1 was addicted to drugs, 3 were spouses and 2 were professionals. Of the 14 members with a drink or drug problem, 9 had been in-patients before joining the group but the remaining 5 had a problem of shorter standing and less severity at the time of joining the group.

Experience Prior to Joining the Group

Supportive networks, both professional and personal do not seem to have been strong in most cases and this applies whether members lived alone or with a spouse and children and irrespective of the type of employment or severity of the drink problem. Most members had had several contacts with professional agencies relating to drink or drug problems. Eight of the nine with in-patient experience of hospital felt that hospitals were only helpful in terms of administering drugs, although one member had a more positive attitude. The one member who had experience of an 'alcoholic unit' felt that the specialist unit was not desirable. Everyone had encountered one or two helpful doctors or nurses but many complained of lack of interest or understanding amongst professionals. Only four out of fourteen felt that their contacts with GPs had been helpful. GPs were seen as useful in giving out pills but rarely in giving any other kind of help. One had had contact with a social worker who had been helpful in practical matters but in no other way. Five members had had contact with AA and felt that the organisation helped many people but had not helped them. The criticisms of AA were that it was 'a bit sanctimonious'; that members took the view that all drink is evil and abstinence is the only answer; that they encouraged excessive recounting of drinking exploits and also that AA insisted on anonymity and often increased guilt feelings.

On the whole members felt their families to be unsupportive, although six found their families to be supportive at times as well as destructive at others. Factors believed to contribute to the drink problem included ill-health and boredom (3 members); their job (5 members); unspecified aspects of their personal lives (every member). The response of members suggests that if families are to support a problem drinker they need a source of support and advice themselves. The Libra group aims to provide this.

The Value of the Group to Members

Group members valued the group for a number of reasons but of overriding importance were:

(a) The feeling that each member derived from the group that he was not the only person with a drink problem (emphasised by all the members).

(b) The opportunity to help others, which made them feel they had a worthwhile role to play (emphasised by 12 members).

(c) That their own recovery is a valuable contribution to the group in showing others, and in particular new members, that recovery is possible (mentioned by 4 members).

(d) The opportunity to meet people whom one can see outside the group meetings. Ten members see at least one other group member frequently outside the group meetings and all the other members contact others by phone or meet them sometimes. The frequency of contact with other members is probably affected by the wide geographical area from which members are drawn.

(e) The informal atmosphere in which some members (10) felt able to talk about themselves, many for the first time in their lives.

(f) The opportunity to learn about alcoholism and the problems causing and arising from it, and to understand both themselves and others better. In particular, members with a less severe drink problem have discovered the effects of alcohol from more hardened drinkers. This learning process has had a valuable preventative effect (10 members).

(g) Crisis prevention — 8 members felt that the group had prevented hospitalisation or family break-up and one member felt that by encouraging him to enter hospital, the group had prevented him collapsing totally (the group does not reject hospital facilities when these are needed).

Not only group meetings but also the leader's offer of temporary accommodation in times of crisis and his visits and telephone conversations with members at times of stress were mentioned by members as having prevented collapse, hospital admission or re-admission.

Negative Aspects

1. *The need for more general discussion*
All members felt that there was not sufficient discussion on topics of general concern where all members could join in. Five members stressed the fact that there is too much time devoted to individual therapy at group meetings. The result has been that three or four members have emerged as being good at the counselling role while others felt somewhat inadequate and became bored. The majority of members suggested discussing a set topic for about half of each meeting, allowing the remaining time for the discussion of individual problems. (Since this report was written, the group leader has begun working full time for Libra. He now has the time to give individual or family counselling on a more regular basis to more members, thus relieving the pressure to use group meetings as counselling sessions to the degree previously necessary.)

2. *The lack of adequate confrontation*
Six members (including three spouses) felt that the group tends to 'avoid painful areas' and 'skirt round things'. However, others believed that confrontation could be harmful. Clearly this is a

difficult area but as individual counselling becomes a more regular feature of Libra the leader can, perhaps, try and obtain the agreement of individual members for a full discussion of a particular issue within the group when this would be valuable. He could try and satisfy himself before the meeting that a member could tolerate an open discussion of a problem.

3. *The need for more availability*

All members, including the three spouses and two professionals, felt that the group needed to reach more people and to help existing members more adequately. The full time availability of the leader (since this report was written) will transform this situation. Nevertheless, over half the members felt that other members should be more involved in the support function in the interests of greater participation, quite apart from the need to extend the service.

4. *The need to be articulate*

One member pointed out that many people would not attend group meetings because the discussion would 'go over their heads'. Not only lack of education but also the type of background might be an inhibiting factor. The group includes a cross-section of educational backgrounds but it is probably true that less articulate members contribute less to discussions than others. Here again the greater availability of the leader and other members for individual counselling and support will to some extent meet this criticism.

5. *The depressing effects of the group*

Three members felt that constant reminder at group meetings of the failure of other members to keep their resolutions weakened their own confidence. It is undoubtedly true that some members feel the need to put the whole period of their bad times behind them, including the group. Others find that as they overcome their drink problem they need the constant reminder of the danger of relapse and the support and facility to help others which the group provides.

Changes in the Pattern of Professional and Personal Support Systems

When looking at the professional contacts members have had

since joining the group, it is noticeable that there have been far fewer contacts compared with the pre-group period. All members had some contact before joining, whereas 5 have needed no contact at all since joining. Nine had been in hospital before joining, whereas only 4 had in-patient treatment since joining. However, 6 were receiving regular support from such sources as GPs and out-patient clinics before joining and this number has only dropped to 5 since joining. It is hard to draw any conclusions from these findings for the variables that affect the need for help are so complex that it is impossible to attribute directly decreased professional contacts to the effectiveness of the group.

Turning to personal supports, the same number of members found family and friends supportive and unsupportive or both, since joining as before joining. However, 4 members have found jobs supportive and only one member has found his job unsupportive compared to one member with a supportive job and 5 members with unsupportive jobs before joining, and 5 members have found part-time occupations or hobbies supportive since joining, whereas this category was not mentioned at all for the pre-group period. Only one member and one spouse felt they had no supports outside the group since joining, compared to 6 members and 1 spouse before joining.

Amongst the 14 members and 3 spouses, 34 unsupportive elements and 35 supportive elements were mentioned since joining compared with 35 unsupportive and 15 supportive elements before joining. Again one can draw no firm conclusions but it is possible that the group experience helps increase the ability to find personal supports outside as well as inside the group, and may decrease the need to ask for professional support."

Development of Libra with and without funds

The earlier part of the exercise is one that can be launched and maintained without funds. It depends, however, upon the goodwill of patients, friends, relatives and colleagues. There seemed to be no shortage of this as evidenced by the hospitality of people offering their homes and the willingness of people in the community to tolerate the venture. However, once the development had reached the stage of requiring a telephone answering service, funds were needed which were more than could be raised through our weekly collection. This extension of the activities of Libra was only possible through the financial help provided by the Mental Health Foundation.

Reproduction possibilities

Any approach such as this could hinge upon the single, individual personality of the leader of the group. If this were the case, the possibility of being able to reproduce the method would be extremely limited. This aspect of Libra is particularly important for it is only by the identification of individual principles of function that can be produced elsewhere that the approach is other than of local significance. Libra started in the county town of Lewes and, later, developed a second group in Eastbourne. Subsidiary groups are planned elsewhere and, at the present stage of development, the method is applicable to a community of a little over 200,000. It is at an interesting stage of development in that it is showing evidence as to its possibilities of being reproduced by the active involvement of other members as group leaders. These have shown themselves through their performance in counselling sessions of the acute crises.

Director

The director of the Libra group has been spending less time in leading groups so that he is able to devote more of his energies to organising new groups in the greater part of East Sussex. This exercise is seen as a necessary precursor to determining ideal plans for dealing with alcohol and drug problems. Whether, for instance, it is necessary to have an in-patient unit or, if as believed, a better service can be provided by a community-based group experience.

In considering the change in functions of the director, thought has been given to his need to maintain contact with treatment situations. If, as is believed, these have played a part in his improved health, it would be important that these should be maintained. The development of his roles has allowed his continued involvement, particularly in small group activities.

Transport

Transport has proved to be of great importance in the life of the group. It is not uncommon for people with alcohol problems to be in a penurious state and most seem to be without cars. Besides serving an urban and rural area with poor public transport systems, some patients have suffered from phobic symptoms that have prevented them from travelling alone. Members have, therefore, shared expenses and the East Sussex Social Services have given invaluable help in defraying some travelling expenses.

In-patient care

In-patient care has only been used for the following purposes:
(a) Detoxification in the presence of a confusional state;
(b) Preventing or dealing with withdrawal symptoms in people who asked for this help or in whom the intake of liquor was such that withdrawal symptoms were anticipated;
(c) The presence of a psychiatric illness requiring in-patient treatment.
Edwards and Guthrie[1] had shown that in-patient care had no advantages over out-patient care. It would be our contention that to admit a patient to hospital will prevent him from dealing with the problems that existed in his immediate environment and, for this reason, in-patient treatment is avoided wherever possible.

Group analytic methods and Libra

Walton[9] has given a description of the group analytic method upon which the development of Libra has taken place. Its manifestation in the weekly large, open-ended group is clearly different from that which exists in the closed, small group sessions but the principle is firmly present in both. To quote Walton: "A new treatment potential is considered to exist in small psychotherapeutic groups which is not to be found in the two-person treatment situation of conventional psychotherapy." From a very natural progression of events and the nature of the origin of Libra, the emphasis has been upon a low key professional input although one which is always available from multiple disciplines. The bias of the group activity is towards a pragmatic consideration of complex life situations on the basis that sharing and thinking anew will result in the emergence of more effective approaches to the human problem. Once these approaches have been defined, the member is able to act upon them and the progress is reviewed at subsequent meetings. By this technique, good use is being made of any determination to learn by any member of the group, professionals or non-professionals, and a feedback to the group of the life situation has a very sobering effect! The testing time of both the large and small group activities comes when the sufferer seems not to be able to understand or to be lacking in motive and perhaps on these occasions the basic principle that we have of "no rejection" comes under great pressure but its very existence is of importance.

In the large group situation, there has been a tendency for the group to ask for didactic sessions on drugs and their effect on the body and, likewise, questions have arisen as to the way in which the body deals with alcohol. Many discussions have taken place on controlled drinking and the use of chemical deterrents has come up time and time again. It would be noted from Lucy Younger's analysis of the way in which the group functioned during its first three or four years, that in the large group there were problems in coping with individual life situations. This is not surprising, particularly in view of the tendency for large groups to split off into smaller ones with resultant chaos. For these reasons, particularly since the director has committed himself full-time to the work of the group, it has been possible to set up more small group activity which is already proving to be more productive.

In either of the group situations presenting, there are abundant opportunities for professionals to learn more about some of the reasons why motives for treatment seem to be so low and the difficulties that exist in analysing and understanding what the goal or attitude of a particular sufferer at one moment might be towards drinking compared with his attitude a day or so later. It has to be emphasised, however, that the Libra process is a developmental one and it is our intention to make whatever changes are necessary in the light of practical experience, for the group is essentially a pragmatic one.

Future assessment

This commentary on Libra is essentially a descriptive one. The intention has been to describe the origins, the developments and present state of the Libra organisation. Very little has been said about the detailed operation of it, nor has there been an analysis of its results in terms of success or failure. Hill and Blane[7] have described in detail the problems linked with such an exercise and favour a comparative approach evaluating treatment and non-treatment groups rather than using the individual as his own control. This analysis of Libra function is an exercise that will have to be done for the findings of an assessment are of direct relevance to the subsequent plans that the East Sussex Area Health Authority will be making for people with alcohol and drug problems. Sufficient has, however, been said to show from the experience gained during the past five years that the Libra approach breaks new ground, destroys some long-held beliefs and perhaps, most important of all, offers hope and a way ahead when other methods have failed.

Summary

A community-based self-help group analytic method of dealing with alcohol and drug problems is described. It functions upon the basis of a weekly large open-ended group, backed by small closed groups, the latter being specially selected. The large open-ended group allows early involvement of the sufferer, encourages education and allows a sufferer to see that it is possible to move from the sufferer to a helper role. The smaller closed group is selected for specific tasks and acts as a catalyst on occasions for the weekly open-ended group.

Libra has three principles inherent in membership that allow people, who have rejected Alcoholics Anonymous or other methods or who are not sure as to their goals regarding abstinence, to participate.

A telephone answering service encourages early involvement and provides an opportunity for sufferers to give a counselling service, so allowing a move to be made from a sufferer to a helper role. A training programme for counsellors is necessary. Professional input is low key but is readily available for any crisis situation.

Acknowledgments

I would particularly like to thank Mr. E. G. Evans for having allowed Libra to gain from his personal experience. Whilst neither he nor I believe that his experience is unique, nevertheless, I would like to acknowledge the special place that he has, and the part that he continues to play. As Director, he would be very happy to answer any questions regarding Libra. His address is 19 Lansdowne Place, Lewes (tel: Lewes 5298).

I should also like to thank the Mental Health Foundation, particularly Mrs. Molly Meacher,* who have made the financial grants that have allowed the work to go forward.

References

1.   Edwards, G. and Guthrie, S. (1966) *Lancet,* 1, 467.
2.   Willems, P. J. A., Letemendia, F. and Arroyave, F. *et al.* (1973) *Brit. J. Psych.,* 122, 637.
3.   Sigerist, H. F. (1941) *Medicine and Human Welfare,* New Haven.
4.   Lancet (1977) *Leader in Community Health Care,* Vol. II, 8048, 1114-5.
5.   Illich, I. (1976) *Medical Nemesis, The Expropriation of Health,* London.
6   Katz, A. (1970) Self-help organizations and volunteer participation in social welfare. *Social Work.* 15, 51-60.
7.   Hill, M. J. and Blane, H. T. (1967) *Q. Jl. Stud. Alcohol,* 28, 76.
8.   Younger, L. (1977) *An Experimental Approach to the Problems of Alcohol Abuse.*
9.   Walton, H. (ed.) (1971) *Small Group Psychotherapy,* Penguin, Harmondsworth.
10.   WHO (1967) Report of the 14th World Health Organization Expert Committee on Mental Health.
11.   Whitney, E. D. (ed.) (1970) *World Dialogue on Alcohol and Drug Dependence,* Boston Beacon Press.

*Projects Organiser.

Appendices to Part II

Appendix I

ROLF OLSEN

A Model of Emergency Management

At present our understanding of the aetiology of the psychiatric crisis is meagre and our management of the situation remains primitive. With one or two notable exceptions our solution to the emergency situation which cannot be contained within the living group is to remove the person defined as the patient to hospital, no matter whether the cause is thought to lie within the person himself, the nature of his relationships, his social environment, or in disease processes. This cannot be regarded as satisfactory, and we must ask ourselves whether it is possible to intervene more thoughtfully and with greater efficacy. From several points of view the personal, social and economic gains to be made by interventive strategies which do not rely solely on hospitalisation appear to be considerable.

In spite of this understanding social work has paid scant regard to its own role and contribution to the successful management of the psychiatric emergency. This neglect gives cause for concern, particularly as the utilisation of the crisis in the mental health emergency as the optimum moment for social work intervention is a concept, if not a technique, which has been known to social workers for more than twenty years. However, in spite of its long pedigree, the notion has received little attention in social work literature and there has been little systematic evaluation of its application or its effectiveness in practice.

An exception occurs in a study undertaken by John Clarke[1] in which he recorded his analysis of crisis management by six mental welfare officers. Clarke found that this group of social workers were anxious during their management of the psychiatric emergency and, in consequence, were unable to offer much constructive help to their client or his family. This finding supports an earlier view put forward by Grace Jackson,[2] who stated that many mental welfare officers saw their casework skills to be of little value in the crisis situation, with the result that they approach the psychiatric crisis in a state of confusion, reluctance and apprehension.

In contrast to this situation, the American social work and medical literature continually reports on the successful application of the strategy. Howard J. Parad, widely considered to be one of the major crisis theorists, in a recently published paper[3] considered that in the USA crisis intervention with the mentally ill has now reached the situation where it is "no longer an experimental fad but is now a generally accepted mode of social work practice in a wide variety of settings" (p.41). Parad goes on to report that the results of these theoretical and practical developments are reflected in a number of legislative changes. These include the provision in the Federal Community Mental Health Centres Act of 1963 mandating 24-hour emergency services. Secondly, some states, such as California, have passed legislation giving preference to the development of emergency services over hospitalisation, residential care and other forms of traditional out-patient care.

As indicated, the evidence which supports the use of this strategy in mental health emergencies is included in a number of papers. Parad considers that perhaps

"The most important and rigorous investigation into the effectiveness of family crisis intervention as a means of avoiding hospitalisation has been conducted by Dr. Donald Langsley and his former colleagues at the University of Colorado, Department of Psychiatry, Denver.[4,5] In this landmark study, 300 patients, all diagnosed by psychiatrists as requiring immediate hospitalisation, were randomly assigned to either a family crisis intervention treatment approach (experimental group) or to immediate psychiatric hospitalisation (control group). Follow-up interviews, after treatment, indicated that patients treated with a family crisis intervention approach were significantly less likely to be re-hospitalised than those who were initially hospitalised. Further follow-up studies at six and 18-month intervals indicated that the crisis intervention patients in the experimental group were faring as well as the hospitalised subjects, with respect to both social adaptation and ability to cope with life's crises. Moreover, those who were treated through out-patient family crisis intervention — when needing re-hospitalisation — were hospitalised for a significantly shorter period of time. Thus, the costs of mental health care are, in this era of cost-benefit consciousness, much reduced by family crisis intervention activities as compared with the expenses of hospitalising the patient. In addition, we cannot overlook the substantial social and other human costs in terms of the social stigma still associated, even during our current era of enlightenment, with the experience of hospitalisation."

Given this kind of evidence it becomes abundantly clear that we need to radically change the emphasis in our legislative framework as well as our methods of coping with the psychiatric emergency. *In toto*, the situation demands that we promote systems which stress "growth and development" rather than "illness and treatment".

To achieve this aspiration we need:

(a) To enable the "patient" and his living group to interpret their understanding of the meaning of the crisis and to mobilise their own resources for coping with the event.

(b) To achieve this first aim we need to concentrate resources upon the individual and his living group rather than upon hospital-based services. Given the present economic situation, this will require greater political commitment than has so far been shown, and a substantial redirection of the scarce resources at present allocated to hospital services.

(c) We must also develop legislation which aims at relieving the stress within the situation, rather than concentrating upon removing the individual to hospital. If removal from the living group is necessary, then we must recognise that this may be achieved in a number of ways and by removal to institutions other than hospital.

(d) To enact this last belief BASW recommends the introduction of a Community Care Order which would give an "approved social worker" the compulsory power to determine that a person reside or attend at specified places for specific purposes, and/or require that a person receive visits at his residence or elsewhere.

(e) Such a strategy will require that responsibility be placed on local
authorities to provide the treatment, care and control recommended under the Community Care Order.

This will require that social workers maintain a 24-hour service. This could
be provided in a number of ways, and the local solution should reflect the
particular circumstances. I think, however, that a great deal could be
achieved through the establishment of the proposed "crisis centres",
inter-professionally manned, conveniently located, and through which all
psychiatric emergencies would pass for screening, evaluation, management
and/or appropriate referral.

Social Work's New Role

There is no doubt that these radical recommendations have serious
implications, not only for legislative and organisational change, but also for
the practice of social work.

This view is supported by the considerable body of opinion which
upholds that the successful management of the mentally ill (particularly
within the community) and support of their living groups, requires the
provision of inclusive social work services. In relation to psychiatric
patients, "social work services" is a descriptive term used multifariously to
describe an assortment of supportive arrangements provided to
in/out-patients and their living groups. In its total sense it is meant to
embrace a variety of evaluative, therapeutic and supportive strategies
which include some twenty-one different treatment approaches[6] as well
as the full range of local authority provision of residential care, training
centres, occupational and sheltered workshops, day care, support for
self-help groups and voluntary workers, etc.

However, in spite of proven need, it remains a fact that the efficacy of
the social work services in relieving the mental, personal and social
maladies which impinge upon the patient and his significant others, rests
upon a shaky framework built by theoretical assumption, central and local
government policy, and agency dictate, rather than upon carefully
collected and assessed data.

This opinion was confirmed in my own study into the personal and social consequences of the discharged long-stay psychiatric patients.[7] Whilst the number of patients who received post-discharge social work support was higher (68 per cent) than that reported in other studies, there was little evidence that the social worker made a clear assessment of client need or of the strategies to be adopted to relieve them (pp. 450-61). In many instances he was uncertain of his role not only with the patient but also with living group members and relatives outside his living group. Equally important was the finding that nearly half (48 per cent) of the patients, 42 per cent of the landladies, and half of the other caring persons were unable to identify the social workers' objectives (pp. 453-5). It was concluded that in many instances the meeting between social worker and client represented no more than "contact", in which there was no clear agenda or understanding of purpose.

The conclusion to be drawn from this situation is that we urgently require a theory of the purpose and process of the social worker's intervention in mental health. As Whittaker points out[8] "whilst elegant theories, for example general systems theory, may be intrinsically interesting and marvellously well suited to developing an overall conceptualisation of practice, they will in the long run prove of precious little value to the practitioner unless they are also capable of yielding practical, concrete suggestions for helping clients overcome real life problems" (p. 14).

If we are to make good the current unsatisfactory situation and develop our social work services for the mentally ill, our primary task is to develop a theory in the service of practice. Therefore we need to proceed inductively and to build an overall theory of practice, which is based upon case experience and an evidence orientation.

The proposed model of emergency care would appreciably increase the powers and responsibilities of the mental health social worker. It is essential, therefore, no matter how contentious the debate, for BASW to prepare a code of practice for social workers in the mental health field, and to devise a system of accreditation, possibly by the establishment and maintenance of a register of social workers with the necessary level of training and experience to competently undertake these responsibilities.

132   *Rolf Olsen*

References

1. Clarke, J. (1971) An analysis of crisis management by mental welfare officers, *Brit. J. Social Work*, **1**, No. 1, 27-39.
2. Jackson, G. (1967) Authority and the mental welfare officer, *Brit. J. Psychiat. Social Work*, **9**, No. 1, 22-4.
3. Parad, H. (1976) Crisis Intervention in Mental Health Emergencies: Theory and Technique in Work with the Emotionally Disturbed and Mentally Disordered, In *Differential Approaches in Social Work with the Mentally Disordered*, M. Rolf Olsen (ed.), Brit. Assoc. of Social Workers.
4. Langsley, D. G. *et al.* (1971) Avoiding mental hospital admissions: a follow-up study, *Amer. J. Psychiat.*, **127**, 1391-4.
5. Langsley, D. G. and Kaplan, D. (1968) *The Treatment of Families in Crisis*, New York: Grune and Stratton.
6. Whittaker, J. K. (1974) *Social Treatment: an Approach to Inter-personal Helping*, Chicago: Aldine.
7. Olsen, M. R. (1976) *The Personal and Social Consequences of the Discharge of the Long-stay Psychiatric Patient*, Ph.D. Thesis, Univ. of N. Wales.
8. Whittaker, J. K. (1976) Treatment of Choice or Chance? In *Differential Approaches in Social Work with the Mentally Disordered*, M. Rolf Olsen (ed.), BASW.

Appendix II

JOHN GLEISNER

An Experimental Crisis Centre, Tameside, Greater Manchester

The experimental project is probably in the poorest of all the Area Health Authorities in the Country. It has only been open for a month at the time of writing, and the following information is necessarily therefore in the nature of an introduction to the project.

The Centre serves a catchment sector of 70,000 population (approximately one third of Tameside) and is co-terminus with the area of one sector of the local District General Hospital, and of two Social Services' Area Offices. It is the base for the major part of the area's secondary care supported by in-patient hospital care; and is financed under joint funding, each authority paying half. It has a maximum of 40 places per session — clients coming for anything between one and ten sessions per week.

The Centre has adopted a psychosocial rather than a medical model as a basis for its work. Many psychiatric conditions do not easily fit the medical model and many psychiatric patients are often regarded as a nuisance in a traditional hospital setting: people with labels such as personality disorder, neurotic or alcoholic, for example. Moreover, in that setting there is ample opportunity for collusion with consequent amplification of the sick role.

Whilst historically there have certainly been advantages to patients and psychiatry as a whole, to have come within the medical ambit, it is ironical that people have to learn illness behaviour and the appropriate language and symptoms in order to get help for what may often be at root, forces within their family or social network which they cannot understand, or for which they haven't learnt the psychological or social skills to cope.

The model is also better suited to chronic handicaps, particularly chronic schizophrenia.

By using psychosocial methods, the Centre's clients are encouraged to learn how to help themselves rather than to expect treatment being given to them. Clients still need a diagnosis but one which takes in the family and social stresses and the psychological strengths and weaknesses of the individual. It is an analysis of the situation rather than the symptoms, and the staff use a problem orientated record which is well suited for this purpose.

Clients are very much included in the on-going assessment and they have access to their files. It is accepted that the majority of clients are taking medication and staff advise the GPs on this when necessary but drugs are not prescribed on the premises nor is medication supervised directly by the staff.

In order to make adequate assessments and to offer a range of solutions, the staff is a multidisciplinary team with psychologist, doctors, social workers and general therapists, supported by an administrator and clerical staff. Each member of the team takes his or her share of the responsibility, and decisions on the running of the Centre are made jointly. Because there is shared professional responsibility for clients on a democratic basis rather than the normal hierarchical basis of a day hospital, not all clients will be seen by medical staff. Great care, however, is exercised to avoid, for example, a person with anxiety secondary to thyrotoxicosis simply being treated by psychotherapy.

The staffing costs are shared on a 50–50 basis by the Local Authority and the Area Health Authority. They are currently about £55,000 per annum and the Centre has its own budget for running costs of £8,500 per annum. The Centre is sited near the middle of town within fairly easy reach of the bus station. It consists of two large houses with gardens and out-buildings. It was regarded as important to have a house rather than a purpose built centre, not only was it cheaper but impressive, expensive new buildings may easily overwhelm a client who is already lacking in confidence. To create a more homely environment, a considerable amount of secondhand furnishings were bought. The buildings, with alterations and equipment cost £58,000.

Though the team is based at the Centre, much of the work is done in people's homes. Crises are on the whole better assessed there and some family work is also better done at home.

The Centre itself can accommodate up to forty clients in any one session and serves as the first step in containing people whose problems are too complex or too severe for them simply to be treated at home. One of the team is on duty each day so that it is possible to run a small walk-in clinic. Some members of the team are also responsible to the hospital psychiatric service or the sector and clients who cannot be managed on a day time basis but require 24-hour hospital care, are admitted without any difficulties.

At present the Centre is open for some evening activities which are expanding with the help of voluntary bodies, such as Mind, Alcoholics Anonymous and the Tameside Council on Alcoholism.

Finally, as some clients have problems specifically relating to their children, the Centre has a small nursery which can take up to eight pre-school children.

For the past two years a case register of contacts of psychiatric patients has been kept for the sector. It will be used to monitor the changes in the service as a result of the Centre, and it is hoped that this will also be used as a sampling frame in comparing the benefits of such a form of care to the more traditional one.

The aims of the project are firstly to provide a more appropriate kind of help than hospital psychiatry and secondly, to develop an effective working partnership with social services, recognising that specialisation in social work is essential. The staff hope to demonstrate not only a reduction in admissions, but more importantly a reduction in morbidity among the clientele without any increase in burden on their families.

PART III

Care and After-Care in Psychiatry

CHAPTER 9

A Brief Hospitalisation Policy: the Effect upon Patients and their Families*

STEVEN R. HIRSCH, STEPHEN PLATT, ANN WEYMAN and ANGELA KNIGHTS
Charing Cross Hospital Medical School

Since the declaration of a new policy for mental health in 1962, there has been a gradual shift towards treating acute psychiatric patients in District General Hospitals. A critical difference in the management of patients in District General Hospitals as opposed to Mental Hospitals, is the length of time patients stay as in-patients. The change from large remotely located hospitals to small units within the community based on a low patient per population ratio has meant that pressures are put upon psychiatrists to discharge their patients as quickly as possible even if this would not otherwise be their inclination. The high cost of private medical care in General Hospitals in Europe and the US and the scarcity of psychiatric beds in developing countries have increasingly led to a policy of shortening the patient's stay in hospital even for floridly ill schizophrenic and manic depressive patients. Given a variation in practice in different countries and the pressures upon us to reduce our reliance on in-patient care, as well as the possibility of achieving significant economic savings if the length of stay in hospital can be shortened, there is a real need to consider whether the amount of time patients stay in hospital is a critical clinical variable. We must test whether brief hospitalisation has untoward effects on the patient, their families, or the community.

If patients having only brief hospitalisation do less well clinically or prove to function socially at a lower level than those remaining in hospital

*This chapter reports the results of a collaborative study on a grant provided by the DHSS.

139

longer, or if the patient's family experience an undue burden by having patients return to their home too quickly before their clinical condition has fully recovered, the policy of reducing psychiatric beds and minimising length of stay will have to be reconsidered. On the other hand, if brief care proves to be as effective or better than current standards of hospital stay then further financial savings can be made for the Health Service, and the pace at which we move trom a mental hospital to a District General Hospital based service might be speeded up.

The purpose of this chapter is to report our attempt to evaluate the effect of brief care on patients' clinical and social functioning, and on the material and subjective distress which might be caused to their families by patients returning home quickly.

All admissions coming from the catchment area of a 40 bedded London District General Hospital Psychiatric Unit were randomly allocated to either Brief or Standard Care after excluding patients under 16, or those suffering from a diagnosable severe brain or physical disorder.

In order to avoid any chance of bias occurring, allocation to brief or standard care was done the moment patients were admitted to hospital. No restriction was put on Standard Care — patients were to be kept in hospital as long as the clinical team felt necessary. The brief care patients and their families were given to expect that the patient would probably be discharged within a week. (We supplied wine and sandwiches to junior medical staff at a weekly review to encourage this process.)

The Research Design

The research design was to take measurements of the patients and their most affected relative or closest informant just after admission and three months later to see if the Brief Care group had improved to the same extent as the Standard Care group over this time period. In order to measure clinical symptoms all patients were given the MRC Present State Examination (PSE) 5-7 days after admission to rate the patients clinical symptoms during the previous four weeks. A second PSE was performed three months later. Information about the behaviour and effect on others were obtained by an interview with the close informant 12-14 days after admission and three months later. For this purpose we developed our own semi-structured standardised interview called the Patients Behaviour Assessment Scale (PBAS). This enabled the research worker to assess, as reported by the key informant, the patient's behaviour, the patient's performance of social roles, such as working, helping around the house and engagement in leisure activities, and a third dimension — the adverse effects that the patient had on the informant or others in the household such as loss of their leisure time, or decrease in their income.

Further, for each item of behaviour or social function that revealed deterioration or absence of performance, the interviewer enquired whether the informant had experienced any distress or emotional burden, but they only rated Distress if it was definitely present to a moderate or severe degree.

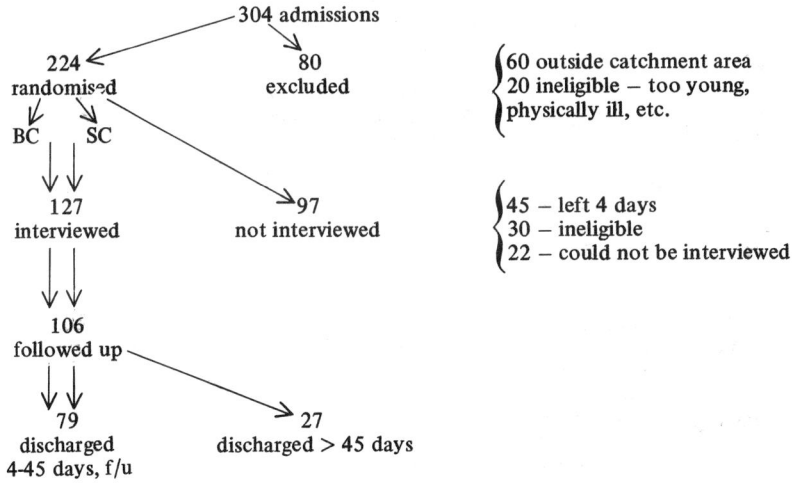

Fig. 1. Selection of Patients: 1975 Study.
(BC = Brief Care; SC = Standard Care)

Selection of Patients

Figure 1 indicates the selection of patients from all admissions in 1975 to the psychiatric service.

Of 224 admissions from the catchment area 50 were excluded because they were too young, physically ill, or demented. Only 10 per cent were missed because of failure to obtain or complete an interview, 45 patients or 20 per cent of patients randomised to Brief or Standard Care were excluded because they left hospital in the first three days, as we did not think this group would in any case be affected by the Brief Care policy; this was borne out by the fact that equal numbers left in less than four days from each group.

The first two tables support our conclusion that the groups were equally distributed between Brief and Standard Care without clinical or social bias. Table 1 shows there was very little difference between Brief and Standard Care on sex, age, marital status, education or occupation.

TABLE 1
Social Factors
Brief and Standard Care (Patients interviewed
at admission)

	% Standard care n = 57	% Brief care n = 70	Sig. <.05
Males	40	47	n.s.
Age distribution	(similar)		,,
Marital status:			
Single	35	31	,,
Married	46	50	,,
Widow/divorced	19	19	,,
Living alone or in institution	19	17	,,
Educational level	(similar)		
Last occupation:			
Non-manual	51	49	,,
Manual	37	41	,,
Not known	12	10	,,
Unemployed at admission	26	17	,,

Similar non-significant difference for patients discharged <45 days.

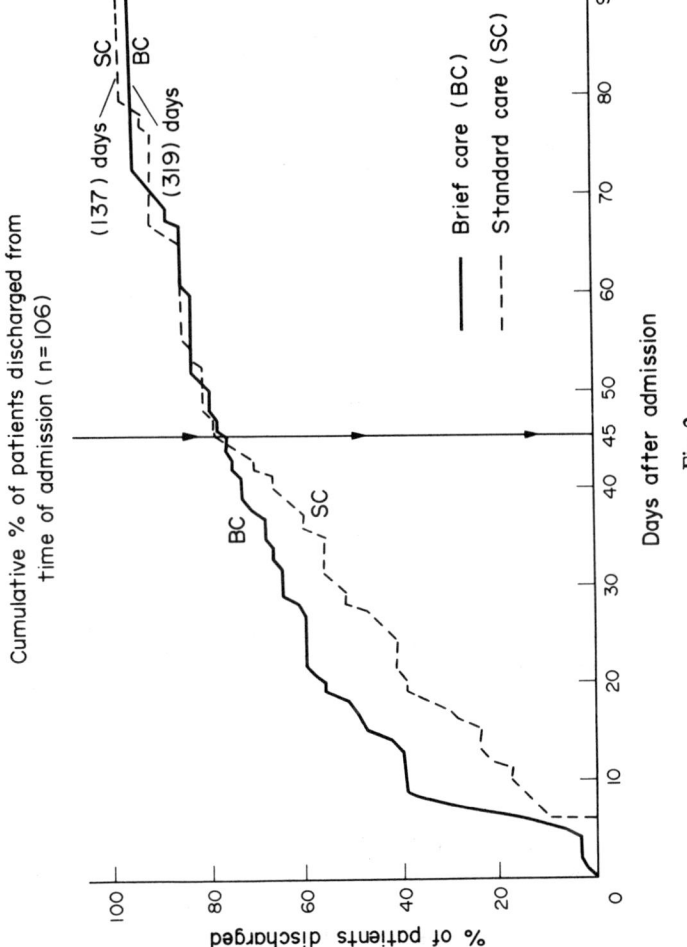

Fig. 2.

TABLE 2
Clinical Factors
Brief and Standard Care (Patients interviewed at admission)

	% Standard care n = 57	% Brief care n = 70	Sig. <.05
Admitted on Section	11	11	n.s.
Total previous admissions:			
None	37	33	,,
< 1 year	44	50	,,
> 1 year	20	17	,,
Diagnosis:			
Manic/depressive	39	41	,,
Schizophrenic	19	24	,,
Neurosis	23	19	,,
Other	19	16	,,

Similar non-significant difference for patients discharged at < 45 days.

Table 2 as well fails to reveal any significant difference between groups for the number admitted on section, previous time in a psychiatric unit, etc. and diagnosis distribution. Other comparisons not shown here including clinical symptoms measured on the Present State Examination, and some forty items of behaviour and social functioning measured on the PBAS failed to show any important or statistical differences between groups.

Results

How successful were we in shortening the length of stay for the experimental "brief care" group? Figure 2 shows the percentage of patients who had left hospital as time elapsed after admission, omitting patients who left in less than four days unless they had been transferred to the day hospital as a result of being assigned to brief care. At any point in time up to 45 days after admission a greater proportion of the brief care group had been discharged from hospital.

By 45 days 86 per cent of all randomised eligible patients had been discharged;* after that point the "brief care" policy made no difference to the length of stay. Note that the two groups did not differ for patients remaining in hospital more than 45 days. We have called this "less than 45 day group" who experienced a real difference in length of stay between the brief and standard care, the "target" group. This "target group" which excluded patients leaving in less than 4 or more than 45 days provides the best test for a comparison of the effect of brief care on patients and their families, because this is the part of the sample which actually showed a shortened length of hospitalisation for patients randomised to brief care.

TABLE 3
Time as In-patient

	Days Standard care n = 109	Days Brief care n = 115	Significance
All patients (n = 224) median	17	9	.05
mean	28	22	n.s.
< 45 days, interviewed group-			
mean (n = 99)	21	16	.01
Discharged within 9 days (n = 224)	34%	54%	.01
Re-admitted in year after discharge	42%	34%	n.s.
Days as in-patient on subsequent			
admission	13.8	13	n.s.
Total days during index admission	3006	2375*	
Total days in hospital during year			
from admission	4508	3840*	

*Adjusted for difference in n.

Table 3 shows the results of the experimental procedure. The median is a better measure of the difference between groups in length of stay. A significantly greater proportion of the brief care group left hospital quickly having a medium length of hospitalisation of 9 as compared to 17 days. The brief care group had a significantly shorter stay in hospital and the saving is most marked for those leaving hospital in under 45 days.

*Figure 1 excludes the "less than 4 day" patients from the calculation.

Outcome — Clinical and Social Measures

Now we can turn to the critical measures of outcome: change in the patient's clinical and social functioning during the three month period after admission and change in impact of the patient's behaviour on significant others. Is there a disadvantage to brief hospitalisation? Table 4 is based on a comparison of Present State Examination rating the patient's mental state over the month prior to admission, and three months later. About 80 per cent of the patients in each group are improved after 3 months regardless of length of stay. As we can see in Table 5, there is little

TABLE 4
Clinical Improvement:
Overall Change at Follow-up
(%)

	Standard	Brief
Numbers	47	60
Improved	37 (79)	48 (80)
Unchanged	7 (15)	9 (17)
Worse	3 (6)	2 (3)

TABLE 5
Change in
Neurotic Symptoms
n = 107

	Standard	Brief
Improved	34 (72)	46 (77)
Unchanged	9 (19)	9 (15)
Worse	4 (09)	5 (08)
	47 (100)	60 (100)

( ) = %

difference between groups in the proportion improving on neurotic symptoms. Table 6 shows that there is little difference between groups when we look at psychotic symptoms alone. As we might expect, psychotic symptoms improved to a lesser degree than neurotic symptoms but there was a slight but non-significant advantage for patients in the brief care group whether measuring symptoms which were psychotic or neurotic. These tables relate to all patients who were interviewed and followed-up, including those who were staying more than 45 days. Results are very similar if the comparisons are restricted to those in the "target" 45 day group for whom the difference between brief and standard care was most marked. The brief care patients did just as well clinically as those staying in hospital longer.

Improvement in symptoms and in behaviour reported by relatives tend to go together, and both change more rapidly than measures of social performance or adverse effects on others, or distress resulting from these. Remember that I said relatives were interviewed two weeks after admission and separate enquiries were made about behaviour occurring before the patient came into hospital, and about the patients function two weeks later at the time of the interview.

TABLE 6
Change in
"Psychotic" Symptoms
n = 86

	Standard	Brief
Improved	20 (54)	31 (63)
Unchanged	16 (43)	15 (31)
Worse	1 (03)	3 (06)
	37 (100)	49 (100)

( ) = %

The next three tables list the main items measured by interviews with the informant.

TABLE 7

Patient's Behaviour

Misery	Worrying	Violence
Withdrawal	Fearfulness	Suicide
Slowness	Obsessionality	Offensive behaviour
Forgetfulness	Odd ideas	Heavy drinking
Underactivity	Overactivity	Self-neglect
Overdependence	Unpredictability	Bodily aches and pains
Indecisiveness	Irritability	Odd behaviour
	Rudeness	

TABLE 8

Patient's Social Performance

Household tasks	Everyday conversation
Household management	Support
Child care	Affection/friendliness
Interest in child	Sexual relationship
Discipline of child	Work/study
Spare time activities	Decision making

TABLE 9

Adverse effects on informant

Physical ill health	Work/educational performance
Emotional ill health	Time off work/studies
Social life	Household relationships
Leisure time	General disruption
Disposable income	

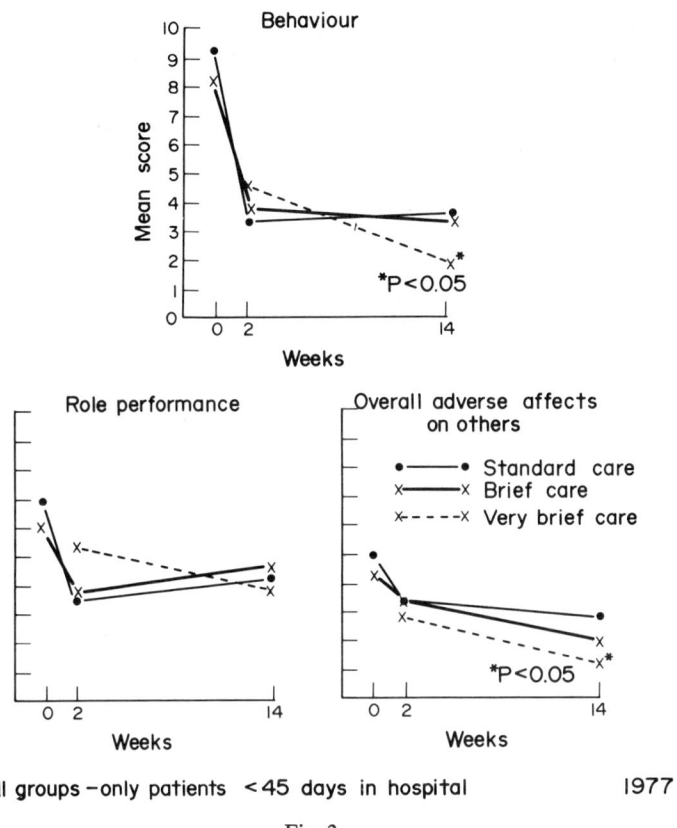

Fig. 3.

Figure 3 shows the change in mean scores for patients who had brief and standard care in the "less than 45 day" target group. It can be seen that on each measure, behaviour, social performance, and adverse effects on others, there was a dramatic difference between behaviour reported just prior to admission, and that present at the time of interview two weeks later. In fact there was no significant change between the two week and three month interview on any measure. The dotted line indicates change in score for a *very* brief care experimental sub-group, patients who were actually discharged in less than 8 days.

Note that the most marked change has already occurred by the end of the second week after admission, whether the patient is in brief or standard care. It is interesting that more than 54 per cent of those having brief care, compared to 34 per cent of those having standard care had already been discharged 5 days or more prior to this two week evaluation.

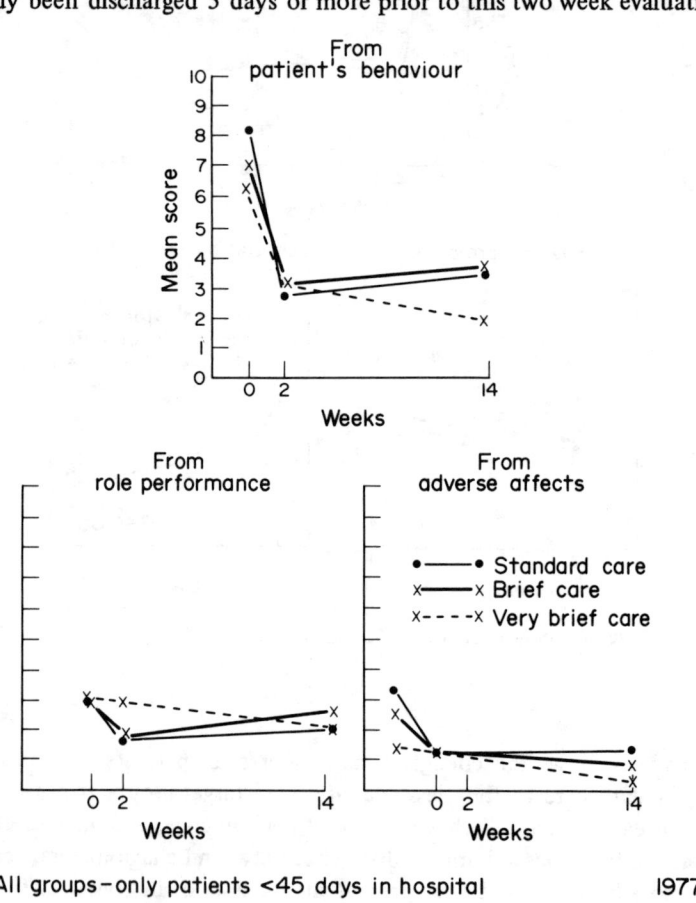

Fig. 4.

Figure 4 shows the change in the informants reported distress on the same three measures. As a generalisation we can say that there are no important or consistent differences which favour either group though the overall mean scores tended slightly to favour the brief care group. Our failure to find a significant difference between groups was true even after a co-variant analysis was carried out, which enabled us to make a statistical adjustment taking into account the small differences between the groups at the beginning of the study when comparing their scores at the end.

TABLE 10
Per cent Improvement in Social Functioning over 3 months

	n*	Standard	Brief	Sig. <.05
Behaviour	105	76	83	n.s.
Role performance	105	55	49	n.s.
Adverse effects on:				
children	17	100	90	n.s.
informant	89	68	76	n.s.
all adults	98	65	69	n.s.

*Patient not included if no abnormality appeared.

Another way of looking at these results brings out the fact that the percentage of patients improving varies considerably according to what is being measured. Table 10 shows the percentage improved for various measures of social function. We can see that the greatest improvement occurs in the informants report of the patient's behaviour; this correlates most closely with improvement on the PSE. Role performance shows the lowest level of improvement and adverse effects to the informant falls somewhere in between. Table 11 shows the percentage improvement in the informant's distress, again showing the least change in distress scores as occurring in relation to the patient's social performance.

TABLE 11
Per cent Improvement in Informant's Distress

	n*	Standard	Brief	Sig. <.05
Behaviour	100	82	70	n.s.
Role performance	78	27	37	n.s.
Adverse effects	63	48	47	n.s.

*Patient not included if no abnormality appeared.

There were no large or significant differences between brief and standard care for the percentage of patients showing improvement. More detailed tables would reveal some differences between groups without any consistent trend favouring brief or standard care. (For example, there were more patients both improved and more who were worse on the behaviour score in the brief care group while more patients were unchanged in the standard care group; paradoxically the distress scores showed just the reverse with more patients showing both improvement, *and* deterioration respectively in the standard care group and more unchanged in brief care. Just the reverse occurred on the Role performance measure, more were improved and worse on social performance in standard care but distress due to social performance was more improved and rose, respectively, in brief care, and more unchanged in standard care.) With so many statistical analyses the importance of a few relatively minor statistical significances which appeared to have occurred randomly in opposite directions can be disregarded.

The Effect on the Community and Supporting Services

I think we have satisfactorily shown that neither the patients nor their families suffer if the patient's stay in hospital is, at it were, administratively shortened. However, an unanswered question concerns the effect on services — did the brief care group consume more resources in hospital or in the community? Was the hospital saving in the short run lost in the long run because of longer or more frequent subsequent admissions?

First let us consider the saving of time as an in-patient, then the readmission rates and the effect on other services. As we see from Table 3, inspection of the number of days spent in the hospital on the index admission reveals a saving of 631 days or 21 per cent. If we take the number of days spent in hospital over a year from day one of the index admission, then the brief care group saved 668 days or 15 per cent. Note that more brief care patients were discharged in less than 9 days and fewer readmitted in the year after discharge. The number of subsequent days as an in-patient was the same, 13–14 for both groups. Table 12 summarises the effect of brief care on other services. The effect of applying a brief hospitalisation policy does not lead to differences in the number of out-patient attendances for the year from the first day of admission, or to

TABLE 12
*Differences Between Brief and
Standard Care
One year from admission day*

	p <.05
No. outpatient appointments	n.s.
No. Psych. Comm. Nurse visits	n.s.
No. local social service visits	n.s.
Hospital social worker time	n.s.
Social security benefits	n.s.

an increase in the number of attendances to their general practitioner. The groups did not differ on the number of local social service attendances or the amount of social benefits received to themselves and their families. While in hospital, and subsequently, there was no difference in the number of patients who saw the hospital social worker or the number of hours spent in contact with the hospital social worker.

The only service which the brief care group made significantly more use of was the day hospital. Unfortunately, due to an unexplained error at the hospital, the attendance records of the day hospital were destroyed covering half the period of this study. However, an estimate based on an extrapolation of available data suggests that the expected number of days spent in day hospital over a year beginning with the index admission was 523, which nearly makes up for the 668 days saved as in-patients by the brief care group during the same period. "Brief care" in this study really means shortening in-patient stay and replacing it with day-patient care for about half the patients; 47 per cent of the 45 day group were admitted to the day hospital at some time during the year compared to 34 per cent of the standard care group.

Is it realistic to expect clinicians to change their habits when the pressure is off, the research team has disappeared, and wine and sandwiches on Fridays have been discontinued? Table 13 shows that the decrease in the mean and median number of days as an in-patient during the study year, 1975, was maintained the following year after the research team had moved off the scene.

One of the most difficult problems in conducting this research was to establish and maintain a difference in length of stay between the brief and standard care groups. There were five part time consultants and several changes of junior staff in the unit during the study period and we found

TABLE 13
*Length of Stay Before and
After Study Year 1975*

	1974 n = 222	1975 n = 224	1976 n = 244
Mean	33 days	25 days	26 days
Median	24 days	15 days	18 days

$\lfloor$_p <.01_$\rfloor$ $\lfloor$_p <.01_$\rfloor$

that while we were able to reduce the stay of the brief care group a halo effect resulted causing the length of stay of the standard care group to fall as well. From a practical point of view in terms of implications for the Health Service, a better estimate of the saving in days as an in-patient is a comparison of the brief care group during the study year, 1975, with the length of stay of all in-patients the previous year, 1974. The mean number of days fell from 33 for all admissions in 1974 to 22 for brief care patients in 1975 — an overall saving of 33 per cent. For the majority of patients the saving was even greater because the median fell from 24 days to 9 — a reduction of 63 per cent. The saving could be substantial.

However, from the point of view of testing the effects on patients and relatives, though we achieved a significant difference between groups, it could be argued that a 9 day difference is clinically not very great; our standard care group would be thought by some to have had relatively brief care as well.

Fortunately, our results replicate a very similar study carried out in New York City by Herz, Endicott and Spitzer* which was published during the time our data was being collected. Though they used different instruments and excluded patients who could not return to families, as well as patients who suffered from alcoholism or psychopathy (so that they had more schizophrenics in their sample) the variables they measured and the strategy of their research was very similar to our own and their results are similar as well. Table 14 compares their results for length of stay and subsequent re-admission with ours. Median length of stay is the most salient variable because it is not affected by the small group of patients who stay a long time and markedly increase the means. Their brief

*Marvin I. Herz, Jean Endicott, and Robert L. Spitzer, Brief Hospitalisation: A two-year follow-up, *Am. J. Psychiatry*, 134, 5, May 1977, pp. 502-7.

TABLE 14
Use of Hospital Beds
US vs English Study

	US Brief Day	Eng. Brief Care	US Brief Out	Eng. Standard Care	US Standard Care
n	61	115	51	106	63
Days : Average	27	33	47	42	115
Days : Median	11	9	16	17	46
% Readmission	45	34	55	42	45

(U.S. data based on 2 years from date of admission; U.K. data on one year.)

out-patient group is very similar in terms of length of stay to our standard care one, and their brief day patient group, 53 per cent of whom subsequently had day patient care, compares most closely to our brief care group, 36 per cent of whom had subsequent day patient care in the year after admission. However, their study nicely supplements our findings by testing the value of more prolonged care in their third group which they identified as having "standard care" with a key admission which lasted on average 115 days, the median length of stay being 46. Because our other results are so similar, I think we can reasonably look to their study for an indication of the benefits of keeping patients for a considerably longer period in hospital.

They compared their patients on a group of variables which were very analogous to the ones used in our study, and their follow up period was extended to two years. At no point in time after admission did they find any large or significant difference between the three groups in their study, thus they found no benefit to the group which we might regard as having prolonged hospitalisation. Given this mutual replication of findings and the additional comparison for the group having prolonged hospitalisation which Herz's study offers, I think we are in a position to conclude that a general policy of brief hospitalisation, regardless of diagnosis,* but allowing for clinical discretion to keep selected patients in hospital as long as necessary, offers no discernable disadvantage to psychiatric patients. On the contrary, both our study and the New York one would support the view that the major benefit to hospitalisation was during the first two weeks when the most dramatic reduction in clinical symptoms and the major improvement in social performance takes place, as well as with a

*Confirmed by further analysis to be published elsewhere.

reduction of distress experienced by the family. Given current standards and practices, which I believe are reflected in this study, the reduction in in-patient beds would need to be matched by a corresponding increase in day places, at least in the first instance. Herz actually reports a significantly better return to work record for those who had brief care than those who had standard care within the group that could be expected to be re-employed. We have not yet done this analysis for our study though we can, nevertheless, reach the conclusion, contrary to what might have been expected, that the effects of a brief care policy, if anything, appears to be beneficial to the patient and family, not to mention those who have a fiscal concern for the health of the NHS.

CHAPTER 10

Employment Problems and Prospects for Chronic Patients

PHILIP COOPER

Department of Social Statistics, University of Southampton*

One of the greatest needs of any individual and, no less, the chronic patient, is for useful employment. And yet psychotic symptoms and in particular their fluctuations from one day to the next or from one week to the next, give rise to considerable problems in the field of employment. What are the effects of unemployment for the chronic patient? How effective are existing rehabilitation schemes and in what ways could these be improved? Is it possible to predict employability and what are the main factors determining the employability of a chronic psychiatric patient? What are the advantages to the patient of the enclave scheme? In the following pages these questions will be discussed in the light of the latest evidence available.

The Chronic Patient

Most psychiatric disorders are not handicapping and 95 per cent of people with psychiatric disorder are treated by general practitioners, social workers and others, and never come near a psychiatrist.[1] Only a proportion of the 5 per cent who do see a psychiatrist ever become disabled and it is this small fraction of patients with whom we are concerned here, who present difficult medical and social problems. In the

*This chapter is written from contributions by Dr. Douglas Bennett (Maudsley Hospital, London), Dr. Donal Early (Glenside Hospital, Bristol) and Dr. W. B. Spry (Bryn-y-Neuadd Hospital, Llanfairfechan).

past, little effort was made to rehabilitate them and instead, they were shut away in large mental hospitals for many years and often for life. Those hospitals are still with us today and account for about 40 per cent of all hospital beds in this country. Some psychiatric disorders are more disabling than others. At one time, neurosyphilis — the so-called general paralysis of the insane — disabled many patients. With treatment this illness has all but disappeared. Schizophrenia is still a disabling psychiatric disorder although not so seriously disabling as in the past (see Chapter 7). One of the new causes of psychiatric disability is senility; a disease of medical progress, which, although a major psychiatric problem, is not a problem of employment.

When speaking of chronically disabled psychiatric patients, one is not only considering those who still reside in mental hospitals. Today, many of these patients are in day centres, day hospitals or their own homes.

Psychiatric Disability

When disability is mentioned we think of physical disability. We are familiar with it and it is visible, whereas psychiatric disability is rarely visible and hence, more difficult to appreciate. The physically disabled person, by and large, has difficulty performing tasks in a physical world whereas the psychiatrically disabled person is largely handicapped in his performance of roles in a social world. To perform life roles satisfactorily a person needs knowledge about the expected performance; the ability to perform properly and the motivation to do so. As we go through life we add to our repertoire of roles.

Mental illness, if it is disabling, impairs role performance either because the person does not know what is expected of him or his ability to play the role is impaired, or because he loses his enthusiasm.[2] This impairment of role performance is an important factor influencing employability.

Of course some of the physically disabled have difficulty in performing roles just as some psychiatrically disabled patients have difficulties in task performance. But it is the psychological and not the physical problems of task performance which handicap the psychiatric patient.

Some psychiatric patients are slow workers and have difficulty in dealing efficiently with the more complex psychomotor tasks. But in a study undertaken in an Employment Rehabilitation Centre in 1964,[3] it was found that when schizophrenic patients were compared with non-schizophrenic entrants, they were not significantly different in terms of good manual dexterity, taking trouble or in the completion and finish of the work. Task performance does influence the employability of some, but it seems that for most psychiatric patients, role performance is more important.

The Need for Employment

Since the late 18th century we have reports of attempts to employ the mentally ill, but these attempts have rarely been sustained. It has, nevertheless, been widely accepted since the 1930s when Jahoda made his study in Austria[4] that unemployment is a social evil. He found that when unemployed over a long period, the men lost their sense of reality; they also lost their sense of time. The clocks in their homes were not wound. They were unpunctual for their meals. Rationality disappeared from their expenditure. They bought trinkets when they should have bought food. Even though they had on their hands so much time which they could have devoted to reading, they did not do so, and the local library became almost deserted. When they had no attachment to work, they had little or no attachment to leisure either.

In a more recent study, 81 per cent of those unemployed for more than six weeks complained of depression, sleeplessness, nervous breakdown or physical illness during their period out of work.[5] Further evidence of the psychiatric implications of long term unemployment was provided in a study by R. N. Antebi in 1970.[6]

The mentally disabled who are unemployed suffer in the same way. The disabilities described compound the handicaps caused by their illness and not only by addition. For we know that the psychiatrically disabled are not only more prone to desocialisation than their so-called "normal" fellows but that a lack of occupation makes their basic disabilities worse. For the mentally disabled, as well as the rest of us,

> "Working for a living is one of the basic activities of a man's life. By forcing him to come to grips with his environment, with his livelihood at stake, it confronts him with the actuality of his

personal capacity — to exercise judgement, to carry responsibility, to achieve concrete and specific results. It gives him a continuous account of the correspondence between outside reality and the inner perception of that reality, as well as an account of the accuracy of his appraisal of himself. In short a man's work does not satisfy his material needs alone. In a very deep sense, it gives him a measure of his sanity."[7]

Of course there are many other reasons why we should provide employment for the psychiatrically disabled; such as their need to be linked into the fabric of society or their need to structure time.

Employability of the Chronic Patient

Our premise then is that open employment, if it can be achieved, is best for the patient (and the taxpayer). The experience is that many — perhaps 25-40 per cent — can be employed in open economic employment. That percentage only indicates that there are employment possibilities for the chronically disabled psychiatric patient. It does not tell us what any particular patient or any particular employer can expect in different parts of the country.

So less than a half of our chronically disabled patients of working age could be useful employees. How many will secure employment depends not only on our treatment, but on how well we prepare them and how carefully we assess them for employment. Much depends, too, on the nature and severity of their disabilities, and how they adapted before they were ill. Disabled patients' chances of employment will also be influenced by the nature of the work available, where they live, the prevailing economic climate, their personal circumstances and a certain amount of luck.

Schemes of Supported Employment and Training

It is the transitional phase back to open employment which can be crucial for the patient's eventual success in obtaining and continuing in employment. A bewildering and ever changing array of schemes, statutory and otherwise, are available to provide training and rehabilitation to acceptable work habits.

Amongst the more important are the Employment Rehabilitation Centres (previously the Industrial Rehabilitation Units), run by the Employment Service Agency and served by the Employment Medical Advisory Service. The first one was at Egham and the aim was primarily that of rehabilitating the war casualties. The number of centres has since increased to 26. A further new one will open in Preston in 1978. Apart from the Egham and Preston centres, all are non-residential though some have limited hostel accommodation. The majority of the centres are situated on industrial estates, though two, (Garston Manor and Birmingham) are situated in close proximity to hospital facilities.

Recently we have seen an increase in the number of chronic psychiatric patients attending the centres following the discharge of considerable numbers from hospitals into the community. The impact has been in the younger age groups where recent psychiatric illness is now the most common disability.

The increasing demand for psychiatric places has to a considerable extent been met, with the proviso that the work place and working environment at each centre must be kept as close as possible to that found in open industry. Practical experience suggests that this is not possible if the psychiatric population of the centres rises much above 25 per cent.

Other rehabilitation facilities available to psychiatric patients are Industrial Therapy Organisations (ITOs) and Local Authority Rehabilitation Centres which receive rehabilitation grants from the Employment Service Agency for patients attending recognised courses. Such courses are longer than the usual 7–9 weeks of the ERC course. At the ITOs the course may be up to 6 months and exceptionally it may be extended to 1 year.

Schemes of a more experimental nature include recognised sheltered workshops and more recently sheltered group working ("Enclave" working). Currently only few of these "Enclaves" have been formed.

Another development has been the job rehearsal scheme arranged through the Disablement Resettlement Officer. The DRO makes arrangements with a prospective employer for the individual to be taken on for some weeks at Government expense to rehearse him for his employment and to demonstrate to the employer whether or not the person is adequate for the task to be undertaken.

The Assessment of Employability

A study by Fraser Watts[8] concludes that satisfactory predictions of employability can only be made when a patient's work performance is directly observed. While such assessments are subjective, this may not matter, since most decisions about promotion or dismissal in employment are themselves made on the basis of such subjective assessments. This means that whatever assessments one tries to make of a patient's specific disabilities in hospital, one also needs an assessment of his work performance in a realistic work situation. It is almost impossible to judge a person's capacity for work in a ward or in an occupational therapy department. Hospital staff are knowledgeable about what sick people cannot do. To predict employability one must assess the former patient in a vocational or industrial unit run on industrial lines by people from industry, who are better able to judge what the person can do in work and how this measures up to the demands that he will meet in employment. To some extent Employment Rehabilitation Centres (ERCs) enable this to be done.

An interesting experimental scheme has been developed at the Egham ERC. The closure of an industrial therapy organisation at Epsom led to the transfer of a number of the patients involved to Egham and a separate work preparation unit was set up adjacent to the ERC facility. This experiment has now run for nearly two years and the preliminary results are very encouraging. The numbers at the unit have varied between about 30 and 40 with an average length of stay of about 9 months. They now come from various areas and several different psychiatric hospitals are concerned. The rate of return to open employment following the course was 43 per cent during the first year of operation. This figure is good in the light of the current economic situation and compares well with that of ERC attendance at the present time. However, it must be borne in mind that these rehabilitees stayed for an average of 9 months at their course compared with the 7 or 9 weeks at a normal ERC course.

The Maudsley Hospital has its own Vocational Resettlement Unit (VRU). This has an added advantage since information about the patients' vocational assessments is fed back to the hospital rehabilitation service and, one hopes, leads to improvements in that service.[9]

Factors Influencing Employability

The VRU has also been a useful setting in which to study problems of assessment and employability. A succession of psychologists working there have developed and refined an instrument for assessing work behaviour. At present it predicts a person's suitability for resettlement in employment in 75 per cent of cases.[10] It predicts failure rather better than success. Of course it is only useful for measuring behaviour in a realistic work situation. When it is used to study the characteristics of those chronic patients who succeeded in employment this rating shows that keenness for work and a capacity for good work relationships in the work situation are rather more important than actual task performance. These findings are in agreement with earlier research.[11,12,13]

Fraser Watts[14] has suggested that employment depends on the employer accepting the employee and the employee tolerating the job. Little is known about how these attitudes interact but it is doubtful whether the worker's unacceptability to the employer is always the primary reason for his dismissal, or his intolerance of the job the main cause when he leaves a job voluntarily. Watts suggests too that such aspects of work-role behaviour as poor relationships and low levels of drive and initiative are more often responsible for unemployment than poor task performance. In support of this view he quotes his own findings and a series of studies which show that employment is not correlated with performance in the interview situation[15] or with measurements of level of intelligence or results of aptitude tests.[16,17]

The former patient's keenness for work, good personal relationships and task performance are not influenced by psychiatric disability alone. They depend too, on aspects of his personality and his previous ability. His tolerance for work is similarly related to his previous inclination, modified by the effects of psychiatric illness. Fraser Watts and Douglas Bennett[18] have recently examined various factors relating to the patient's employability prior to his illness. The work history of forty-four patients entering the VRU were examined. This history covered the ten-year period after leaving school. The duration of the longest job, mean job length, longest time in a single type of work and other summary statistics were noted. These were related to the patient's subsequent employment history. It was found that if before rehabilitation the patient had been recently employed, he was likely to be successful in returning to work. But recent employment did not predict a person's stable resettlement at work. This was more likely to be related to his occupational stability in the ten years after leaving school. The mean job length, the mean time in each type of work seemed most likely to predict stable employment for psychotic patients. On the other hand the longest time at one type of work and the total time spent in jobs lasting two years or more seemed to be the best predictors for non-psychotic patients. Too much should not be made of these differences between psychotic and non-psychotic patients at present for the sample is small. The results, however, do show that it is not the patient's psychiatric disability alone which determines his re-employment after rehabilitation but also his social adaptation to employment in terms of an orderly work career before he became disabled.

The Development of Rehabilitation Programmes and Policy

It is only about twenty years since some psychiatrists began to recognise that many of their patients were disabled rather than ill. In the years since then, they have been preoccupied in bringing this fact to the attention of their colleagues, in setting up rehabilitation programmes in the mental hospitals and trying to delineate disabilities. More recently as the emphasis has shifted from the care of the mentally ill in hospital to care in the community, psychiatrists have had to readjust their views and their practice. They are no longer concerned solely with the "late" rehabilitation of patients who have been disabled for years and who have acquired additional disabilities during a long mental hospital stay. Instead they have had to pay attention to the "early" rehabilitation of patients who are disabled, but who have never had a long hospital stay.[19]

Studies in the Vocational Resettlement Unit at the Maudsley Hospital have been unable to show that patients improved during rehabilitation. This is not surprising since it seems unlikely that severe psychiatric disabilities can be changed; anymore than one can change blindness or paralysis. Rehabilitation is readaptation. So we have to help psychiatrically disabled people to fit in and cope with society or employment in spite of their disabilities. To do this one has to assess the patient's handicaps, his capacities and the requirements of employment. It is apparent that the time needed for the psychiatric rehabilitee to progress adequately to hold down work in open or sheltered employment is considerably longer than that found for many other conditions.[20] The current Employment Services Agency (ESA) centres are not geared and cannot really become geared to lengthening their courses and thus there is a need to bridge this gap by developing special services for the psychiatric rehabilitee to offer him a longer period of rehabilitation, possibly of a year or even longer.

Industrial therapy departments at various psychiatric hospitals in many instances offer first rate rehabilitation, although the standards are quite widely divergent. However good these are, they do not really compare to realistic work in open employment. There is a need for some form of intermediate facility which would bridge this gap between the hospital type centre on the one hand and the short intensive Employment Rehabilitation Centre (ERC) facility on the other. This would still be primarily geared as a work orientated and employment situation, but would need considerably more medical and social support than that found in the usual ERC facility. Individual schemes of this nature already exist under the auspices of the Industrial Therapy Organisation (ITO). It is instructive to examine in some detail the development and working of a scheme for sheltered groups in open industry operated in Bristol.[21]

In 1962, ITO (Bristol) demonstrated that a group of 12 psychiatric hospital patients could raise their earning capacity three to four-fold within six weeks of starting to work on an open factory floor. Having repeated this experiment, the industrial and trade union directors of ITO suggested that this approach would be more appropriate to the needs of rehabilitation and sheltered employment. In the same year, the organisation negotiated with the Ministry of Labour to obtain deficiency payments (similar to those applicable to Sheltered Workshop employees) for groups of severely disabled people working in open industry and employed by ITO. In 1963, the Ministry agreed to the scheme on the following terms:

(a) ITO should make itself responsible as the employer in every respect for those persons in the outworking groups, and should continue to pay wages until further employment could be found if the work on which a group was engaged came to an end.

(b) ITO should be covered by a comprehensive insurance policy covering employer's liability.

(c) Workers should be tried out in the ITO training factory at Bristol for at least six months before allocation to one of the outworking groups, with the two-fold purpose of establishing that they were unlikely to be capable of open employment within the reasonably near future, but that they were likely to be sufficiently productive to justify their moving into sheltered employment.

(d) The Department would have to be generally satisfied with the arrangements with each firm to which an outworking group was to be sent; in particular, the firms would be expected to provide continuous employment for at least three months, subject to satisfactory standards of working being maintained by the workers concerned.

(e) Each outworking group should consist of at least 10 workers to ensure that adequate supervisory arrangements could be made.

(f) Unless there were very exceptional circumstances, only those patients should be included in the outworking groups who were sufficiently recovered from their illness to be able to live outside the hospital, and for whose accommodation firm arrangements had been or were being made.

The scheme ran under these rules from 1963 to 1969 during which time 58 workers were employed, of which 26 per cent gained individual employment, 12 per cent retired on pension, 5 per cent died and 21 per cent remained in the sheltered groups after six years. 16 per cent relapsed and required admission to hospital. The main drawback of this scheme was that it militated against the employment of men since few employers can supply work for groups of 10 or more men. In 1969, following prolonged negotiations, the Department of Employment and Productivity "approved a scheme whereby a group of 8 or 10 workers distributed among factories in a given area would have the care of a nurse who would keep in constant touch with all workers in a group". This meant that in any single work-place there could be groups of workers less than the previously stipulated number of 10 and that supervision would, therefore, be peripatetic. In the next five years, industry was in a decline and the numbers employed in the scheme were reduced. Thirty-six workers were employed between 1st January, 1970 and 1st January, 1975. Nineteen (53 per cent) remained in the group at the end of this period. Seven (19 per cent) had gained open employment and only 2 (6 per cent) had relapsed to in-patient status. The employment situation has threatened the sheltered placement scheme which has become increasingly difficult to sustain during the past 2–3 years.

At the end of 1976, there were 17 workers in the ITO sheltered placement scheme. When the national economy improves, it will expand again. Schemes of this nature have several characteristics of note: [22]

(i)   They show that rehabilitation and assessment of employability are intermingled.

(ii) They indicate that the organisation and running of the programme cuts across many statutory and institutional boundaries — employment and health are not mutually exclusive concepts.

(iii) They show that poor risk groups or individuals can perform satisfactorily and even beyond what was expected.

(iv) They reject the usual assumptions about competence, readiness and capability of psychiatric patients.

(v)   They assume the value of real work for real pay.

(vi) They treat work as part of the restoration process and concentrate on maximising abilities and adjusting to disabilities.

(vii) They demonstrate that expectations and attitudes greatly determine performance and outcome.

(viii) They demonstrate that with poor risk patients the best way to evaluate performance is by placing the person in the real work situation or by simulating a real work situation.

(ix) They are in the main examples of the utilisation of intentional social support systems as curative agents in guiding the individuals involved.

(x)   They recognise and accept that the employer is in business and that the employee has to meet his expectations.

(xi) They allow former patients unsuited to open employment to find their appropriate niche over an extended period of time. Some will need sheltered *work* (not *employment*) in day centres. Some, particularly women, may find voluntary jobs. Some will be community invalids and a few — fewer than in past times — will require the shelter and support of a hospital or some similar residential facility.

(xii) They recognise open employment for what it is and do not ask that the patient should be given special consideration because he is sick or disabled. Such arrangements never work.

Official policy has endorsed this approach to rehabilitation and resettlement since the Department of Employment's consultative document of 1974 (Department of Employment 1974). This introduces the concept of the "enclave" (this is unacceptable civil service jargon for the sheltered group in open industry!) An "enclave" is defined as "a group of severely disabled people working together under special supervision in an otherwise ordinary and undifferentiated environment" (but defined by the Oxford Dictionary as "territory surrounded by foreign domination"). The Department accepts that the sheltered group approach is preferable to other methods of employment of disabled persons and, more important, now proposes a revolutionary change in previous policy in that "eventual rehabilitation to ordinary industry for all who may become capable of it should be made a statutory aim".

The consultative document discusses the problems involved in establishing sheltered work in open industry but concludes that the cogent objections to direct subsidy in employment do not apply where "workers are employed by the independent voluntary body which is paid by the firm concerned for all the work done". The document describes the financial, social and medical advantages of such schemes in a way that has been urged for 14 years by ITO.

Actual statistics of the potential demand for such services are very difficult to come by. Inferences that one could reasonably draw from the figures that are available would suggest that there is a considerable unmet demand and that the offering of a bridging facility between employment and hospital is a very necessary development to fill a gap into which a number of patients now fall often never to be recovered. It is clear from the literature that the results obtained directly reflect the expectations and attitudes of those concerned in operating the system, and unless one has in some way built into the system these favourable expectations and attitudes of mind it is unlikely that it will be satisfactory. Even with modern buildings, modern machinery and every modern convenience, a project will not produce the desired results if the people running the system lack the necessary drive and enthusiasm. Legislation cannot put this degree of personal commitment into the service. We must therefore look to those with such a degree of commitment who are offering exceptional work and see if their work can act as a catalyst to further schemes in other areas.

Conclusions

In rehabilitation it is always important to accept the patient's limitations — but only after assessing them carefully. There is a large element of uncertainty about the likely success of any patient, but with careful attention to detail in rehabilitation, good communications and cooperation with employers and the employment services, and a realistic appreciation of the demands of various forms of employment, the element of uncertainty can be reduced.

We have indicated that many chronic psychiatric patients who previously mouldered in mental hospitals can be employed. Our present techniques of rehabilitation are progressing slowly from "hit or miss" methods to more refined and precise techniques. We are beginning to differentiate those chronic patients who can manage open employment from those who need other forms of assistance. Only in this way shall we be able to improve the employment prospects of our patients and secure the confidence and good will, as well as the cooperation of employers.

References

1. Shepherd, M., Cooper, B., Brown, A.C. and Kalton, G. W. (1966) *Psychiatric Illness in General Practice*, OUP, London.
2. Brim, O. G. and Wheeler, S. (1966) *Socialization after Childhood: Two Essays*, John Wiley, New York.
3. Wing, J. K., Bennett, D. H. and Denham, J. (1964) Industrial rehabilitation of long-stay schizophrenic patients, *MRC Memo* No. 42, HMSO London.
4. Jahoda, M., Lazarfeld, P. F. and Zeisel, H. (1972) *Marienthal, The Sociography of an Unemployed Community*, Tavistock.
5. Meacher, M. (1971) *Scrounging on the Welfare*, 55, Arrow.
6. Antebi, R. N. (1970) *State Benefits as a Cause of Unwillingness to Work*.
7. Jaques, E. (1960) Disturbances in the capacity to work, *Int. J. Psychoan.*, **41**, 357-67.
8. Watts, F. N. (1978) A study of work behaviour in a psychiatric rehabilitation unit, *Brit. J. Soc. Clin. Psych.*, **17**, (in press).
9. Bennett, D. H. (1972) Principles underlying a new rehabilitation workshop, In *Evaluating a Community Psychiatric Service: The Camberwell Register*

170   *Philip Cooper*

1964-71, 275-82, J. K. Wing & A. M. Hailey (ed.), OUP, London.
10. Griffiths, R. D. P. (1973) A standardized assessment of the work behaviour of psychiatric patients, *Brit. J. Psychiat.*, **123**, 403-8.
11. American Medical Association Joint Committee on Mental Health in Industry, JAMA, 1962, **181**, 1086-9.
12. Paridexter, W. R. Screening ex-patients for employability, *Mental Hospital* (1963), **4**. 444-7.
13. Plas, J. A. and Arthur, R. J. (1965) Psychiatric re-examination of unsuitable naval recruits in a two-year follow-up, *A. J. Psych.*, **122**, 534-41.
14. Watts, F. N. (1974) *Social treatments. A Textbook of Human Psychology*, H. J. Eysenck & G. D. Wilson (eds.), Academic Press, London.
15. Sandler, J. (1952) Vocational Guidance, *Social Psychiatry: a Study of Therapeutic Communities*, M. Jones (ed.), 147-55, Tavistock, London.
16. Allen, R. V. and Loebel, R. (1972) Work assessment of psychiatric patients: a critical review of published scales, *Canad. J. behav. Sci.*, **4**, 101-17.
17. Taylor, F. R. (1963) The GATB as a predictor of vocational adjustment by psychiatric patients, *J. clin. Psych.*, **19**, 130-1.
18. Watts, F. N. and Bennett, D. H. (1977) Previous occupational stability as a predictor of employment after psychiatric rehabilitation, *Psych. Med.*, **7**, 709-12.
19. Bennett, D. H. (1975) Techniques of industrial therapy, ergo-therapy and recreative methods. In *Psychatrie der Gegenwart: Forschung und Praxis*, **3**, 743-8, K. P. Kisker, J. E. Meyer, C. Müller & E. Strömgren, (eds.), Springer Verlag, Berlin.
20. Patterson, C. H. (1962) Evaluation of rehabilitation potential of the mentally ill patient, *Rehabilitation Literature*, **23**, 162-72.
21. Early, D. F. (1975) Sheltered groups in open industry, *Lancet*, 1370.
22. Daniels, D. N. (1966) New concepts of rehabilitation as applied to hiring the mentally restored, *Community Mental Health Journals*, **2**, 197-201.

CHAPTER 11

The Employment Patterns of Former Psychiatric Patients

NANCY WANSBROUGH, PHILIP COOPER
(University of Southampton)

and

BETTY MITCHELL
(Medical Adviser, Harrods)

For any patient leaving a psychiatric hospital, one of the hurdles he has to overcome is the understandable but possibly unjustified anxiety of any employer about accepting him for employment; anxiety which is felt quite regardless of the severity of his illness, the length of his stay in hospital or the existence or non-existence of residual symptoms. If a body of knowledge can be developed about the performance of people with a schizophrenic, depressive or alcoholic history in different kinds of work, it is hoped that employers will be enabled to make employment decisions on the basis of factual information about the requirements of a job and the likely capacity of the applicant to fulfil those requirements.

The results presented below are of a six year study of former psychiatric hospital in-patients; people now working whose illness has previously necessitated in-patient treatment and which was therefore not trivial, but neither was it invariably chronic.

The aim of the research has been to see what happens when these people go or return to work, to try to identify any pattern of occurrences or behaviour which would enable employers to make more skilled placements and know what to expect, while at the same time enlightening those engaged in rehabilitation in the psychiatric hospitals about what happens to their patients. Our trademark has been the approach through

171

employers rather than to patients. Our premise is that open employment, if it can be achieved, is best for the patient and best for the tax-payer.

A Description of the Groups Studied

The data were collected by postal questionnaire from respondents who reported on the situation at work of ex-patients in their organisations — hundreds of respondents, over a thousand ex-patients (Table 1). We have had two rounds, a retrospective survey reported on in 1974[1] followed by a prospective study still being analysed. We have also used visits and a little clutch of case studies.

TABLE 1

Sample respondents	Old employees	New employees
A. 42 Remploy managers	45	142
B. 92 Concerned employers	54	242
C. 92 Occupational health doctors	405	148
D. 59 Occupational health doctors	180	
Total of 285 record keepers	Total of 1216 subjects	

In Sample A, 1974, there were 42 Remploy Works Managers and the employees were the sheltered workers for whom Remploy exists.

In Sample B, 1974, the respondents were 92 benevolent employers reported by the hospitals as having helped in resettling patients in employment — a highly selected group. The efforts made by some quite modestly placed employers quite put the large firms in the shade.

Sample C, provided by 92 industrial medical officers in 1974, represented on the whole open competitive labour conditions, the overt bias towards large size and medical awareness in manufacturing industry being manifestly unavoidable.

Sample D, 1976-7, still being analysed, came from 59 firms who for 12 months kept running records of the performance of 180 ex-patient subjects. A few respondents in D were the same doctors as in C, but a scrutiny of subjects' birthdates showed that the degree of overlap in these two samples is so small as to be negligible. Alas, Sample D is not random either, although we tried hard to make it so: this was largely because of the difficulty of identifying all ex-patients in records not flagged for this purpose. But of the 59 firms, 37 kept records on 1 or 2 subjects only, so that the spread among different employers and different industries is quite extensive.

TABLE 2

Number of records kept by firms

1	*24 firms*
2 - 4	*22 firms*
5 - 9	*9 firms*
10 - 12	*4 firms*

The quality and extent of the data are a tribute to the members of the Society of Occupational Medicine. These doctors have done an enormous amount of unpaid extra work because they believed in the importance of this study; and, in fact, one quite unquantifiable research finding is that the potential contribution to the rehabilitation and resettlement of the mentally ill by these occupational health doctors is almost totally overlooked.

The Characteristics of the Different Groups

In the event the diffuse nature of the samples has been very useful in delineating the whole picture as well as providing an element of control where more rigorous analysis has been feasible.

And what is this total picture? It is that Remploy, the state sheltered workshop, provides as is well known insufficient sheltered work places for the mentally ill, currently only some 10 per cent of the total available. What is probably not known is that once they can find a place, they more often appear to be engaged in more complex work such as operating machinery than do the employees in the other samples, despite the fact that Remploy workers come under Section 2 of the Disabled Persons' Register, indicating that they are so severely incapacitated as to be deemed incapable of work in open conditions. The figures are: 36 per cent of Remploy's skilled and semi-skilled mentally ill workers operate machines; 16 per cent of Sample B do so; and 18 per cent of Sample C.

Turning to Sample B provided by the compassionate self-selected group of employers, what are the characteristics of this sample? They are that it is barely recovered at all. Let us consider one index, that of surviving in a job. We looked at all the new employees in all the samples engaged within the preceding three years. We found that 18 per cent of Sample C had left, but that no less than 38 per cent of Sample B had; two-thirds of them for reasons connected with their illness such as being re-admitted to hospital or failing to turn up at all. In our internal shorthand we call them the Trial Balloons.

And how can we best describe the outstanding features of Sample C? These employees result from what we have identified as the prevailing ethos among the big employers with the big medical departments. It is "Don't take the mentally ill on in the first place if you can help it, but once they belong to the company, treat them with consideration as you would treat an employee who has broken down physically, especially if he has many years' service." In our most recent Sample, D, only 16 per cent had been recognised as having a psychiatric history at the time they were taken on. For 80 per cent the discovery was made subsequently i.e. the employers did not hire them knowingly. Our open employment Samples C and D, therefore, are largely long service; though not necessarily a long time out of hospital.

Diagnosis

The difficulties of the very concept of diagnosis in mental illness, together with the limitations imposed by our method of collecting information at several removes, make us hesitant to be too categorical in this realm, but a remarkable congruence of percentage distributions does rather excite us. The data derive from the open employment samples C and D, plus a small case study sample provided most kindly (again after a lot of work) by a large manufacturing company.

Percentages of a total of 31 are not usually quoted but we shall do so here to point out the striking similarities.

One is tempted to feel on safe ground in commenting that, of all known former mental hospital in-patients now working in large scale industry, nearly 1 in 5 is likely to have been psychotic. In our categorisation of diagnosis, psychosis is almost synonymous with schizophrenia, as all forms of depression have been classified together.

TABLE 3
Diagnosis : Percentage distribution of ex-patient employees in four samples

Diagnosis	Case Study A 1973 n = 31 %	Sample C 1974 (i) n = 396 %	Sample C 1974 (ii) n = 138 %	Sample D 1977 n = 180 %
Psychoses	19	18	20	18
Depressions	58	58	42	59
Neuroses	16	14	17	19
Personality disorders	3	2	7	2
Alcoholism and addiction	3	6	9	2
Other, the residual category comprising disorders of organic origin, subnormality, epilepsy, etc.	0	2	5	0

The Relationship of Diagnosis to Employment Conditions

Diagnosis is significantly correlated with certain conditions at work, and also with the propensity of our subjects to attract complaints, a factor which we have utilised as an index of "failure" and "success". For instance, overtime seems to be taken in their stride by everyone whereas shiftwork often presents difficulty to employees diagnosed as depressive or psychotic. As to complaints about slow work, absenteeism and behaviour, the few employees with a personality disorder diagnosis were complained about most. Those diagnosed as psychotic and alcoholic came next, attracting only slightly more complaints than depressives. Neurotics were complained about least. Overall, dangerous behaviour complaints turned up least often; slow work and odd behaviour complaints most often, so that the violent characteristics portrayed on stage and screen in real life obtrude the least. Rather the complaints are of inadequacy and oddity. And we found that employers could tolerate oddity. People did not get sacked for it. And throughout, the "old", long service employees get taken off their shifts, persist with their odd behaviour, and are kept on, while a more rigorous standard is evidently demanded of newcomers.

The Sickness Absence of Employees

We have found that one of the most frequent complaints amongst employers was that of excessive sickness absence.[2] It is also an index that can be objectively and easily measured. We have used two sets of data to identify characteristics of the sickness absence pattern exhibited by former in-patients, and to compare these with the features exhibited by a sample of employees suffering from coronary disease (a chronic organic condition), and also with the sickness absence patterns of employees at large.

With the cooperation of a large employer in manufacturing industry certified sickness absence data for the calendar years 1966–1974 were collected for the three groups of employees. The first group consisted of 54 men who, whilst in the employ of the company, had received psychiatric hospital in-patient treatment and had then returned to employment. Some had returned to their old employment but the majority were working in a specially equipped workshop undertaking simple repetitive tasks. The second group contained 71 men, who at some stage had suffered from coronary disease, 23 of them dying during the observation period. In the main these subjects were treated as normal healthy workers in respect of job placement. The third group was a randomly chosen sample of 92 men from the company work force.

The second study was a prospective one. The 59 employers of Sample D kept monthly records for a year of the sickness absence by cause of 180 employees (139 men and 41 women) who had previously been psychiatric hospital in-patients, and of 180 controls matched as far as possible for age, sex, duration of employment and type of job. This analysis was confined to certified absence, although shorter absences were also recorded.

Though in both studies a distinction was made between absences attributed to recurrence of the chronic condition, and absences due to other causes, this refinement is not normally that which most concerns the employer. His interest is in total absence, and it is the characteristics of total absence which we shall examine.

It is known that sickness absence varies markedly with age and sex. The "classical" analysis[3] is to produce a set of rates in working days per year exposed-to-risk by age and sex. However, it is possible to decompose these rates into three components and to examine these with a view to gaining more insight into the nature of sickness absence. The decomposition takes the following form:

Total working days of sickness	Years of exposed to risk with sickness	Total spells of sickness	Total working days of sickness
Total years of exposed to risk (generating the sickness)	= Total years of exposed to risk	$\times$ Years of exposed to risk with sickness	$\times$ Total spells of sickness

which may be expressed as:

Sickness rate = Proportion falling $\times$ Mean number of spells $\times$ Mean length
sick of those falling sick of spell

or symbolically:

$$S_x = P_x.N_x.L_x$$

Sometimes a decomposition into two components: $P_x.N_x$ and L_x is used. The product $P_x.N_x$ is then termed the inception rate.

The first study within the single company has the advantage of a large number of years exposed to the risk of sickness – resulting in small sampling errors of the estimates; however, the samples from the coronary and control groups have not been matched. Thus we must be cautious in making comparisons between the groups. Looking at the overall sickness rates, S_x, for the Psychiatric and the Coronary groups we can see that there is little to choose between them, but they both definitely experience much higher rates of absence than the work-force at large in the factory. Whilst the Psychiatric and the Coronary group overall rates are similar, the characteristics of absence are different. About 55–65 per cent of the psychiatric group will fall sick in any year, having an average 2 or 3 spells of sickness, each lasting for an expected 12–15 working days. However, in the coronary group only 35–45 per cent will fall sick in any year, having an average 1–2 spells of sickness, but each lasting for an expected 25–35 working days. These differences are to some extent accentuated by the fact that coronary disease is an affliction of middle-age which is eventually fatal in many cases, whilst psychiatric illness is rarely fatal and has an incidence in the main independent of age. We can compare the characteristics just observed with those of the control group within the same factory: 20-30 per cent falling sick each year, having an average 1-2 spells of sickness each lasting for about 10-15 working days on average.

TABLE 4
Study I: Manufacturing Industry 1966-74: Certified Sickness Absence

Psychiatric (54 men)					
Age, x	Exposed to risk	P_x	N_x	L_x	S_x
16 - 30	74.0	0.66	2.7	15.4	27.4
31 - 40	161.5	0.65	2.2	14.5	20.9
41 - 50	119.0	0.46	1.7	14.1	10.7
51 - 64	76.5	0.56	2.6	11.6	16.9
16 - 64	431.0	0.58	2.2	14.1	18.5

Coronary (71 men)					
Age, x	Exposed to risk	P_x	N_x	L_x	S_x
16 - 30	–	–	–	–	–
31 - 40	21.0	0.42	1.1	21.7	10.4
41 - 50	128.5	0.38	1.8	24.4	15.6
51 - 64	272.5	0.38	1.9	35.1	25.3
16 - 64	422.0	0.41	1.7	32.2	22.1

Control (92 men)					
Age, x	Exposed to risk	P_x	N_x	L_x	S_x
16 - 30	197.0	0.19	1.8	7.2	2.5
31 - 40	229.5	0.27	1.4	10.8	4.2
41 - 50	143.0	0.31	1.5	18.9	8.8
51 - 64	93.5	0.21	1.3	11.4	3.1
16 - 64	663.0	0.25	1.5	12.1	4.5

We might summarise the situation of the former psychiatric patients in this company as being more likely to fall sick more often, but each spell being no longer than those of the average employee.

The second study has fewer years of exposed to risk resulting in larger sampling errors; however it has the advantage of matched controls, making for a more valid comparison between groups; and also of a small group of females — all subjects in the first study were male. Again the overall sickness rates, S_x, show a marked difference between the subjects and the controls for both males and females. Looking in more detail at the

TABLE 5

Study II A: 59 Companies 1975-76 (139 men and matched controls): Certified Sickness Absence

Age,x	Psychiatric					Control				
	Exposed to risk	P_x	N_x	L_x	S_x	Exposed to risk	P_x	N_x	L_x	S_x
16 - 30	13.0	0.76	1.8	12.3	17.1	11.8	0.23	1.8	5.4	2.3
31 - 40	24.8	0.58	4.2	9.7	23.9	25.7	0.43	1.8	5.8	4.5
41 - 50	43.8	0.65	2.2	11.8	16.7	46.3	0.42	1.8	11.4	8.4
51 - 64	42.2	0.59	2.9	21.7	37.0	40.0	0.41	1.7	19.5	13.6
16 - 64	123.8	0.63	2.7	14.6	25.3	123.8	0.40	1.8	12.4	8.9

Study II B: 59 Companies 1975-76 (41 women and matched controls): Certified Sickness Absence

Age,x	Psychiatric					Control				
	Exposed to risk	P_x	N_x	L_x	S_x	Exposed to risk	P_x	N_x	L_x	S_x
16 - 30	6.2	0.68	2.9	13.1	25.6	9.2	0.78	1.7	5.6	7.3
31 - 40	5.2	0.58	3.0	3.7	6.5	2.2	–	–	–	–
41 - 50	15.3	0.52	3.3	9.8	16.7	12.3	0.65	2.0	4.2	5.4
51 - 59	10.1	0.79	3.8	9.0	26.7	13.1	0.46	1.8	5.6	4.7
16 - 59	36.8	0.63	3.3	8.9	18.7	36.8	0.42	1.8	5.0	3.8

components of absence we see that as in the first study about 55–65 per cent of former in-patients — males or females — will fall sick in any year, males having 2 or 3 and females 3 or 4 spells of sickness, lasting in the case of males about 15 working days and in the case of females slightly shorter. The pattern is similar to that observed in the first study. The components of the controls' sickness absence in the second study are similar to the first: about 30–40 per cent falling sick each year having an average of 1–2 spells of sickness, each lasting about 5–15 working days.

These tentative results lead us to conclude that former psychiatric patients do experience more sickness absence than an average employee; however, it is no worse than at least one chronic condition namely coronary disease. The excesses of the absence record are brought about by more former in-patients falling sick more frequently but only for slightly longer each time than the average employee.

Conditions and Patterns of Employment

In designing the study for Sample D, we became more cunning, more specific, in our questions about the jobs themselves. It was Sample D that produced the following indicative patterns. In respect of training we found that 60 per cent were trained on the job; 13 per cent not at all. For only a quarter was a special course required. This is an indication of the simple (and sometimes repetitive) nature of the tasks performed. One might hypothesise that repetition implies boredom and dissatisfaction, whilst discretion involves stress and possible relapse. This dilemma of job placement remains to be resolved.

This pattern repeats itself in the statistics of pay. We found that 70 per cent received regular salary or wage, or flat rate plus overtime; only 14 per cent had to withstand the pressure of personal or group incentive bonus.

We looked closely at the work environment. Few were bottled up in their own office, slightly more shared with up to 4 others, but the largest group, nearly half, worked not in isolation but on their own particular pad in office, shop or factory. What does seem of particular interest is the quite high proportion of 37 per cent who do neither, but circulate about. So many psychiatrists seem to think that industrial work is performed solely tied to a conveyor belt or at an assembly bench.

TABLE 6
Communication Patterns
Percentages of subjects in communication

	Face to face %	Telephone %	Written %
Superiors	80	49	45
Colleagues	80	46	35
Subordinates	20	16	10
Public	14	17	14
None of these	0.5	45	50

We examined patterns of communication, particularly having in mind comments from employers about the inadvisability of ex-patients working in contact with the public. It is certainly the case that ex-patients communicate less often with the public and with subordinates than they do with their superiors or their colleagues. Of course, by no means everyone has *got* a subordinate: nor does the public penetrate most factories. Nor have we got controls. But the picture is not without interest, even raw at this stage.

"Face to Face Communication with the Public" has also been broken down by diagnosis. A very slightly lower percentage of psychotics are in jobs necessitating face to face contact with the public than the percentages of depressives and neurotics, but the difference is not significant. It would seem that employers do not consciously use diagnosis in job placement.

TABLE 7
Face to Face Communication with Public by Diagnostic Group

	Percentages within diagnostic category			
	Psychoses	Depressions	Neuroses	Other
Public	13	15	18	6
No public	83	79	75	94
Not applicable	4	6	7	0

Relapse into Hospital Care and Subsequent Return to Employment

Some of our subjects were "old" employees i.e. they had been employed by the company prior to their most recent hospital admission. It was possible to obtain data of a before/after sort in these cases. Five out of six employees in Sample C and four out of five in the Sample B, returned to their own jobs. Of the remainder, the majority drifted "downwards" as expected, but a substantial minority moved "up" the Registrar General's socio-economic group scale. This, of course, related to a single episode of illness for each individual, and no doubt re-admissions repeated too often will try the patience of any employer beyond endurance. We found that those who underwent the most pronounced occupational drift were the skilled workers.

The Role of the Occupational Health Doctor

It is not easy for managers or workers to accept the idea that work can adversely affect both mental and physical health. Although stress at work is accepted as a definite entity the stresses are often difficult to define. Unemployment, redundancy, long hours, physical discomfort, emotional upset — these are blamed but they rarely produce disability or clearly disordered health. Situations of a more subtle nature more often command our attention and we have to narrow the focus on to which factors at work, and which reactions of a person to something in his job, actually trigger mental disorder.

Most stresses seem to involve change of varying degree:

(a) The environment at work changes, e.g. closure of factory, disordered leadership, inappropriate job placement.
(b) The environment at home changes — by birth, marriage or death for example.

The vulnerability of the individual changes with age, occupation, level of education. Day by day events, conflicting attitudes, lack of participation, moods, lack of recognition, all these may increase tensions.

The stressed and vulnerable employee may react with anger and frustration or by withdrawal or disordered interpersonal relationships.

Excessive drinking may occur. All result in low morale, high absenteeism. Low productivity and accidents can be by-products of individual reaction to subtle and/or more obvious stress.

When an individual is unhappy, a nuisance in the department, shifting from job to job, quarrelling with spouse, drunk in charge, unable to relax, he requires help and insight into the causes of his disorder. If many employees are in this condition, a state of industrial unrest will develop which can only be treated by good mental hygiene and correction of cause of the breakdown. In the case of the individual it is necessary to help him and his manager to understand what is happening.

The Health & Safety at Work Act deals largely with protection from physical hazards. But the time consuming and unrewarding job of trying to educate managers and workers to their social responsibilities is a subject which is not mentioned. It is however the thorn in the flesh of every doctor in industry for managers change and the staff of medical departments keep changing and education must go on — the doctor must be unrelenting in assessing his own attitudes, be aware of changes around him and must sense the social climate where he works. This is not easy and requires time and much communication with all levels of those employed.

It has been suggested that workers and management should participate in monitoring attitudes and social climate. Hygienists are appointed to assess the toxicity of the atmosphere polluted by vapours and dusts of every kind — so why not monitor the social atmosphere? Occupational health and counselling programmes and the example of committed doctors and nurses who can sympathetically judge the difficulties of both employee and employer will contribute to better understanding.

The monitoring of the health and progress of the employee requires regular contacts with the employee's manager/supervisor. In doing this it is found that the interest of the manager is crucial to the health of the patient. The attitude of the managers changes when enquiries into the rehabilitation of the patient are made on a regular basis. The patient instead of a burden which they would gladly have shed after the previously disordered conduct which had disrupted the work of the department, is now a human being dependent for stability on the insight of the manager — a challenge to his/her ability. The establishment of this rapport depends to a great extent on the help of those who are not medically qualified — the Chaplain, the Welfare Officer, the Members of the Health & Safety

Committee, the Personnel Manager and the Shop Stewards. Their various insights and ideas contribute greatly to the work of the nurses and doctor in their efforts to maintain the health and happiness of the worker and the general good of the whole organisation.

Finding a New Job after a Spell in Hospital

Whilst we have found that, on nearly every criterion, to return to a previous job is the most successful course for the formerly mentally ill, there remains a large number who because of their length of hospital stay or for other reasons have no employment to which they can return. We have looked at the "new" employees in Sample B and C i.e. those not previously employed in the firm before their breakdown, and in particular to a line of enquiry which we believe had important results. This centres on the methods of introduction of ex-patients to their employment and the immediate background from whence they come.

A pattern emerged whereby ex-patients taking a job direct from hospital fared worse in terms of keeping it, than those coming from the employment exchange, even if these latter had been unemployed. This appeared to indicate that hospital preparation alone is less good than real life experience and that ex-patients may take years to settle down in employment. Emerging contemporaneously with the Department of Employments' Consultative document on Sheltered Employment, this finding slotted in well with the document's renewed emphasis on the rehabilitative component of sheltered work which in recent years has become in practice overlaid if not denied. Our own previous study[4] of Dr. Donal Early's pioneer sheltered working groups had shown how sheltered workers in existing "enclaves" had progressed, given a strong incentive and in particular a financial one, from sheltered to open conditions, thus effectually achieving their own rehabilitation.

An Experimental Scheme for the "New" Employee

In early 1976, the Manpower Services Commission commissioned an experimental "Enclave" Project in the Southampton area.

The essence of the research plan was to set up sheltered working groups, under the auspices of Professor Hugh Glanville's Wessex Rehabilitation Association, and compare the performance of Section 2, psychiatrically disabled workers with the performance of randomly selected long term unemployed workers, who — such was our hypothesis — might be suffering from covert personality difficulties which impeded their job-getting but which might be helped by "enclave" working — particularly by special supervision.

The project is in mid-term. Much the easiest to deal with have been the psychiatrically disabled, probably because this is where the expertise of our team lies, consisting as it does of: consultant psychiatrist in rehabilitation, Dr. Brenda Morris; psychiatric charge nurse in charge of the hospital Works Bureau; and very competent young DRO trained on the mental health side. Despite this, there have been four breakdowns, illustrating yet again the difficulties of prognosis with regard to schizophrenia. The unemployed were originally a 1 in 5 random sample of 80, all of whom had been out of work for over a year. Finally, 28 subjects were selected on the basis of the clinical judgement of a psychiatrist, following an extended interview. They have presented quite a different picture. Of the 28, 10 have refused offers of jobs — 4 we believe for psychiatric reasons and 3, all married men, because they were better off under social security. In some cases we thought both factors operated.

The results so far confirm our opinion that supported working groups offer a good method of resettlement for appropriately assessed severely psychiatrically disabled, and we applaud the fact that the Department are officially encouraging their extended establishment. But for the long-term unemployed — despite their undoubted hang-ups, the picture is more confused. All these people have at one time worked to qualify for benefit — but it does seem as if the experience of long-term unemployment accentuates latent inadequacies, immaturities, and disabilities so that, under present government policies, an unfortunate submerged section of the population is not only unemployed but becoming barely employable. So far we have got so few of them into jobs that it is impossible to say whether enclave working would help them or not. Similarly, we would enjoin caution before expressing premature eulogies on the value of enclave working for the disabled. We hope that ex-patients, chronic ex-patients, will be rehabilitated by this sensible method, but many more experiments are needed together with progress in psychiatric assessment, before such results can be confidently expected in even the majority of cases.

References

1. Wansbrough, S. N. (1974) *Employment Experiences of Ex-psychiatric Hospital Patients: the Employers' Standpoint*, Research Report to DHSS, May 1974.
2. Wansbrough, S. N. and Cooper, P. J. (1977) Psychiatric diagnosis in relation to some aspects of employment, *J. Soc. Occup. Med.,* 27, 50-7.
3. Benjamin, B. and Haycocks, H. W. (1971) *The Analysis of Mortality and Other Actuarial Statistics*, OUP.
4. Wansbrough, S. N. (1971) Interim report on schemes in open industry for the resettlement of ex-psychiatric patients, Unpublished Report to DHSS.

CHAPTER 12

A Positive Approach to the Care of Old People with Mental Disorders

TOM ARIE

Nottingham University Medical School

Over the last decade the number of old people in England and Wales has increased by around another million. We now have nearly 7 million old people, which is about equal to the entire population of this country a couple of hundred years ago. This great increase in the numbers of our old people is continuing through times when it is difficult, and often frankly impossible, even to maintain services at their existing levels; moreover we are faced with a great increase in public expectations of help — not so much on the part of the elderly themselves, for on the whole they expect very little, but chiefly from those of us who are their children and who have grown up in prosperous times and have come to take so much for granted.

Yet the extra demand generated by increased expectations is still relatively modest, though it can be critical; anyone working with the elderly knows how little most people ask and how huge are the burdens they carry without seeking relief, or indeed without awareness that sources of relief exist. The care of the elderly rests largely on the shoulders of lay people — families, neighbours, friends — and it is inconceivable that things can ever be otherwise, however great the much needed expansion of professional resources. Some 95 per cent of old people remain in private households, and increasingly services are reaching them; yet even with the great increase in services over recent years, successive surveys show how much these fall short of even the most moderate estimates of need.

The critical nature of the balance between the overwhelming majority of the elderly who are at home, and the mere 5 per cent or so who are in institutional care poses great problems: for example the roughly 2-3 per cent of the elderly who are in hospitals occupy half of all hospital beds. Even a marginal shift of the distribution between home and institutions, or between different compartments of the institutional sector, would have the most far reaching consequences for the balance of the caring system. Hence much of the anxiety and friction that bedevils care of the elderly and particularly when they move, or attempt to move, across the compartments of the care system.

These problems are compounded by the rapid increase in the numbers of the very old, and it is they of course who are most subject to degenerative disorders of body and mind, and above all to that greatest of all generators of disability and dependence — dementia. Dementia is literally a disruption of the "nerve centre" of the individual and it affects practically all aspects of function. Above all dementia erodes the awareness of one's own disability, and so the demented depend not only on the availability of others, but on constant surveillance since they themselves will not detect danger or forestall crises. No wonder that dementia is the biggest single user of institutional care, and probably the bigger trigger of socio-medical crises.

But the psychiatry of old age is by no means merely a matter of dementia. Pretty well the whole range of mental disorders occurs in the elderly. Depression is the commonest and it is in general eminently treatable. Suicide grows more common with increasing age, and the diagnosis of depression is crucial; in old people this can be a very tricky business, for it masquerades in many physical and confusional guises.

Neurotic and personality difficulties loom large; so far from being, as is sometimes comfortably believed, less troublesome in old age, they are in fact often much more insistent, for it is no longer possible to accommodate to them through work or even through family and social relationships. For in old age there is usually no work and sometimes no family or no effective family, and health may be poor and mobility restricted; and money is likely to be short, for half our old people live at or near the poverty line. It is in old age that many people come for the first time face to face with themselves, and in that predicament their needs are quite central to what psychiatry is about. Unfortunately, in our youth orientated society, psychiatrists are as likely as everyone else to place old people at the end of the queue in the inevitable competition for scarce time and resources.

In a way the most important thing that has happened during the past decade is the evolution of a coherent and basically sensible government policy for the care of the elderly with mental disorders. This has been promulgated in a series of guidance documents which are summarised in circular HM (72) 71 on *Services for Mental Illness related to Old Age*[1] and in *Better Services for the Mentally Ill.*[2] These offer on the one hand a rational basis for collaboration and distribution of functions between services, which in this context is no mere modish retailing of current "multi-disciplinary" ideology, but the very essence of the work – and on the other hand, estimates (and here the policy is probably at its weakest) of the scale of resources needed. Above all the "psychogeriatric" problem has been recognised and placed firmly on the map.

At the same time, psychiatric services specifically designed for the elderly have developed in many varied centres throughout the country, in part stimulating and shaping government policy, in part as a response to it. We now have a growing group of psychiatrists who have identified in the care of the elderly a fascinating and urgent task of psychiatry. The Group for the Psychiatry of Old Age in the Royal College of Psychiatrists has over the last 4 or 5 years gone from strength to strength, numbering its members in hundreds but with a nucleus of a few dozen people for whom old age psychiatry is their main professional concern.

Connoisseurs of government policy pronouncements will see a growing and gratifying acceptance of the idea, urged by many of us over the years and now accepted as the official policy of the Royal College of Psychiatrists, that in each Health District there should be a special sector of services for the elderly under the leadership of a consultant specifically appointed for this work; in a background paper[3] prepared by the Department for a conference on the elderly earlier this summer this policy was given firmer endorsement. The twenty or so main centres in which this work is now well developed have also an important role as models, and as teaching centres (though many are not formally in teaching districts); above all they have shown that this work is capable of engaging the professional interest and enthusiasm of the brightest of our young people in all the health professions. Formidable problems of "image" and recruitment remain, but there is cause for modest optimism that with good sense and above all with acceptance on the part of the universities of the need to place this work firmly in the "shop window" of undergraduate and postgraduate education these problems can be solved. Unfortunately teaching on these matters is still extremely meagre in the curricula of all the health professions, and not a single university department exists devoted specifically to this work, despite general acknowledgement that the care of the elderly with mental disorders poses perhaps the biggest challenge to health services for the rest of this century and well into the next.

One of the difficulties encountered in making out the case for specialist "psycho-geriatric" services has been that those services that have been set up have often lacked a framework for data collection capable of reflecting their impact across boundaries of psychiatry and geriatric medicine, health services and social services, institutional and domiciliary care. The emergence of a case register in association with the service in South Manchester may help to fill this vacuum and at the same time attract people in training posts to undertake research projects. This may tempt them to further commitment to work with the elderly.[4]

Some principles of a "positive approach" were set out in the report of the first year's work of Goodmayes Psychiatric Service for Old People.[5] They may bear repeating, and can be updated in the light of subsequent experience:

(1) *Availability.* A service for old people is nothing if it is not readily available to all who need it — patients, their families, doctors, social workers. Among potential "case-finders" health visitors have been an underused resource in the past. Klaus Bergmann has argued that theirs should be an expanding role with the elderly and they are likely to become cornerstones of the interplay between primary and secondary care systems in the support of families with elderly disabled members much as they have fitted easily into work with mothers and babies when relationships are strained by emotional problems.[6]

There must be the minimum of fuss and when the situation demands it, a crisis must be quickly met. Rapid response has proved one of the most effective weapons in our armoury. A service which is ready to respond promptly, even at some inconvenience to itself can often achieve more and give families more sense of support than might be achieved by offering other resources, which may not exist. It follows that the urgency of a problem depends not only on objective factors, but equally on the subjective sense of urgency of those seeking help. Therefore, it is almost always right to accept the referrer's estimate of the urgency of a problem even if it turns out later that in objective terms things weren't all that urgent after all.

(2) Such a service must be *flexible*; one must be prepared to try any solution, however unorthodox which seems sensible and with which resources can cope. Now that resources are even tighter, flexibility and willingness to try novel solutions is not only desirable but indispensable.

(3) All work must be based on *assessment*, whenever possible at home, before any plan of action is undertaken; patients must never simply arrive in the hospital.

Here we have had to make over the years a few compromises, but we have maintained the principle that first contacts should always be seen at home by a psychiatrist, or in whatever setting they are at the time; we have had to be a little less rigorous in relation to patients re-referred in the face of our fast increasing referral rate. Our excellent community nurses have increasingly been involved with this work, though we have maintained the principle of initial assessment by a psychiatrist. The benefits in terms of assessing the old person's capacity to function in her normal setting are overwhelming, and of course the consequences of moving an old person from her normal setting can be correspondingly catastrophic; it may prove impossible to re-establish her at home, and the very act of moving her to unfamiliar surroundings may induce confusion and irreversible deterioration.

(4) *Communication* and collaboration must be open and effective: situations should not collapse for want of the right hand knowing what the left hand is doing.

(5) One must take *responsibility* for every solution that one formulates, and always be ready to think again.

We have learnt from Albert Kushlick to distinguish between "hit-and-run" people like doctors, social workers, psychologists, administrators and many others, and continuing care people like nurses, and above all families, who are with the patient around-the-clock.[5] There is little place in this work for the "hit-and-run" doctor if by "hit-and-run" we mean simply that he makes a brief descent and diagnostic formulation, and then disappears. Probably the most basic principle of all in work with the elderly is to *carry problems through* — of course not necessarily by constant personal presence, but by willingness to come back to the problem, to pick it up when things go wrong, and to think ahead and wrestle with the complications.

"Seeing people through", to use an entirely happy phrase of Eric Wilkes', is really what it is all about. This is an age of chronic disease and chronic disability where lightening cures are few, gratifying though they are both to patient and therapist; most medical work today is continuing care, what Maurice Backett has called "maintenance medicine". Nowhere is this more apparent than in the care of the elderly and in psychiatry, yet the same is true of most of the work of what we might call the greater health profession. Part of the challenge and fascination of psychiatric work with the elderly is that it is just like the rest of psychiatry and the rest of medicine — only much more so!

References

Sources of figures, and more detailed data, together with further discussion of some of the issues raised in this paper can be found in Arie, T. "Issues in the Psychiatric Care of the Elderly", a chapter in *Care of the Elderly*, edited by A. N. Exton-Smith & J. Grimley Evans, Academic Press, 1977.

1. DHSS (1972) *Services for Mental Illness Related to Old Age*, Circular HM(72)71.
2. DHSS (1975) *Better Services for the Mentally Ill*, Comnd. 6233, H.M.S.O.
3. DHSS (1977) *Conference on the Elderly*, July 1977, Mimeographed background paper.
4. Jolley, D. J. (1977) Psych-geriatrics — Making out a case, Unpublished paper presented at the Mental Health Foundation Conference on New Methods of Mental Health Care, Oxford, September 1977.
5. Arie, T. (1970) The First Year of the Goodmayes Psychiatric Service for Old People, *Lancet*, 2, 1179-82.
6. Egdell, H. G. (1977) The health visitor and community psychiatry, Unpublished

paper presented at the Mental Health Foundation Conference on New Methods of Mental Health Care, Oxford, September 1977.

7.   Kushlick, A. (1975) *Some Ways of Setting, Monitoring and Attaining Objectives for Services for Disabled People*, Health Care Evaluation Research Team, Highcroft, Romsey Road, Winchester, Hampshire, Research Report No. 116.

CHAPTER 13

All is not lost: New Approaches to the Management of Old People with Mental Disorders in Continuing Care Settings

DAVID JOLLEY
Withington Hospital, Manchester

When no effective physical treatments were available to ease the management of the functional psychoses, mental hospitals offering early admission and a vigorous nursing policy that emphasised the importance of work and freedom of movement were seen as worthy ventures and likely to improve the lot of the mentally ill.[1] Unfortunately county mental hospitals grew to be enormous, were often ill-sited and frequently became overcrowded and understaffed. In these far from ideal circumstances their therapeutic potential was reduced and indeed they may in many instances have developed regimes of care that compounded rather than reduced the incapacities of patients.[2] The past 30 years have seen a vigorous movement to reduce the size and overcrowding of mental hospitals and to manage people disabled by chronic mental disorders in the community, in private households or smaller group settings. Whilst there have been great achievements attributable to this policy of extramural care, there have been sobering lessons to learn. In particular many of the disabilities that some had naïvely supposed due to "institutional neurosis" are commonly seen in chronic schizophrenia wherever it is managed. The uncertainties of provision associated with moving from a "mental hospital" pattern of care

*This chapter includes contributions by Dr. Roger Morgan (St. Wulstans Hospital), Mr. Frank Parker, formerly of Craven Lodge School, Leicester, Mr. N. C. Marston, Social Services Department, Northampton and Dr. Colin Godber, Consultant Psychogeriatrician, Moorgreen Hospital, Southampton.

to "community care" have sometimes exposed patients to the likelihood of neglect or care that falls short of being optimal: "Many schizophrenics need and benefit from prolonged care in special environments with special facilities". "By the same token the community . . . in which the patient first broke down . . . is not by definition a health-giving place and good for him to remain in."[3]

Mental Health Services have become preoccupied in defining the best way to serve their traditional clients, patients with major functional psychoses, or alternatively seeking more acceptance in general medical circles by the practice of "psychological medicine". Meanwhile a rising tide of elderly people with its accompaniment of mental disorders many of which are chronic or progressive has received less attention than is its due. Mental disorder in late life combined with the social vulnerability of being old and liability to physical frailty often reduce an individual's ability to cope with matters required to keep body and soul together within a home. Thus it is that in places of safety: mental hospitals, geriatric hospitals, Part III accommodation, private nursing homes etc. mentally disabled old people come together in alarming numbers.[4] This is in every way a new challenge to the resources of a developed society such as ours, but a challenge which is too readily dismissed with the comment that "there is nothing that can be done for them". Attitudes as much as lack of resources explain why the elderly within mental hospitals are the least likely to receive occupational therapy of any sort.[5]

Yet there is a great deal of evidence that social and psychological manipulations have a tremendous impact on the style of life and achievements of even the most severely demented.

It was the observation of Dr. Brian Lodge, Consultant Geriatrician at Carlton Hayes Hospital, Narborough, Leicester that the deterioration of memory and understanding of the elderly was in many ways not dissimilar to the slower than normal growth of memory and understanding of the ESN child. It was likely, he thought, that although each condition was at the opposite end of a theoretical continuous growth curve, principles governing the treatment which were successful in improving the ESN child might equally successfully arrest the deterioration and may well improve the mental well-being of confused, forgetful old people.

From this premise the invitation was made to proffer principles of education and management of ESN children to Dr. Lodge and the staff at

Carlton Hayes Hospital so that these could be learned by them and applied to patients.

Much of the presentation seen in the daily living of elderly patients appeared to accord with that in some ESN children. Patients did not expect to be involved: they did not expect to be spoken to: they did not help as opposed to doing what was required. Patients appeared unaware of a place for them in the order of things — they "didn't matter". The appearance of the patients suggested a slow moving aimlessness. Apathy appeared paramount. All this could be found in admission children at school. So could the attitudes of the patients to staff — there was either a dependence on or an irksomeness to Authority. Further looking at the pre-hospital and hospital histories suggested that:

(1) For a long time no demands were made upon patients to remember.
(2) Their every day life had not been pleasurable and they had sunk their identity to avoid "pain".
(3) Their identity had been lost in the group identity of institutional living.

Again, all conditions noted in examined histories of ESN children.

The problem then was to define educational aspects of treatment suitable for aged patients who have become confused. The secondary problem which would become the primary need would be to translate the practices of this treatment to nursing staff whose training had been, like teachers, first to observe the patients/pupils but thereafter had diverged almost totally. For nurses the route was via restrictions of prescription, procedure and palliative, whereas for teachers experiment, empiricism and exhortation provided open ended travel.

Discussing patients' confusions with hospital staff it became apparent that some of the difficulties were hospital induced. At its most simple the fact that patients failed to identify ward toilet doors may well have been because all doors were identical in shape and colour and that for different purposes patients were periodically directed through different but similar looking doors. Such observations emphasised the need for basic consideration of the nature of the problems and the ways in which solving them would be educationally sound. As a starting point for teaching and discussion with ward staff the following was offered as a proposition:

Memory recall demands that the happening will have been understood and will exist for recall.[6] (The child in school/patients in hospital require to know what occurs within the context of their comprehension before logical recall can be expected from them.) Memory of an event, however important or trivial, is only structured to be understood, appreciated, available for recall if the event has been communicated to the person. The communication demands that the recipient of the event is conscious of the "persona" and that the event is not unpleasurable to a high degree.[7]

It became evident at this time that staff at all levels were feeling threatened by what they conceived would be happening. Concern was expressed that behaviour modification techniques of a doubtfully ethical nature were being constructed. This questioning of method and motive provided the opportunities to suggest that a transfer of work orientation and demand from a routine dominated by the clock and the kitchen to one of care and communication with the patients' real needs was the intention. That it was, for example, desirable for patients to be motivated to dress themselves and come to breakfast rather than to be helped to feed whilst lying in bed was self-evident only to some. Such proposed interference with routine was evident to all and unwelcome to many.

From the outset it was emphasised to hospital staff that ideally educationally based treatment would be continuous daily — not sessional, that it would be structured in the smallest steps; that it would never allow failure and its reinforcement of unpleasure to the patient. It was emphasised that treatment would initially concentrate on recall of small aspects of daily living (say dressing sequence, names of garments, colours). It was explained in detail that the patient's five senses were the only pathways available, supported by their voices (talking *with*, not *to*) and their movements. The greater amount of learning by children who move around compared to those who don't and whose needs of say materials are met by a monitor distribution was the foundation for requiring voluntary self help — however limited.[8]

The diagrammatic presentation served to emphasise the desirability of spectacles/hearing aids if needed being clean, comfortable and worn. It offered opportunity to consider the consequences of seating patients (a) side by side all facing the same way, and (b) having them looking out of windows into strong light for long periods.

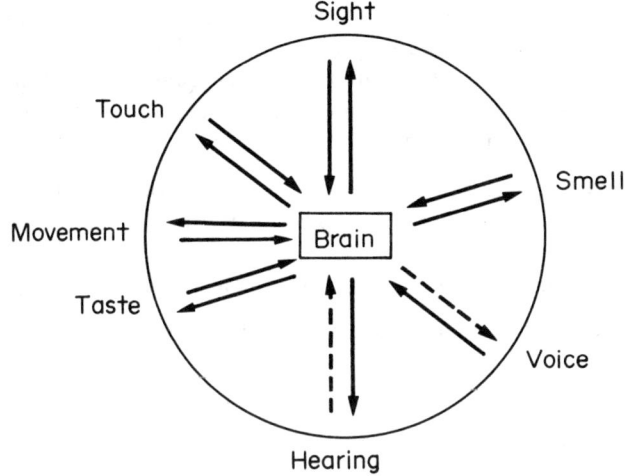

Impediment in reception produces
impediment in execution

Fig. 1.

The use of voice to modify emotion — and the necessity of emotional response and rapport was a further area in which the chart helped.

The pattern of personal educational treatment used was:

— to identify the patient	— "John",
— to create rapport	will you put this crayon in the
interdependency	box for me?
opportunity for praise	"Well done: you did move well
— to leave space to extend	and quietly."
— to provide teaching opportunity	"John —
— to allow language development	what colour was the crayon etc.
be it nominal or qualitative.	OR can you find that crayon
	again for me please? It is called
	green/light green etc.
— to allow opportunity for praise	"Well done John"
— never to be designed to cause	
failure.	

The emphasis was "patients cannot be overpraised for successful achievement within the structured programme". Reference to work done showing increased perception in adults who were praised and supported, led to simple experiments amongst staff. The procedure was to provide a variety of interesting experiences

— limited not to confuse	structured to avoid over stimulation
— simple not to confound	presented systematically enthusiastically
— pleasurable to encourage	offered cheerfully

The experiences were to be talked about and provided:

presentation of whole,
analysis, $\Big\}$ verbal and kinaesthetic
re-synthesis

Equipment and other provisions aimed at unlocking or jolting personal awareness were requested:

Mirrors large enough to allow full length viewing. It was disturbing to realise that there was no hospital provision for these old people to regularly see themselves in mirrors. Following their installation there were several reports of patients being disturbed by their reflections which they initially failed to understand.

Clock

Calendar: / menu: / static items — pictures, news illustrations (changed often) live and moving items — fish, plants, seed growing.

A place of one's own for personal storage. This should be private to the patient and cleaned etc., with her present: not "anybodys" but lent to her and not gone to at random by staff.

Physical room in which to operate. (If material is issued and collected the patient will assimilate less quickly than if he collects and returns it.)

The "personalising" of items of equipment and possessions.

Variations in decoration of rooms/areas. (A common colour key for toilet doors for example.)

Provision for personal progress to be appreciated.

The consequent development of altered relationships between staff and patients received support and guidance along the following lines:

— acceptance   A total acceptance in human terms of the patients as
they were. (A common early staff response was "if only
... was — or was not — so bad in degree then I could
etc. ....") The starting point had to be, as with children,
acceptance of the person as they are now. [9]

— affection   Aim to induce self respect with its attendant pride and
pleasure. Respect for own property, then other people
and their possessions can follow.

Staff were made aware that the response to any educational dialogue is
pre-determined by the attitudes of the teacher regarding the pupil.

This is pre-eminently the significant determinant in the success or
failure of learning. (Shaw's Eliza Doolittle talking to Colonel Pickering,
points out that to him she would always be a lady because he'd always
treated her as a lady, whereas to Professor Higgins she would never be one,
for he never saw her as one.)

Staff were guided not automatically to make self limiting prognosis and
achievement targets. They were helped to understand that these achieved,
become self fulfilling prophecies and each re-inforces — justifies — the next
limited prophecy. They were also encouraged to accept that varying
emotional "climates" were desirable rather than a bland atmosphere of
controlled institutional low key responses to routine demands.

In Practice

The approach was for the medical staff to nominate 6–8 patients whose
conditions of senility and dementia were moderately severe. Those
patients selected to form the pilot group were then considered:

Medically: physical, psychiatric, performance;

Socially: attitudes, habits;

Intellectually: recall, response, orientation (time and place).

The patients selected were then moved to live in side rooms off from a
communal ward. The rooms were each equipped with the usual bedroom
provisions for sleeping, dressing and clothes storage.

A separate dining area and sitting area was established for the group. It proved administratively impossible to provide patients with personalised clothing or crockery.

The nursing staff were encouraged to verbalise with each patient every procedure. Where the patient had forgotten, then an immediate response was sought, i.e. "These are your stockings". "What are these?" "Yes, stockings". "Two stockings", and so on. Staff were also instructed to encourage patients towards independence. They were told that in some instances it may be necessary to put patients into situations wherein they would miss some established part of daily routine unless the patients made efforts to help themselves. This made it necessary occasionally to, for instance, leave the patient to dress and prepare themselves for breakfast rather than to aid a reasonably competent but recalcitrant person. If in the process the patient was very late indeed for breakfast then the ward routine had to allow for this. Where patients wrongly considered themselves incapable it was not easy to encourage ward staff to be a little "difficult" and for example put a drink sufficiently distant so that the patient had to make an effort to get it — rather than to stand and aid them with it. These procedures all needed nurses to talk the patients through their routines.

Outside ward routines the nursing staff said that they found patients' ward time difficult to occupy.

The non-availability of material to use was evident. Teachers have a "treasure chest" of material personal to them and built up over time. The nurses had none and almost no means were known to them of getting one.

It was desirable — and is still — that nurses should identify with patients. There seemed more reasons why nurses could not eat food from the same serving bowls as patients together with them in work time than there are choices of menu. Educationally it is desirable for a teacher to eat meals similar to children's together with children. Why administratively could this not happen in hospitals? Throughout the exercise staff involved showed considerable unease at their "good fortune" — support accorded and the regard paid to them. They felt guilty at their colleagues in the same ward·areas having so much physical work to do. Staff not involved showed evidence of feeling threatened by this new pilot scheme and the broadly advertised proposals arising from it. Frank Parker's final report to Dr. Lodge and the hospital staff read:

"At the beginning all the patients were unresponsive, apathetic, perseverating and vacant. None was an individual person viewed from the door, all were a ward group. Some needed much help.

In eight weeks mannerisms had minimised, folk looked to see who had come into the ward, they moved within the ward, incontinence did not exist.

In twelve weeks all were said to be eating less, all had lost weight and were judged to be in better physical shape.

In eighteen weeks occupations had been established about which some could converse. Greater recall was evident in all patients.

At the end of the six months no patient had died. Chair-bound patients were moving voluntarily, self help at meals was established and an identity within the group and of the group plus its nurses distinct from the rest of the community at social functions outside the hospital was well established."

What had begun as an interesting comparative exercise in philosophy became a successful route by which to increase job satisfaction for those who work with people needing care.[10] Yet this "educational" framework is unlikely to be the only one to find validity in this field, indeed Woods and Britton[11] in reviewing recent publications identified at least four main themes among successful programmes: stimulation and activity, reality orientation, milieu treatment and behavioural approaches. Examples of new enterprises are encouragingly reported in different residential settings in various parts of the country. For example, a loosely structured milieu therapy model found early success in Northamptonshire Old Peoples Homes.[12]

Whilst residential care has demonstrated its ability to cope with the 24-hour needs of very dependent people, the episodic input of domiciliary services can in no way compete.[13] Similarly "sheltered housing" as experienced in most current projects has shown itself a blessing to many fit people in their 60s only to become a nightmare as they become more heavily dependent in their 80s. The basis of the nightmare has been the reliance of schemes on a single warden or a husband and wife team that is expected to provide 9 a.m.–5 p.m. cover and otherwise is available for emergencies only. The presence of 40 elderly couples in their 80s every night is likely to present its own series of emergencies! Yet in Southampton the experimental provision of a three shift system of wardens together with planned cooperation from social services, community nurses, general practitioners and active involvement of the local psychogeriatric team appears capable of transforming potential disaster into a viable support system in which residents own coping abilities are exercised to the full.[14]

The selection of tenants was on primarily medico-social grounds by a panel including the Assistant Director of Housing, the Senior Residential Care Advisor, the General Practitioner and the Community Physician from the steering group. They included people off the Part III waiting list, "problem cases" from existing sheltered housing schemes, and people waiting on the sheltered housing list. A number of suitable existing residents in Part III homes were identified but did not wish to make the move. Those selected included some with well established dementia whose suitability for this form of care would obviously be of crucial interest. There was a fair range of physical disability, though this was limited by Kinloss Court having two floors but no lift. The units comprised 16 flats and 16 bedsitters.

The staff comprised a resident warden, a resident assistant warden (specifically not a joint husband/wife appointment), a non-resident warden and a domiciliary aide. Apart from providing between them twenty-four hour cover their role was to visit the tenants daily watching out for signs of social or medical deterioration and encouraging integration and the development of a sense of community while at the same time fostering the tenants previous ties. The aide would also help with laundry, shopping and the preparation of meals, and at the request of an individual's GP would also check on the consumption of medication. Nursing experience was not a condition of employment and it was recognised that any nursing function would devolve on to the Community Nursing Services, a member of which was specifically seconded to Kinloss Court. Similarly the dependency of the clientele was recognised in the provision of adequate home help; most residents had meals on wheels which were served communally for those who wished it.

This network of domiciliary support was expected to maintain tenants there to quite an advanced level of disability and to tide them through most intercurrent illnesses and crises. In the event, however, of it becoming acutely or chronically overloaded by one or more individuals a vital clause in the operational policy guaranteed immediate admission (if necessary) to a geriatric or psychogeriatric bed or to a Part III home. It was hoped (and has proved to be the case) that experience that this guarantee was honoured would in fact increase the staff's readiness to see people through where they were.

The evaluation of the project has been by a comparison of the Kinloss Court tenants with a group entering a partly supervised satellite complex opening at the same time, and the residents of a recently opened Part III home. Though obviously not strictly comparable groups their levels of dependency were rated at the outset and at three monthly intervals. Subsequently, using a modification of a schedule already under use in a survey of Hampshire Part III residents, the consumption of domiciliary services and movements in and out of residential or hospital care will be compared for the three groups for the period of the study (initially eighteen months, but hopefully longer) and data is also being gathered on the work level of the staff in relation to the sheltered housing groups. A study has also been undertaken by students from the University Department of Sociology on the quality of life of the three groups and it is hoped to repeat this again later when Kinloss Court has established itself better as a community. The value of a comparison between groups of such very different composition is obviously limited and it will be difficult to produce any very clear figure on the costing of Kinloss Court. It will, however, be supplemented by the learning experiences of the staff and the steering group in the problems of this form of care, the sort of people suited to it, and the extra facilities to be incorporated should future complexes be designed for this purpose.

This scheme has been operating now for just over a year and it has been gratifying to see some initially very precarious individuals continuing to cope, with a lot of help from the staff; from the psychiatric point of view this has been notable in the cases of one or two fairly demented ladies who wandered initially but have since settled well. The hospital and residential care backup has worked well and about one third of the residents have had short spells in hospitals, one remaining for long term care and one moving to Part III (where he proved a great handful). About one third of the tenants are on the books of the Psychogeriatric Service and one of the psychogeriatric community team visits most weeks. The supervision of medication has often been of crucial benefit. One gains the impression that the tenants strongly value their own front doors, though it is hoped that as time goes on a stronger sense of community will develop to the benefit of some of the tenants who are still rather isolated.

Thus it appears that this project has got off to an encouraging start and that despite shortcomings of design some (physically and/or mentally) very disabled individuals are being maintained who would otherwise have entered Part III homes. This has partly been due to the extra staffing level and partly to good collaboration between services. One would like to feel, however, that an additional factor in the equation is the harnessing of the tenant's own pride and self-caring effort which is always prone to atrophy in residential care.

The needs presented by mentally and physically frail old people call for the exhibition of the greatest human ingenuity. There are lessons to be learned from the experience of services dealing with the chronic mentally disabled of former generations. There is much to be gained from further investigation of the skills of other disciplines than those traditionally involved in health and social services and in this comparison with patterns of care found to be successful in the management of subnormal individuals appears to be most fruitful.[15] But perhaps the most important step to take is to look at the novel situation created by the presence of disabled old people in such numbers with innocent eyes and minds capable of flexible thought. It is extremely unlikely that arrangements that have fragmented continuing care into "hospital", geriatric and psychiatric, and "social services" will survive the scrutiny that is being forced upon them. A great deal of rethinking is called for, there is ample evidence that it is taking place and what will emerge will be a new order of skills and mutual responsibility.

References

1. Roberts, Nesta (1967) *Cheadle Royal Hospital, A Bicentenary History*, John Sherratt & Son, Altrincham.
2. Wing, J. K. and Brown, G. W. (1970) *Institutionalism and Schizophrenia: a comparative study of 3 mental hospitals 1960-1968*, London: CUP.
3. Morgan, R. (1977) Unpublished paper presented at the Mental Health Foundation Conference on New Methods of Mental Health Care, Oxford, September 1977.
4. Kay, D. W. K., Beamish, P. and Roth, M. (1962) *Some Social and Medical Characteristics of Elderly People under State Care, Sociological Review Monograph*, No. 5, Keele.
5. DHSS (1975) *Statistical and Research Report Series* No. 10, Census of A:

Patients in Mental Illness Hospitals and Units in England and Wales at the end of 1971 (Tables 18 and 19).

6. Cofer, N. F. and Appley, M. H. (1964) *Motivation: Theory and Research*, John Wiley & Son.
7. Stones, E. (1966) *An Introduction to Educational Psychology – reinforcement*, Methuen.
8. Skinner, B. F. (1967) *Teaching Machines.*
9. Rosenthal, R. and Jacobsen, I. (1968) *Pygmalion in the Classroom: teachers' expectations and pupils' intellectual development*, Holt, Rinehart & Winston.
10. Times Educational Supplement (1974) *Second Childhood*, (August issue).
11. Woods, R. T. and Britton, P. G. (1977) Psychological approaches to the treatment of the elderly, *Age and Ageing*, 6, 104-12.
12. Marston, N. C. (1977) Improving the Quality of Life in Old Persons Homes, Unpublished paper presented at the Mental Health Foundation Conference on New Methods of Mental Health Care, Oxford, September 1977.
13. Isaacs, B. and Neville, Y. (1976) The needs of old people, *British Journal of Preventive and Social Medicine*, 30, 79-85.
14. Godber, C. (1977) Kinloss Court – an experiment in sheltered housing and collaboration, Unpublished paper presented at the Mental Health Foundation Conference on New Methods of Mental Health Care, Oxford, September 1977.
15. Kushlick, A., Felce, D., Palmer, J. and Smith, J. (1976) Evidence to the Committee of Inquiry into Mental Handicap Nursing and Care, Mimeographed report.

CHAPTER 14

Comments and Conclusions

J. K. WING

Institute of Psychiatry and London School of Hygiene

The contributions to this volume collectively deal with most of the urgent issues now facing people, whether professional or lay, carers or sufferers, who are seriously concerned with the prevention, treatment and everyday management of the "adult mentally ill". If, as was pointed out in the introduction, their contributions raise as many questions as they answer, this is because the issues are complex and our knowledge about causes and basic mechanisms is limited. To some extent, we are bound to fill in the biggest gaps with untested theories and to make up the rest as we go along. That is the state of the art and there is very little point in trying to apportion blame, any more than it would have been sensible, in the seventeenth century, to attack Newton for not discovering relativity or Harvey for not achieving even greater understanding of physiology than he did. Just as Newton and Harvey stood on the shoulders of their predecessors, so we stand on the shoulders of those who have gone before us. This is how useful knowledge accumulates and we can be sure that much that seems obscure to us will seem simple to our descendants.

Meanwhile, we can try to be as clear as possible about the nature of the theories upon which we base our actions. Kathleen Jones, in her role of historian of ideas, is very helpful here. Many of our current concepts can be traced back to the period of reform in British and American psychiatry that began a century and a half ago. As Foucault[1] and, more particularly, Rothman,[2] have suggested, the principles of "moral treatment" then put forward (which were derived from the ideas of the Enlightenment) became embodied in the institutions which tried to put them into practice, so that the institution became regarded as, in itself, therapeutic, even when the principles were no longer being applied. The custodial era lasted for a century, although there was always an undercurrent of awareness that perhaps it had gone too far. The Mental Treatment Act of 1930, for example, was evidence of dissatisfaction with a purely institutional solution to the social problems of the severe mental disorders.

It was not, however, until after the second world war that, throughout the western world but particularly in Britain, these problems came to be regarded as part of the general "matter of the welfare state". Kathleen Jones argues that the solution eventually adopted here — on the one hand, integration of the public health and psychiatric sectors into the National Health Service; on the other, creation of a network of social services based on a separate administration that is locally rather than nationally financed — had many unanticipated results. Within these new administrative conglomerates "there was no special representation for mental health interests". In the name of integration, the psychiatric expertise that had been built up, on which much of the pioneer enthusiasm for a new order had been based, was absorbed into general medicine or generic social work, leaving only the rump (the large mental hospitals) behind. "There is now no entity at central or local government level which can be called a Mental Health Service."

The reasons for these changes were not wholly administrative. There was an extraordinary change, during the late 1960s and early 1970s, in the attitudes of educated people towards psychological abnormality, which had its effect on legislators and policy makers. The catalysts were sociologists and psychiatrists who adopted the view that severe mental illness did not "exist". Goffman was probably the most influential. He was familiar with the conditions prevailing in the large State hospitals of the USA and his compelling literary style and brilliant polemic convinced many people that such institutions actually created the disorders they were supposed to treat.[3] Scheff[4] extended the theory to conditions outside the institution and suggested that "mental disorders" were simply the product of a process of labelling which had its roots in society itself. Laing[5] and Szasz[6] put forward quite different theories for the labelling process and suggested different remedies; one thinking that the families of afflicted people, the other that State-organised services, were responsible.

These theories had in common a denial that any element of intrinsic psychobiological impairment contributed to the social disablement of "psychiatric patients".[7] Most of the empirically-based investigations of the time came to far more cautious conclusions.[8,9] Wing and Brown[10] at the end of an eight-year study of three English mental hospitals, concluded:

> "New forms of community agency must be developed in which the best aspects of the mental hospital tradition are preserved, even if the buildings themselves are not. The services provided by the various specialised environments of the good mental hospital are still needed. The experience of the rehabilitation team is relevant to the new problems of community psychiatry. If these skills and traditions are lost it will be a long time before they are developed again. . . . The present ferment of change provides an opportunity for further progress but only if the lessons of the past — particularly the state of 'community care' which preceded the foundation of the early hospitals for 'moral treatment' — are remembered and profitably used."

Many of the most skilled clinical psychiatrists, nurses and social workers echoed these sentiments. They had been the pioneers of social treatment and were adapting the techniques developed in hospital for use outside. This was strongly realistic, since the main point of need occurred just before discharge, i.e. while the patient was still in hospital. If this foundation had been built upon it is possible that subsequent developments would have been more favourable. It is tempting to speculate about the influence a Chief Scientist's Organisation, like that set up in the Department of Health following the Rothschild Report, might have had in making planners' decisions better informed. As it was, most of the empirical research was ignored.

The result was that the decision to "run down" the mental hospitals was taken in a climate of optimism that made it appear likely that rather few people would remain handicapped after discharge, and that these could relatively easily be dealt with by the social services. (The term "mental handicap" was officially restricted to the mentally retarded.) A few rather irrelevant articles were quoted by the Department in favour of their point of view. Of course, we know that it was incorrect; that a severely handicapped "new" long-stay group is accumulating,[11] that many handicapped people become destitute,[12,13,14] that group homes, hostels and day centres are filling up with long-stay residents and attenders although often begun with high hopes of resettlement,[15,16,17,18] and that some families experience severe problems.[19,20,21] Social service departments place a rather low priority on work with the mentally disabled and the economic recession has forced them to cut down their plans for expansion.

Meanwhile, changes have continued to take place in the mental hospitals, which still cope with the bulk of admissions since very few District Hospital psychiatric units have been opened. On the one hand, there is a tendency to refuse to admit or retain "difficult" patients on the grounds that they should be in regional medium-security units. On the other hand, the fine traditions of social care and rehabilitation that some hospitals had established are being forgotten; partly because of a generally low morale due to the threat of eventual closure, partly because of a feeling that hospital treatments ought to be "medical". Recent reports from the Hospital Advisory Service have emphasised some of the deficiencies of the large hospitals and these have been highlighted by several Commissions of Enquiry.

Somehow, we seem to have made the worst of both worlds. Nevertheless, there are positive features in the present situation and several of the contributions to this book bring them out. The rational combination of in-patient with day-patient care described by Steven Hirsch has more than economic savings to recommend it, particularly if the idea could be extended to the rational coordination of a wider variety of services. It is, of course, important to remember that the fact that in-patient stay can be reduced without risk, does not mean that the total time needed for recovery is reduced. Services of another kind may continue to be needed.

Coordination is the main theme discussed by Peter Jeffreys in Chapter 2. He lists all the many difficulties that stand in the way of planning teams consisting of members of different professional and administrative hierarchies. One of the main problems is that the health and social services are financed in different ways. David Goldberg at the Mental Health Foundation Conference on which this book is based argued strongly that a single method of financing was needed and the Secretary of State seemed to go some way towards accepting the idea in principle. Meanwhile, Peter

Jeffreys' suggestion of a standing joint committee on mental health, on which senior representatives of the AHA and the SSD sit, deserves consideration, particularly if jointly available funds can be stepped up considerably.

There is still the difficult problem of deciding where clinical responsibility lies. Theoretically, this can be decided by "the multidisciplinary team", which appoints one of its members to take the lead in any particular case, depending on the nature of the action needed. A great deal of common training of the different professions represented will be necessary in order to get them to accept and act on this principle. The danger is that the team will wish to assume some sort of collective responsibility, which might sometimes mean that decisions were not executed at all. The problem is compounded when the services of voluntary organisations are considered.

What is needed is not so much extra health or social services staff who will look after coordination, but the devolution by each authority of specific responsibility to named individuals who will undertake certain duties. One obvious need, administratively and clinically, is to appoint officers in every district who are responsible to both types of authority; who will ensure that a case-conference is held whenever anyone becomes "new" long-stay (i.e. stays more than a given time, such as six months) whether in residential or day accommodation and whether in property belonging to the NHS, SSDs or voluntary organisations; who will see that all likely interests are represented at the conference, including where necessary employment, housing, and other relevant staff; and who have sufficient power to be able to turn their recommendations into solid action.

Another prominent theme which provides some hint of future progress concerns vocational rehabilitation and resettlement. Nancy Wansborough and Philip Cooper indicate that there are many new avenues to be explored, particularly in the utilisation of sheltered workshops (why could not one day centre in each area be upgraded to the status of a Remploy Factory?) and in the introduction of sheltered sections into large industrial firms. Russian psychiatrists claim that they are able to place substantial numbers of handicapped people into factories. Many such schemes have been successfully launched for the physically handicapped in this country. Here is a large area for future experiment. Both authors re-emphasise the old observation that the longer an individual has been socially disabled, the less likely is he or she to do well in future. It may be that we shall find ways of changing this situation but, meanwhile, it is necessary to recognise that concepts of shelter are still important.

Another large area, not much discussed in this book, concerns the "management" of handicap. Although the term sounds rather authoritarian, the idea behind it is the very opposite. Much progress has been made with helping individuals to understand their handicaps, the situations that make them better or worse, the reactions of other people, and the services available. The general aim is to minimise the disadvantages of being disabled and maximise any compensating talents.

The example of diabetes is often used. Although there are difficulties in applying exactly this model to conditions like schizophrenia (notably because of the problem of insight), useful analogies can be drawn — in particular, the recognition that relatives need almost as much help as the affected individuals themselves. Useful progress has been made in the field of mental retardation and childhood psychosis[22,23,24] and well-established voluntary societies (e.g. the National Society for Mentally Handicapped Children and National Society for Autistic Children) have consciously adopted a role similar to that of the British Diabetic Society. In the case of conditions such as schizophrenia it has been much more difficult to establish an equivalent body, partly because of the prejudice of the public in general and professionals in particular, and partly because of the problems of diagnosis.[25,26] Nevertheless, even here, the foundation of a National Schizophrenia Fellowship has attracted wide support, and the opportunity to develop a programme of self-help is being eagerly accepted.[27,28] The principles of management, based on empirical research, are beginning to be laid down.[29]

Research into the equivalent problems of the elderly mentally infirm is urgently needed. What are the real problems of dealing with such people at home and how can they be overcome by the selective provision of realistic advice about behavioural problems, help with extra chores, adaptations to the home, counselling about family problems, and occasional relief from burdens? The chapters by Tom Arie and David Jolley set out the priorities and the opportunities with considerable clarity.

A further area in which pioneering efforts could well be rewarded is that of the creation of new forms of sheltered community. One of the functions of the large mental hospital was to provide facilities for residential care, occupation, and recreation, for people who could not achieve such conditions for themselves. The disadvantages of the large mental hospitals are evident and the challenge is to find ways of eliminating these without, at the same time, eliminating the advantages. It is not sufficient to discharge someone "into the community" and to think that this act alone is a form of "community care". The concept of community is an artificial one when applied to people with no social roots, few social skills, and an inability to make useful social contacts for themselves. "Hospital hostels", which provide accommodation on a domestic scale but also have spacious grounds, and a generous enough staff ratio to ensure that withdrawn and handicapped people have a well-structured and socially stimulating environment, are one possibility, but there are others.

In all these ways, the present state of services offers opportunity for new ideas, for experiment, and for evaluative research. The Mental Health Foundation has supported several such ventures which it sees as pointers towards a more satisfactory future for people with severely handicapping disorders and for their families.

The remainder of the book is concerned with a different though inter-related set of problems. Even when they were at their largest, mental hospitals never admitted more than a tiny fraction of those who could be given a diagnosis of some sort of psychiatric disorder. Most people with anxiety states, depressive disorders, alcohol or drug addiction, or personality problems, were never referred to a psychiatrist. This is still true today.[30] General practitioners and generic social workers see most such people who seek professional help. Others look for advice to a wide variety of unofficial or semi-official agencies. These conditions do not so frequently lead to severe social disablement as do the schizophrenias and dementias, although they do so occasionally, but they are frequently distressing and handicapping.

Since everyone becomes depressed or anxious in response to the common personal or social stresses of everyday life, it is not surprising that the so-called "minor" neuroses are commoner among people who are isolated or unprivileged or who experience particularly difficult social problems.[31,32,33,34] These people are often least able, for a variety of reasons including prior deprivation ("learned helplessness") and possible constitutional disadvantages, to cope with their problems alone.

Geoffrey Marsh and Malcolm Lader express the reasonable view that medication with analgesics or minor tranquilisers or antidepressant drugs is unlikely to be a sufficient response to such conditions. A more thorough training of general practitioners in the psychosocial aspects of their work is one solution advocated. The establishment of primary health care teams (including not only health visitors and psychiatric nurses but also social workers and counsellors) is complementary to this. Experiments to show how successful such schemes are, compared with the traditional visit to the family doctor, or with no professional contact at all, are much needed. Matilda Goldberg has shown what can be done. Another promising line of development is the introduction of therapists trained in the use of behavioural methods of reducing disablement due to phobias, "learned helplessness", psychophysiological symptoms and poor social skills.

Susan Holland puts forward an approach based on informal contact with people in high-risk situations, such as a housing estate in a poor area with few amenities. The attractiveness of this idea is that it does not depend on the formal declaration of a health or social problem that a visit to a doctor or social worker entails. She is frank about the difficulties encountered, particularly the fact that the more educated and less deprived clients more easily became involved and could therefore divert attention from the less socially accessible group. Similar problems have been met in the United States when attempting to counter the effects of a deprived environment on children.[35,36]

Matilda Goldberg's chapter presents some of the results of the latest research into social work practice, a field of work that has expanded rapidly during the past decade and which contains many of the most promising lines of development for the future. Miss Goldberg takes nothing for granted. She is willing to question the assumptions of her profession as thoroughly as any scientist questions the hypotheses of his predecessors. Even if the results are disquieting it is very unlikely that progress can be made in any other way. I do not doubt she is right to suggest that "a radical redeployment of social work resources" and "the reintroduction of certain forms of specialisation at a post-graduate and non-graduate level" will be needed. (Indeed, one might suggest as a minimal criterion that counsellors should know at least as much about a disability or a problem as those they are counselling do. It is a hard standard to meet.) The corollary is that each innovation should be evaluated, so that we can learn from the experience of the innovators (as in the case of Susan Holland) which are the most effective and useful ways forward.

Colin Parkes tackles the even more difficult problems of primary prevention. He points out that there is already some evidence that sensible advice given during pregnancy, before operations, or before discharge from prison, can significantly decrease the number of problems experienced after the event (or significantly improve the ability to cope with them). The techniques used were simple and it would seem that no extra staff ought to be needed in order to apply them. The best staff probably do so now. The issue of training for prevention runs through many of the contributions to this book and deserves attention in its own right. It used to be said that the nurses in old-fashioned mental hospitals could not undertake the new roles necessary for social rehabilitation and community work. The pioneers showed that idea to be wrong; psychiatric nurses are taking new roles as behavioural therapists, family counsellors on the management of conditions such as schizophrenia, and leaders of therapeutic communities, in addition to their more traditional duties. The same may well be true of other professional groups.

Thus new problems suggest new opportunities. What is needed in order to find the right ways forward is a more open and less authoritarian attitude on the part of the professionals, a new recognition of responsibility on the part of relatives, a realisation on both sides that "management" begins at home rather than in the clinic or office, and an experimental approach to the provision of services so that new ideas can be evaluated as they are put into practice.

References

1. Foucault, M. (1967) *Madness and Civilization: A History of Insanity in the Age of Reason*, Trans. R. Howard, London: Tavistock.
2. Rothman, D. J. (1971) *The Discovery of the Asylum: Social Order and Disorder in the New Republic*, Boston: Little, Brown & Company.
3. Goffman, E. (1961) On the characteristics of total institutions, In *The Prison*, D. R. Cressey (ed.), New York: Holt, Rinehart & Winston.
4. Scheff, T. J. (1966) *Being Mentally Ill*, Chicago: Aldine.
5. Laing, R. D. (1967) The schizophrenic experience, In *The Politics of*

218   J. K. Wing

Experience, London: Penguin Books.
6.   Szasz, T. S. (1961) The Myth of Mental Illness, New York: Hocker-Harper.
7.   Wing, J. K. (1978) Reasoning about Madness, London: OUP.
8.   Brown, G. W., Bone, M., Dalison, B. and Wing, J. K. (1966) Schizophrenia and Social Care, London: OUP.
9.   Catterson, A., Bennett, D. H. and Freundenberg, R. K. (1963) A survey of longstay schizophrenic patients, Brit. J. Psychiat., 109, 750.
10. Wing, J. K. and Brown, G. W. (1970) Institutionalism and Schizophrenia, London: CUP.
11. Mann, S. and Cree, W. (1976) "New" long-stay psychiatric patients: A national sample of 15 mental hospitals in England and Wales, 1972/3, Psychol. Med., 6, 603-16.
12. Leach, J. (1979) The evaluation of a voluntary organisation attempting to resettle destitute men: Action Research with the St Mungo Community Trust, In Vagrancy, T. Cook (ed.), New York: Academic Press.
13. Tidmarsh, D. and Wood, S. (1972) Psychiatric aspects of destitution, In Evaluating a Community Psychiatric Service, J. K. Wing & A. M. Hailey (eds.), London: OUP.
14. Wood, S. M. (1976) Camberwell Reception Centre: a consideration of the need for health and social services of homeless single men, J. soc. Policy, 5, 389-99.
15. Edwards, C. and Carter, J. (1979) Day services and the mentally ill, In Social Care for the Mentally Disabled, J. K. Wing & R. Olsen (eds.), London: OUP.
16. Hassall, C., Gath, D. and Cross, K. W. (1972) Psychiatric day-care in Birmingham, Brit. J. prev. soc. Med., 26, 120-2.
17. Hewett, S., Ryan, P. and Wing, J. K. (1975) Living without the mental hospitals, J. soc. Policy, 4, 391-404.
18. Ryan, P. and Hewett, S. H. (1976) A pilot study of hostels for the mentally ill, Social Work Today, 6, 25, 774-8.
19. Brown, G. W., Birley, J. L. T. and Wing, J. K. (1972) Influence of family life on the course of schizophrenic disorders: a replication, Brit. J. Psychiat., 121, 241-58.
20. Creer, C. and Wing, J. K. (1974) Schizophrenia at Home, London, National Schizophrenia Fellowship, 79, Victoria Road, Surbiton, Surrey, KT6 3JT.
21. Vaughn, C. E. and Leff, J. P. (1976) The influence of family and social factors on the course of psychiatric illness, Brit. J. Psychiat., 129, 125-37.
22. Howlin, P., Marchant, R., Rutter, M., Hersov, L. and Yule, W. (1973) A home-based approach to the treatment of autistic children, J. Autism. Child. Schiz., 3, 308.
23. Wing, L. (1971) Autistic Children: A Guide for Parents, London: Constable.
24. Wing, L. (1973) Children Apart: Autistic Children and their Families, London: MIND.
25. Cooper, J. E., Kendell, R. E., Gurland, B. J., Sharpe, L., Copeland, J. R. M. and Simon, R. (1972) Psychiatric Diagnosis in New York and London, London: OUP.
26. World Health Organisation (1973) The International Pilot Study of Schizophrenia, Geneva, WHO.
27. National Schizophrenia Fellowship (1974) Living with Schizophrenia, NSF, 79, Victoria Road, Surbiton, Surrey KT6 4JT.

28. Wing, J. K. (ed.) (1975) *Schizophrenia from Within*, London: National Schizophrenia Fellowship, 79, Victoria Road, Surbiton, Surrey KT6 4JT.
29. Wing, J. K. (1977) The management of schizophrenia in the community, In *Psychiatric Medicine*, G. Usdin (ed.), New York: Brunner, Mazel.
30. Shepherd, M., Cooper, B., Brown, A. C. and Kalton, G. W. (1966) *Psychiatric Illness in General Practice*, London: OUP.
31. Brown, G. W., Bhrolchain, M. and Harris, T. O. (1975) Social class and psychiatric disturbance among women in an urban population, *Sociology*, 9, 225-54.
32. Hare, E. H. and Shaw, G. K. (1965) *Mental Health on a New Housing Estate*, London: OUP.
33. Wing, J. K. (1962) Institutionalism in mental hospitals, *Brit. J. soc. clin. Psychol.*, 1, 38.
34. Srole, L., Langner, T. S., Michael, S. T., Opler, M. K. and Rennie, T. A. C. (1962) *Mental Health in the Metropolis: The Midtown Manhattan Study*, New York: McGraw Hill.
35. Robins, L. N. (1973) Evaluation of psychiatric services for children in the United States, In *Roots of Evaluation*, J. K. Wing & H. Häfner (eds.), London: OUP.
36. Rutter, M. and Madge, N. (1975) *Cycles of Disadvantage*, London: Heinemann.

Appendix: The Case for Low Cost Solutions

HUGH FREEMAN

Studies of either whole populations or service case-loads emphasise the overwhelming importance of schizophrenia for community-orientated programmes. In view of the likelihood of it arising in early adult life and its low mortality under present-day conditions, there is bound to be a large number of people in every population who are handicapped or vulnerable through schizophrenia. These will require care or treatment, continuously or in episodes, over a period of many years and the number of affected individuals, multiplied by the number of years during which these services may be needed are equivalent to an enormous drain on public finance. In the light of our current values, the alternative of leaving the patients and their families to cope with this hardship unaided (which is still the case in many parts of the world) is now felt to be unacceptable. However, overall performance still falls far short of the clearly identified needs of this group.[1]

Though the management of the acute episodes of schizophrenic illness is reasonably satisfactory overall, residential and rehabilitation facilities for the chronically disabled are relatively poor everywhere and appropriate support and counselling for families has scarcely begun to be available.

This suggests that schizophrenia, together with mental subnormality and the psychoses of old age, must assume a position of great prominence among the medico-social problems for which services have to be further planned and developed. But since resources are limited, there has to be either a search for low-cost solutions or else rather more "benign neglect" of certain other disorders. At a time when expectations are still rising, it is not at all easy to adopt the latter as a positive policy, but perhaps the care of neuroses and personality disorders, for instance, might be firmly pushed back into the primary care sector. Advice and training would still be needed by primary health workers, but it might be better to state frankly that a specialist psychotherapy service for the whole population cannot be achieved in the foreseeable future. Whilst the ratio of one full-time psychotherapist per 200,000 population has figured in national policy discussions, the present provision in the North Western health region is less than one-tenth of that, with little sign of significant increase. Since Ryle[2] has estimated that about a third of the population have serious emotional or interpersonal difficulties, we would seem to be on a hiding to nothing in seeking to have these treated by specialist personnel — particularly doctors.

Recurrent depression and manic-depressive psychosis share some of the same characteristics as schizophrenia, in respect of their demand on services, but this whole problem is of much more manageable proportions. It focuses mainly on those patients who are subject to increasingly more frequent and severe relapse over the course of time; though their numbers are relatively small, they can wreak havoc both with the medico-social services and in the community, causing difficulties that would hardly seem possible from the rather few people concerned. However, technological progress has now made them highly treatable, if compliance can be achieved over prolonged periods.[3] This progress has involved both the development of effective forms of medication and of means of monitoring the regular use of these treatments by particular patients. There is little point, though, in giving therapy during years of quiescence if the system fails as soon as things begin to go wrong clinically, since prophylaxis cannot always be guaranteed.

The conclusion to be drawn from these circumstances is that every psychiatric service needs to maintain a register of those individuals in its population who are significantly affected by psychoses. Such a register must be related to a defined population, which would normally be that of a Health District or Area (depending on size); in urban areas, around 250,000 seems to be the most manageable figure. However, this is not something which necessarily calls for elaborate technology and a premature use of computers, for instance, could well be disastrous, if the organisation does not exist to keep this information continuously up to date. Such resources will be beyond the reach of most health authorities and in any case are not essential for this particular purpose, which is largely one of effective book-keeping. It would be convenient to have the information on-line on a screen in every clinical office, as an airline booking clerk has available — but it is perfectly possible to manage just with a telephone and ordinary clerical methods.

A continuous monitoring scheme of this nature is under pilot investigation at Salford, with the support of the DHSS; preliminary findings suggest that it will not need to intervene very often when efforts have previously been focussed on integration of the different aspects of the mental health service.[4] Such a register will have some inactive names (e.g. long-stay hospital patients) and the rest can be divided into several categories, according to their degree of vulnerability and need for services. Where a long-term pharmacological treatment has been prescribed, the primary objective of the monitoring process must be to maintain unbroken therapy for as long as necessary. We do not yet know how long these periods should be, but current evidence suggests that vulnerability to relapse may still be present with both schizophrenic and affective psychoses after years of freedom from illness. In addition to medication, a register must also try to maintain monitoring of other medical and social measures that have been recommended by the treatment team, e.g. day care or residence in sheltered housing.

In the course of testing this instrument, Cheadle, Freeman and Korer[5] analysed all those patients from a defined population of 124,000 who had a diagnosis of schizophrenia, were aged between 15 and 65, had not been continuously in hospital for over twelve months, but had been in contact with some psychiatric service during 1974. The data base for this sample, numbering 282, was provided by the Salford Psychiatric Case Register;[6] after certain exclusions, 190 individuals took part in the study. These consisted of almost equal numbers of men and women, but significantly more of the men were aged under 45 and more of the women were in their 50s. Much fewer of the men had ever been married, but many of the females' marriages had ended in divorce; far more men were currently living with parents. Forty-nine of the sample were working and this social feature was the one most strongly correlated with a favourable clinical state. A surprisingly large number (152) said they were satisfied with relationships with their families, though 48 complained subjectively of social isolation. Clinical interviews, using the Present State Examination, revealed relatively few patients currently showing active features of psychosis, but many troubled by neurotic symptoms, which were strongly associated with social handicaps.

Out of this group, 156 were taking neuroleptics, and of these 137 were receiving them in the form of depot injections. This is a technological advance which has already been of the greatest significance in the long-term management of psychotic disorders. Studies of the use of hospitalisation[7] have shown that when schizophrenic patients are used as their own controls, they require much less time in hospital when changed from an oral to a depot regime. This is by no means the complete answer — a few patients are unresponsive, others are troubled by major side-effects and more by persistent neurotic or personality handicaps. However, the improvement that has been achieved in the rate of relapse and in the control of psychotic syndromes through the widespread use of long-acting neuroleptics (mainly fluphenazine decanoate) has been dramatic. Britain has probably made more effective use of this therapeutic advance than any other country.

In the case of the affective disorders, long-term use of lithium carbonate and of anti-depressive drugs[8] has brought immense benefit to many patients and their families. Technological help here has come in the form of biochemical recording of the level of therapeutic substances in the patient's blood. In the case of lithium, this procedure is already well developed and most psychiatric services in Britain now have their "Lithium Clinic", as well as their "Modecate Clinic". Things are more complex with the anti-depressive drugs, but there is reasonable hope that further development of serum estimations will allow them to be used much more effectively.

However, the continuity of care which is so essential to the management of psychosis must also be considered in relation to the general organisation of medico-social services. If there are distinctly separate sectors of care, e.g. public versus private or mental hospital versus polyclinic, then consistent and effective management becomes overwhelmingly difficult. This situation may be seen in such different countries as the USA, Holland, West Germany or Poland. However, the NHS now presents no particular problems of this kind, at least so far as medicine and nursing are concerned. Therefore, it should be possible to demonstrate in Britain a model of care for psychosis which could not even be attempted in many other countries.

In the past, psychosis was dealt with by admitting only a proportion of those affected to long-stay institutions, either because they caused unusual disruption or because they lacked supporting relatives. Efforts have been directed in Britain for some time towards dispersing the various treatment and care activities of psychiatric hospitals into the populations they serve. Correspondingly, the former isolation of these institutions is being replaced by a coordination with all related medico-social services, though this process still has far to go in many places. As the intended phasing-out of mental hospitals has receded into the far distance because of its staggering cost, it becomes more than ever necessary to proceed by small steps. Of these low-cost solutions, group homes are one of the most important and will have to replace almost completely the idea of staffed and "purpose-built" hostels, which are now impossibly expensive.[9] We also have to find out what degree of supervision of patients in their own homes is possible or desirable and by whom it should be done. Since Seebohm, whatever care of chronic psychotic patients had been undertaken by social workers has largely been taken over by community nurses — where it is done at all. Yet this is a largely unrecorded change, which was never the subject of a deliberate policy decision.

One of the largest unmet problems, though, in developing the care of psychotic patients is that of regional disparities — both in patients and in resources. On the one hand, the distribution of skilled personnel shows enormous variations between different parts of the country and other facilities tend to vary in the same direction. On the other hand, there is the question of environment (Freeman, 1978); certain areas have overwhelming concentrations of social pathology and may be the focus of drift by handicapped individuals, causing a great local excess over the usual prevalence of psychosis. Compared with many other countries, the NHS has great capacity to overcome such regional inequalities, yet it has not so far shown much evidence of the will to do so. Similarly, the potential benefits of existing new technologies have yet to be fully exploited; the tools are to hand, but there is still much further use to be made of them.

226   *Hugh Freeman*

References

1. Wing, J. K. and Creer, C. (1974) *Schizophrenia at Home*, London: Institute of Psychiatry.
2. Ryle, A. (1967) *Neurosis in the Ordinary Family*, London: Tavistock.
3. Blackwell, B. (1976) Treatment adherence, *Brit. J. Psychiat.*, **129**, 513-31.
4. Freeman, H. L. (1977) Continuity of care in the mental health services, *Int. J. Ment. Health*, **5**, 3-13. (1978) Mental health and the environment, *Brit. J. Psychiat.*, **132**, 113-24.
5. Cheadle, A. J., Freeman, H. L. and Korer, J. R. (1978) Chronic schizophrenic patients in the community, *Brit. J. Psychiat.*, **132**, 221-7.
6. Fryers, T., Freeman, H. L. and Mountney, G. H. (1970) A census of patients in an urban community, *Social Psychiat.*, **5**, 187-95.
7. Johnson, D. A. W. and Freeman, H. L. (1972) Long-acting tranquilizers, *Practitioner,* **208**, 395-400.
8. Mindham, R. H. S. (1977) Long-term prophylaxis of affective disorders, *Int. J. Ment. Health*, (in press).
9. Soni, S., Soni, S. D. and Freeman, H. L. (1977) Group homes for psychiatric patients, *Int. J. Ment. Health*, (in press).

Name Index

Adams, G.   72, 80
Aldrich, C. K.   52, 54, 61
Allen, R. V.   170
Antebi, R. N.   159, 169
Appley, M. H.   207
Arie, T.   192, 214
Arkin, A. M.   61
Arroyave, F.   126
Arthur, R. J.   170

Balint, E.   72, 80
Balter, M. B.   46, 80
Barr, J.   81
Barraclough, B. J.   80
Bartlett, M. K.   61
Battin, D.   61
Battit, G. E.   61
Beamish, P.   206
Benjamin, B.   186
Bennett, D. H.   157, 169, 170, 218
Bhrolchain, M.   81, 219
Birley, J. L.   218
Blackstock, E.   71, 80
Blackwell, B.   226
Blane, H. T.   125, 126
Bone, M.   218
Booth, T.   93
Boverman, H.   52, 54, 61
Bowlby, J.   51, 61
Brill, K.   45
Brim, O. G.   169
Briscoe, M. E.   89, 92
Britton, P. G.   203, 207
Brook, A.   80
Brown, A. C.   2, 19, 31, 46, 169

Brown, G. W.   61, 81, 91, 93, 206, 211, 218-19
Brown, M. J.   81
Butler, H.   46

Caplan, G.   49, 52, 61
Carpenter, J.   52, 54, 59, 61
Carter, J.   218
Catterson, A.   218
Chave, S.   46
Cheadle, A. J.   226
Clarke, J.   127, 132
Clyde, K. B. J.   45
Cofer, N. F.   207
Cole, J. O.   45
Cook, T.   218
Cooper, B.   31, 46, 81, 169, 219
Cooper, J. E.   218
Cooper, P. J.   186, 213
Cooperstock, R.   46
Copeland, J. R. M.   218
Corbett, J. A.   31
Corney, M. R. H.   89, 92
Cree, W.   45, 218
Creer, C.   218, 226
Cressey, D. R.   217
Cross, R. W.   218
Curry, S. H.   46

Dalison, B.   218
Daniels, D. N.   170
David, H. O.   14
Davis, J. M.   46
Davison, K.   80

227

Denham, J.   169
Deniker, P.   45
Dimitz, S.   46
D'Mello, A.   46
Dohrenwendt, B. S.   61
Doll, R.   46
Dunnell, K.   46

Early, D. F.   157, 170, 184
Edwards, C.   218
Edwards, G.   107, 123, 126
Egbert, L. D. 52-53, 61
Egdell, H. G.   74, 76, 81, 192
Ennals, D.   32
Epps, B. M.   32
Evans, E. G.   126
Ewalt, J. R.   8
Exton-Smith, A. N.   192
Eysenck, H. J.   170

Fairbairn, E. M.   81
Felce, D.   207
Finlay, B.   46
Flowenhaft, K.   62
Forman, J. A. S.   81
Forrest, F. M.   46
Forrest, I. S.   46
Foucault, M.   209, 217
Freeman, H. L.   46, 226
Freudenberg, R. K.   50, 218
Fruin, D. J.   92
Fryers, T.   226

Gath, D.   218
Gerard, R. W.   45
Gerber, I.   61
Gillison, K.   46
Gittleman, R. K.   45
Glanville, H.   185
Gleisner, J.   62
Godber, C.   32, 195, 207
Goffman, E.   14, 207, 210
Goldberg, D.   ix, xii, 31, 80, 212
Goldberg, E. M.   31-32, 81, 92, 93, 216
Goldberg, S. C.   45

Goodman, N.   45
Griffiths, R. D. P.   170
Grimley Evans, J.   192
Gunderson, E. K. E.   61
Gurland, B. J.   218
Guthrie, S.   107, 126

Häfner, H.   219
Hagen, J. H.   57, 59, 61
Hailey, A. M.   170, 218
Halbeck, S. L.   31
Hare, E. H.   219
Harris, T. O.   81, 219
Hart, D.   46
Hassell, C.   218
Hatswell, V.   32, 80
Hawton, K.   71, 80
Haycocks, H. W.   186
Hersov, L.   218
Hewitt, H. S. H.   218
Hill, M. J.   116, 125, 126
Hirsch, S.   212
Holland, S.   216-17
Howlin, P.   218
Hunt, R. C.   6

Illich, I.   108, 126
Isaacs, B.   207

Jackson, G.   128, 132
Jacobsen, J.   207
Jahoda, M.   159, 169
Jaques, E.   169
Jefferys, P.   212
Johnson, D. A. W.   46, 226
Jolley, D. J.   192, 214
Jones, K.   14
Jones, M.   14, 170
Joseph, Sir K.   9, 18

Kaim Caudle, P.   80
Kalton, G. W.   31, 46, 169, 219
Kaplan, D.   132
Katz, A.   126
Kay, D. W. K.   206

Kendell, R. E.   218
Kesey, K.   14
Kessel, W. I. N.   46
Kisker, K. P.   170
Klein, D. F.   45
Klett, J. C.   45
Korer, J. R.   226
Kramer, M.   45

Lader, M.   216
Laing, R. D.   210, 217
Lambo, T. A.   4, 14
Langner, T. S.   219
Langsley, D. G.   58, 62, 128, 132
Lazarfeld, P. F.   169
Lazarus, H. R.   57, 59, 61
Leach, J.   218
Leff, J. P.   46, 218
Lefton, M.   46
Letemendia, F.   126
Levine, J.   46
Lewis, A.   45
Linn, E. L.   45
Lodge, B.   196, 202
Loeb, M. D.   31
Loebel, R.   170

Machotka, P.   62
Maddison, D.   56, 61
Madge, N.   219
Main, T. F.   14
Manheimer, D. I.   46
Mann, S. A.   45, 218
Manning, N. P.   14
Marchant, R.   218
Marsh, G. N.   80, 81, 216
Marston, N. C.   195, 207
Mason, A. S.   46
Mason, R. W. T.   46
McCullock, J. W.   80
McGuinness, B.   92
McNay, R. A.   80
McPheeters, H.   46
McQueen, A.   73
Meacher, M.   169
Meyer, J. G.   170

Michael, S. T.   219
Mindham, R. H. S.   226
Mond, N. C.   46
Morgan, R.   195, 206
Morris, B.   185
Mortimer, A.   93
Mould, G. P.   46
Mountney, G. H.   226
Müller, C.   170
Murdoch, J. C.   80

Neill, J. E.   92
Neville, Y.   207
Nilsson, R.   45
Norell, J. S.   80

Ødegard, Ø.   45
Olson, M. R.   127, 132, 218
O'Neill, D.   46
Opler, M. K.   219

Page, L.   46
Paine, R. E.   32
Palmer, J.   207
Parad, A.   128, 132
Paridexter, W. R.   170
Parker, F.   195, 202
Parkes, C. M.   61, 217
Pasamanik, B.   46
Paterson, J.   81
Patterson, C. A.   170
Paykel, E. S.   52, 61
Pearson, C.   81
Perry, J.   46
Plas, J. A.   170
Pollack, M.   45
Powell, E.   7, 11
Prien, R. F.   45
Pritchard, E. R.   61

Querido, A.   14

Radouco-Thomas, C.   45
Rahe, R. H.   52, 61

Raphael, B.   56, 61
Rapoport, R.   14
Rathod, N. H.   45
Ratoff   81
Rees, L.   ix, xii
Rennie, J. A. C.   219
Roberts, L. M.   31
Roberts, N.   206
Robins, L. N.   219
Rosenthal, R.   207
Roth, M.   206
Rothman, D. J.   209, 217
Rowlands, J. H.   92
Rutter, M.   51, 61, 218-19
Ryan, P.   218

Sabshin, M.   31
Salkind, M. R.   46
Sandler, J.   170
Scarpetti, F. R.   46
Scheff, T. J.   210, 217
Schoenberg, B.   61
Scott, R. D.   58, 62, 81
Sharpe, L.   218
Shaw, G. K.   219
Shaw, M. J.   53, 55, 61
Shepard, M.   31, 45-46, 169, 219
Shneidman, E. S.   61
Sigerist, H. F.   108, 126
Simon, R.   218
Sinclair, I. A. C.   53, 55, 61
Sjöström, H.   45
Skegg, D. C.   6, 46
Skinner, B. F.   207
Slaby, A. E.   46
Smith, J.   207
Soni, S.   226
Soni, S. D.   226
Spry, W. R.   157
Srole, L.   219
Stevens, B. C.   46
Stones, E.   207
Strömgren, E.   170
Szasz, T. S.   210, 218

Tancredi, L. R.   46
Taylor, L.   46
Tidmarsh, D.   218
Troop, J.   53, 55, 61

Usdine, G.   219

Vaughan, C. E.   218
Viola, A.   56, 61

Wah, D. C.   46
Wallace, R. B.   80
Walton, H.   123, 126
Wansbrough, S. N.   186, 213
Warburton, R. W.   92
Watts, F. N.   162-3, 169-70
Weiner, A.   61
Welch, C. E.   61
Wernent, J. J.   46
Wheeler, S.   169
Whitney, E. D.   126
Whittaker, J. K.   131-2
Whurell, J.   80
Willems, P. J. A.   126
Willey, J.   169
Williams, B. T.   93
Williamson, J.   85
Wilson, G. D.   170
Wing, J. K.   46, 169, 170, 206, 211, 218, 219, 226
Wing, L.   218
Wolff, S.   51, 61
Wood, S. M.   218
Woods, R. T.   203, 207

Younger, L.   109, 117, 124, 126
Yule, W.   218

Zeisel, H.   169

Subject Index

Alcoholics Anonymous   84, 107, 108,
    114, 118, 125
Alcoholism   111
    Libra
        evaluation   109, 116-22
        organization   111-13, 115
        principles   110
        self help   112
Anti psychotic drugs
    effectiveness   34-37, 40
    maintenance therapy   38-40, 224
    metabolism of   39

Battersea Action and Counselling Centre
    95
"Better Services for the Mentally Ill"
    25, 189
Brief Hospitalisation Policy   139
British Association of Social Workers
    129, 131
Brunel Working Party   22

Carlton Hayes Hospital   197-203
Case Registers   222-3
Caversham Study   76
Citizens Advice Bureau   88, 90
Community Care   215
Community Health Council   101, 105
Community nurses, role of   225
"Community Psychiatry" definition of
    16
Council of Europe Working Party   60
Crisis Intervention   58-59, 127-31
    Experimental Crisis Centre   133-5

Federal Community Mental Health
    Centres Act 1963   128

Dawson Report   69
Dementia   188

Employment
    Assessment for   162-4
    Conditions of   180-1
    Disablement Resettlement Officers
        161
    Employment Rehabilitation Centres
        159, 161, 162, 165
    Enclaves   168, 184
    Industrial Therapy Organisations
        161, 165
    Maudsley Hospital VRU   162
    Occupational health doctors, role of
        182-4
    Psychiatric history and   175
    Remploy   173
    Sheltered Workshops   213

Figures
    Brief Hospitalisation Policy
        adverse effects of symptoms
            149, 150
        behaviour scores   149, 150
        discharge rates   143
        role performance   149, 150
        selection of patients   141
    Counselling following Bereavement
        56

231

Counselling prior to
    childbirth   54
    openheart surgery   57
    operative surgery   53
    release from prison   55
    Sensory pathways   199
Finance of Mental Health Service   212
    Earmarking of Funds   28
    Joint Financing   27, 29

General Practice
    Counsellors in   77-79
    Health visitors in   74-75
    Incidence of neurosis in   42-43, 70, 83
    Psychiatric nurses in   75
    Social workers in   76-77
    Stockton-on-Tees   73
    Training for   72
    Use of Psychotropic Drugs in   70
Goodmayes Psychiatric Service   190-1
Group Homes   31, 225
Guideposts Trust   xv

"Integration" meaning of   12-14

Joint Planning   17, 26-27

Lithium Clinics   224
Local Authority Social Services Act   9

Magdalen College   ix
Mental Health Act 1959   6, 7
Mental Health Foundation   60, 97, 101, 215
Mental Treatment Act 1930   210
MIND(NAMH)   20, 24
Mobile Psychiatric Teams   4
Modecate Clinics   224
Multidisciplinary Teamwork   22-24
Multiplex Model   4-7

Napsbury Hospital   58
National Council on Alcoholism   114
N.H.S. Reorganisation Act   10, 18
National Society for Autistic Children   214
National Society for Mentally Handi-capped Children   214
National Schizophrenia Fellowship   xiv, 214
Neighbourhood Action and Counselling Centre   216
    child care   101-3
    community involvement movement   95
    multifaceted problems   99
    psychotherapy, use of   99
    use of premises   97
    volunteers   102, 104, 106
New Long Stay Patients   37, 211, 213

Prevention   217
    Council of Europe Report   50, 60
    Developmental Model of   51
    Organisation of Services   50
    Preventive Intervention   52-58
    Psycho-social Transition Model   52
    Royal College of Psychiatrists Report   51
Primary Health Care Team   xii
Psychiatric Nurses, new roles   217
Psychiatric Rehabilitation Association   xiv
Psychogeriatric Services
    Southampton   203-6
Psychotherapy   222
    In action Centre   99, 105

Reorganisation of Services   8-12
    Geographical factors   19
    Joint Consultative Committees   21
    Planning structures   20-22
Royal College of Psychiatrists   10, 16, 22, 51

Samaritans   78
Seebohm Committee Report   8, 18,

225
Services for Mental Illness related to Old
    Age   189
Sickness Absence, study of   177
Social Work   xii, 87-97, 216
    children in care   87
    clientele   85-87
    crisis management   130-1
    disturbed families   86
    the elderly   85
    in general practice   76-77, 88-89
    mental health problems   87
    redeployment of skills   90
    social work tasks   87-88
    training   9, 29

Tables
    Brief Hospitalisation Project
        Adverse Effects on Informant
        148
        Behaviour   148
        Clinical Factors   144
        Clinical Improvement   146
        Follow-up services   153
        Informants' Distress   151
        Length of Hospitalisation   154
        Neurotic Symptoms   146
        Psychotic Symptoms   147
        Social Factors   142

Social Functioning   148, 151
Use of Hospital Beds   145, 155
Employment Patterns
    Communication Patterns   181
    Diagnosis   175
    Groups Studied   172
    Records   173
    Sickness Absence   177-9
High Risk Situations and Prevention
    63-68
Psychiatric Disorder, incidence of
    83
Psychotropic Drug Prescriptions
    71
Sickness Absence   178-9
Wansbrough Study
    Records   172
    Respondents   173
Tranquillisers   40-45, 216
    Alternatives to   44-45
    Usage   41-42

Voluntary Organisations   24-25

Wansbrough Borough Council   101
Women's Aid   103
World Health Organisation   4, 5